9780900952173

D1744695

LONDON RECORD SOCIETY
PUBLICATIONS

VOLUME XVII
FOR THE YEAR 1981

LONDON POLITICS 1713–1717

MINUTES OF A WHIG CLUB 1714–1717

EDITED BY

H. HORWITZ

LONDON POLLBOOKS 1713

EDITED BY

W. A. SPECK

AND

W. A. GRAY

LONDON RECORD SOCIETY
1981

© *London Record Society, 1981*

SBN 90095217 2

Printed in Great Britain by
WESTERN PRINTING SERVICES LTD
BRISTOL

CONTENTS

MINUTES OF A WHIG CLUB 1714–1717

INTRODUCTION

Guildhall Library manuscript 197 consists of the minutes of a Whig political club operating within the City of London during the last months of Queen Anne's reign and the early years of King George I's. The minutes take up eighty-two folios, numbered pages 1 to 164, in a volume $7\frac{1}{2}$ inches high by $5\frac{3}{4}$ inches wide and containing a total of ninety-four folios (three blank at the beginning, nine more at the end). Virtually nothing is known of the manuscript's provenance. The political character of the club is not in doubt: those present at its meetings include numerous Whig notables of the City, and the club was especially active in organising preparations for the annual elections of Common Council in December 1715 and December 1716.

To describe these minutes as the record of a London Whig club only raises further questions. Why do they begin in May 1714 and what does their abrupt termination in January 1717 signify? Why did the club not get involved with some important aspects of the political process in the City during these years—the regulating of the lieutenancy during the autumn of 1714 for one, the parliamentary elections of January 1715 for another? How effective was the club in its areas of activity? Finally, what connection was there between this City organisation and the Whig ministry at Westminster?

The opening pages of the manuscript appear to record the club's beginnings. The first entry is headed 'names of the members of a club', and twenty-two men are listed; the second gives 'the names of the several wards and their representatives'; and shortly afterwards comes a list of additional 'persons recommended to be admitted'. There are also provisions for paying the club's incidental expenses.

However, the group may well have been formed before the minutes start, and on this point some further evidence survives in the Corporation of London Record Office miscellaneous manuscript 166.25.[1] Under this number are filed a dozen or so sheets of notes made by the club's secretary, chiefly accounts of expenses incurred and monies received in his official capacity. Much of the information these sheets contain does appear in the financial entries in Guildhall manuscript 197, but these papers do add to our knowledge on several scores. First, the secretary refers to himself by name as David Le Gros, a little known figure despite his subsequent service as Secretary to the Bank of England.[2] Second, with respect to the club's

---

1. We wish to thank Professor Gary S. De Krey of Colgate University for this reference and for his comments on an earlier version of this Introduction.
2. Le Gros does not figure in the Bank's records until his election as Secretary; this position he retained until his death in 1743. His will is in PRO, PROB 11/728, f. 267,

1

origins, entries in his earliest sheet of expenses, dated 1714 and headed 'HS D[ebto]r to DLG', take us back before 20 May—the date of the first meeting recorded in the minutes. Le Gros's sheet of expenses begins with an entry for 22 April noting the purchase of three quires of ruled paper; the next, dated 20 May, refers to his 'first attendance as Secretary'. It may well be, then, that the club's minutes begin not when the group was formed but rather after it was decided to appoint a secretary and when that secretary began to act.

This supposition is reinforced by consideration of the list of twenty-two members which constitutes the first entry in the minutes. Le Gros's papers include two other lists of members: one has twenty names (with addresses) in much the same order as the first twenty given in the minutes; the second, an account of dues paid from Midsummer's Day 1715 to Lady Day 1716, gives the two names missing from Le Gros's first list (Moses Raper and John Thompson, the last two listed in the minutes), but the twenty-two are not in the order found in the minutes.

Too much should not be made of the differences between the list in the minutes and those in Le Gros's papers, but there are further difficulties with the set of 'founding' members. For one thing, at least five of them (James Fisher, John Hatley, Gabriel Smythe, James Cooper and John Warner) were subsequently issued invitations to join a group they presumably helped to found (9, 37), and three of the twenty-two (Warner, Raper and Thompson) are not recorded as attending any meetings until 1715 when the two latter were formally admitted as members (75). For another, though eighteen of the 'founders' were among the twenty-two most diligent attenders during the club's recorded existence, Smythe, Raper, Richard Houblon and Richard Blowen were not. Joining the eighteen were James Craggs, Sir Gilbert Heathcote, Sir Harcourt Masters and John Egleton, and it is noteworthy that these four only began to attend late in 1715 as the club made preparations for the election of a new Common Council that December.

Just as the list of 'founding' members raises as many questions as it appears to answer, so neither the club's recorded proceedings during its early months nor Le Gros's papers help to supply an explanation as to why the club adopted a formal organisation in May 1714. Le Gros, to be sure, refers to the group as the 'HS' in several of his papers, and these initials might be supposed to relate to the Hanoverian Succession. Certainly, spring 1714 was a time of crisis in national politics, with the Queen's health failing and the succession apparently in doubt, and at this juncture some City Whigs were reported to be preparing to defend the Hanoverians' claim, by force if need be.[3] Yet, there is no evidence in the club's minutes of

but it reveals nothing of his background. He was not among the wave of Huguenot immigrants but he may have been related to the Norfolk family of Le Gros descended from a Flemish ancestor. Le Gros's employment as secretary to the club may have furthered his candidacy for the position at the Bank; two of his four sureties for the post were among the twenty-two 'founders' of the club. We are indebted to the Research Section of the Bank of England for information about Le Gros's service with the Bank.

3. Nicholas Rogers, 'Popular Protest in Early Hanoverian London', *Past & Present*, no. 79 (May 1978), p. 71 and n2.

any concern to secure the succession; between May and November 1714, the only subjects mentioned in the twenty-six meetings minuted by Le Gros were the recruitment of additional members and the preparation of canvassing lists of City householders and liverymen. Even in December, when a new Common Council was to be chosen for 1715, the club took an interest only in the election for the ward of Cornhill (**30**). Perhaps, then, it might be more plausible to expand Le Gros's abbreviation to read the 'H[onourable] S[ociety]', but this is speculation.

In any event, the club's minutes show no great increase in political activity for most of 1715, and only as the time approached for the choice of a Common Council for 1716 were the group's meetings transformed from largely convivial evenings into electoral strategy sessions. It is true that in March 1715 the club took up the important question of the City franchise, in particular whether the Whigs would benefit from a reversal of the Common Council's act of 1692 barring all non-freemen from voting in elections for Common Councilmen (**40**, **62**, **71**, **76**). But until November 1715, the club's other business, apart from renewed efforts to fill its own ranks so that every ward would be represented, was largely prompted by outside stimuli: the selection of commissioners for the land tax in the City, coupled with an attempt to resolve a dispute about the choice of collectors of the tax in Bread Street Ward (**41**, **44**, **48**, **71**); the recommendation of individuals for places in the London establishment of the Post Office (**47**, **52**, **54**, **73**); and the compilation of lists of 'persons disaffected to the government and non-jurors' to assist the lieutenancy in making searches on the eve of the Fifteen (**55–9**, **61**, **64**).

Once, however, the decision was made to take an active role in the choice of a new Common Council for 1716, the club moved into high gear. Lists of recommended candidates were drawn up, the precinct books prepared the previous year were distributed to the organisers of canvasses in the various wards, funds were allotted for expenses in individual wards, and careful attention was given to the selection of members of a crown commission to be appointed to administer the oaths to City inhabitants.[4] Other measures adopted included the preparation of a loyalty association to George I and the mobilisation of various types of 'influence'—that of the Court, the Whig Lord Mayor Sir Charles Peers, the Bank of England and the East India Company (**76** and ff.).

After the election, the club remained busy. During the winter and early spring of 1716, the group worked to gain the choice of its nominees to the principal committees of the City administration (**106** and ff.). Then, during the closing months of 1716, the club again sought to secure the return of Whig Common Councilmen for 1717 (**126** and ff.).

In the light of the club's electoral activities during the closing weeks of 1716, the abrupt end to the minutes in January 1717 comes as a surprise. There is no hint in the minutes that the members were considering the dissolution of their organisation. Nor does lack of space in the minute book account for the termination of the record, for nine blank folios follow the last entry. However, the cessation of the minutes does coincide

---

4. The commission, as appointed, differed only slightly in composition from the club's recommendations: see *The Flying Post*, 22–24 Dec. 1715.

with the commencement of a new stage in Le Gros's career. The last club meeting recorded was that of 19 December 1716; the last entry, which deals with election finances, is dated 2 January 1717. And on 16 January 1717 Le Gros was elected Secretary to the Governor and Directors of the Bank of England. Yet if Le Gros's new position explains the ending of his minutes, it does not necessarily follow that the group broke up when its secretary departed.

Given that neither the origins nor the demise of the club can be determined precisely, the brief summary of its business during Le Gros's secretaryship should make it clear that the bulk of its recorded political activity centered on the Common Council elections of December 1715 and December 1716, coupled with the selection of committees in the City government during the term of the 1716 Common Council. But while the club was principally concerned with City affairs, it did have close connections with the predominantly Whig ministry appointed by George I after his arrival in England. Among the twenty-two most frequent attenders were three current members of the 1715–22 parliament (Charles Cooke, John Eyles and Sir Gilbert Heathcote), and four other sitting M.P.s made occasional appearances. Again, three of the twenty-two were appointed to office under the crown in the early years of the reign, and five other royal officials attended at least once.[5]

The chief link between the ministers and the club was supplied by James Craggs senior, appointed (with Lord Cornwallis) Postmaster General early in 1715. It is no coincidence that the only time the club was asked for its recommendation in matters of patronage was in connection with London places on the Post Office's establishment. Craggs's position carried with it an official residence in the City, but probably more important was that Craggs had a host of business and financial connections in the City going back to his days as an army clothing contractor.[6] Little direct evidence for Craggs's role as 'minister for the City' has hitherto come to light, but one highly suggestive fragment exists among his few extant papers.[7] This is a memorandum entitled 'some heads relating to the common council'; it appears to come from the pen of Thomas Woodford, one of the most assiduous attenders at the club and an appointee to a post in the Customs at much the same time Craggs was named Postmaster.[8] In turn, what is proposed in the memorandum is the compilation of a list of all Londoners (and especially freemen) who held places in the Excise, Stamp, Leather, Navy, Ordnance 'and other offices'—a scheme that re-

5. The four other M.P.s were Sir William Humphreys, Sir Theodore Janssen, Sir Gregory Page and Sir Thomas Scawen. The three officials among the twenty-two were Cooke, Craggs and Sir Harcourt Masters; the other four were Robert Baylis, Roger Gale, Richard Holditch and Samuel Westall.

6. One previous Postmaster General, Major John Wildman (Postmaster 1689–91) had taken an active interest in City politics; he, like Craggs, had a long record of involvement in London affairs prior to his appointment. For later Postmasters' roles in City politics (among them, the one-time club member John Eyles), see K. L. Ellis, *The Post Office in the Eighteenth Century* (London, 1958), pp. 9–10.

7. The indirect evidence is cited in Romney Sedgwick, *The House of Commons 1715–1754* (London, 1970), I, 283 n1.

8. British Library, Stowe MS. 751, f. 179v.; the endorsement on f. 181v. allows identification of the memorandum's author as Woodford.

sembles the list made up by the club in 1715 of 'expedients to be used in the election of Common Councilmen' (**76**).

It is not necessary, however, to rely on indirect evidence to establish Craggs's links with the club. In the first place, Craggs attended some twenty meetings of the club, beginning in November 1715, and even earlier he entertained the club at a dinner (**54**). In the second place, it was from Craggs that the club received £1,000 towards the expenses of the 1715 Common Council election and £700 for the 1716 expenses (**88, 95, 133, 140**). Craggs's disbursements, in all likelihood, were known to and authorised by his colleagues in the ministry. The sums he advanced were unlikely to have come from his own pocket, London was of sufficient importance to account for the ministry's interest in and support for the City Whigs, and contemporary observers noted an especial interest on the ministry's part in the December 1715 election of Common Councilmen. Thus, the young Dudley Ryder recorded in his diary that it was said that 'my Lord Townshend and Secretary Stanhope came . . . into the City about the choice of common council and went among the dissenters and chief of the Whigs'.[9]

The reason for the ministry's unusually great interest in the choice of the Common Council can be briefly indicated. Since the civil wars, conflict between the Common Council and the Aldermen had been intermittent, and in the dispute over the statute of 1690 restoring the City's charter and in the quarrels over controverted elections during the last years of Anne's reign, the Aldermen's use of their authority had become a partisan issue. In both controversies, Whig majorities on the aldermanic bench had been pitted against Tory majorities on the Common Council, and the outcome of the second clash was Common Council's passage of an act to simplify the procedure for choosing Aldermen—an act which had the effect of reducing the bench's power in that process. Since 1689, the Whigs for the most part had been able to maintain a majority among the Aldermen, but their strength on the Common Council had fluctuated considerably. In 1714, of the 158 Common Councilmen (about two-thirds of the total of 234) whose partisan leanings can be ascertained, 104 (66 per cent) were Tories and only fifty-four (34 per cent) were Whigs. Furthermore, though the Whigs easily carried the parliamentary election for the City in January 1715, only seventy of the new Common Council elected in December 1714 can be identified as Whigs (38 per cent) as against 113 Tories (62 per cent).[10]

Now, Tory control of the Common Council was, at the least, a source of discomfort: it could frustrate the activities of the City's standing committees (composed of both Aldermen and Common Councilmen); it might also encourage the renewed pursuit of the long-standing grievances of the Common Council against aldermanic prerogatives. At the worst, Tory

9. *The Diary of Dudley Ryder 1715–1716*, ed. William Matthews (London, 1939), p. 153.

10. Identifications of partisan allegiances have been made on the basis of the party ascriptions given by the *Post Boy*, 19–21 April 1716; this list is printed as an appendix to the minutes of the club (**146–8**). See also the notice of the December 1714 elections for the Common Council in *The Weekly Packet*, 18–25 Dec.: 'there has been very great endeavours used in all parts to throw out the old ones; but, as far as we can hear, very few new ones have obtained their end.'

predominance on the Common Council gave them a base to organise a campaign to undo the Whigs' majority on the aldermanic bench by further electoral reforms and also a platform from which to challenge the ministry's claim to speak for the realm. To avert these dangers and to join a Whig majority on the Common Council with the Whig preponderance among the Aldermen and on the newly-revamped lieutenancy was, then, the joint aim of the City Whigs and the ministry.

As the club's minutes indicate, the Whigs did not succeed in their objective either in 1715 or in 1716. A month before the elections were to be held on St Thomas's Day 1715, the minutes include 'a computation of the Whigs . . . and the Tories . . . which may be elected in the next Common Council' (**82**). The Whigs, it was reckoned, might hope for 111 of the 234 seats. On the club's assessment, the outcome was reasonably close to the forecast: some 100 Whigs were returned (47 per cent of the members whose partisan inclinations were identifiable) along with 114 Tories (53 per cent) and twenty men designated as doubtful (**113**). However, the club's analysis was rather more favourable to the Whigs than that published in the *Post Boy*: this detailed report (**146–8**) gives a total of ninety-five Whigs (42 per cent), 132 Tories (58 per cent) and seven uncertain.

The *Post Boy*'s tabulation differs from the club's computation in another respect. The club's computation was by ward only, while the newspaper's was by individual, and so it is not possible to be sure which individuals were assessed differently. However, it would appear that sixteen of the eighteen additional Tories listed by the *Post Boy* were reckoned as uncertain by the club, that three accounted Whigs by the club were designated uncertain by the newspaper and that another two were listed as Tories.

Despite these divergences over individuals, it is apparent on either reckoning that the Whigs failed in December 1715 to achieve their expected total of 111, much less a majority. Never the less, the club began, almost as soon as the results were in, to mount a campaign to gain the selection of Whigs and moderate Tories to the key City standing committees—one for City lands, another to direct the Irish Society. Lists of nominees were prepared, arrangements were made to lobby Tory Common Councilmen thought to be susceptible to personal or official influences, and already in early February 1716 it was noted that seven Tories had been 'made good' and that two more had promised to absent themselves at the crucial May meeting (**109**). But again, the Whigs were unsuccessful. Of the twelve Common Councilmen the club sought to place on the committee for City lands, only three (all incumbents) were chosen. Similarly, only eight of the Club's nominees for the eighteen councilmanic seats on the committee for the Irish Society were selected, and six of these were incumbents.[11]

These setbacks did not, it is true, deter the club from making a new effort in anticipation of the December 1716 election. During the six weeks before the election, the club met frequently and organised canvassing in almost

11. Corporation of London Record Office: City Lands Committee Journals, vol. 13, f. 216v., vol. 14, f. 1; Irish Society Minutes, vol. 7, pp. 60. 124.

half the wards. However, as the returns came in, it was the Tories who claimed victory: the *Weekly Packet* informed its readers 'it is computed the High Church have gain'd a greater Majority by thirty this year, than they did the last'.[12] Such Tory claims must be received with caution; so large an increase in their majority would have required that the Tories gain fifteen additional seats from the Whigs, and all told only thirty-three new members were chosen. Of the 201 incumbents returned, seventy-nine (41 per cent) can be identified as Whigs, 115 as Tories (59 per cent) and seven as uncertain. Thus, incumbent Whigs and Tories would seem to have fared almost equally well, and Tory claims of an increased majority can not be substantiated. Even so, the Whigs can hardly have done more than hold their own, for all the club's efforts as well as the £700 advanced by Craggs.

Whether the club, despite this new defeat, continued to function after Le Gros's translation to the Bank is unclear. But in any case, the club's extant record reveals much about the state of London politics during the early years of George I's reign and also draws attention to several notable features of national political life at this juncture.

To begin with, the lists of 'disaffected persons' for five City wards that are preserved in the minutes can be compared with the lists of 'popular protestors' in and about the City that have been compiled by Professor Nicholas Rogers. Surprisingly, none of the individuals named in the club's minutes can be traced in the judicial records of the City, Westminster or Middlesex.[13] Granted, the club's lists cover only a portion of the City, but it is also likely that the relative prominence, or at least reasonable prosperity, of many of those listed by the club is relevant to any explanation. Among the 190 individuals named, at least twenty-three were former, current, or future Common Councilmen, not to mention two senior officials of the Navy Board. A substantial proportion of those whose occupation is specified seem to have been men of some substance, ranging from goldsmiths, vintners and grocers to barbers, coffeemen and victuallers. Perhaps, then, the club members listed a stratum or several strata of disaffected individuals in those five City wards socially distinct from, though politically akin to, the rioters and Jacobite blasphemers whose names figure in the judicial records.

It is easier to demonstrate that the club's minutes isolate a cadre of Whig activists within the City. Some eighty-seven men are recorded as attending at least one of the club's ninety-one meetings, with twenty-eight attending only once and an additional twenty-three attending no more than four times. Of the thirty-six present at five or more meetings, no less than sixteen were serving Common Councilmen and two were sitting Aldermen; six others had been or were to be elected to the Common Council. Furthermore, four of the thirty-six were sitting Members of Parliament. Nor were the less frequent attenders less substantial men: six were sitting Aldermen (including the Lord Mayor), three others were serving as M.P.s, and at least fourteen more were Common Councilmen. The club's members, then, included many of the leading City Whigs;

12. 22–29 Dec. 1716.
13. This comparison was carried out by Professor Rogers at our request; we are most grateful for his help.

7

among them, the more active members were distinguished chiefly by their zeal to further the Whig cause.

Yet, zeal was not enough, even when reinforced by systematic organisation and ministerial subsidies. The nature of the club's electoral preparations and the results of its analysis of election returns help to explain why. Professor Rogers has already shown how disaffected to the Whigs and to the government popular feeling in the metropolis was during George I's first years on the throne. Organised Jacobitism might be in decline, but there was little love for the Whigs, especially among 'the petty tradesmen and craftsmen of the industrial suburbs' who were 'the main sources of disaffection'.[14] Perhaps, the disenchantment of the less prosperous with the Whigs was not quite so novel a phenomenon as Professor Rogers's account might appear to suggest. Already in William III's reign, the Whigs had the upper hand in the wards within the City's walls with the highest proportions of ratepayers at the upper end of the assessment scale (the 'inner city'), while the Tories fared better among the poorer wards within the walls (the 'middle city').[15] Yet, in the 1690s the correlation between the social character and the political complexion of the City wards was only partial; the wards outside the walls ('without walls'), though they contained a lower proportion of highly-assessed ratepayers than both Whig and Tory wards within the walls, inclined to the Whigs. The change by 1715 is marked. In 1715, as in 1693, the Whigs won ninety-four seats in the 'inner' and 'middle city' combined, but in the wards 'without walls' the Tories captured thirty-one seats in 1715 as compared to seven in 1693. In this fashion, a Whig majority in 1693 of twenty-one (leaving aside twenty-seven Common Councilmen whose allegiances are uncertain) was transformed in 1715 into a Tory majority of nearly forty (excluding seven uncertain members). Without pollbooks, it is impossible to argue convincingly from constituency level results to the supposed behaviour of particular types of voters in those constituencies, and the difficulties are heightened by the likelihood that many of the disaffected craftsmen and traders in the outer wards were not freemen. None the less, it is suggestive that in those wards where Rogers's analysis would indicate the most anti-Whig sentiment, the Tories had the advantage in 1715, though not in 1693. Moreover, it is noteworthy that in 1715 the Whigs, though bested in the 'middle city', did better in those wards than they had earlier, collecting a total of thirty seats in 1715 as compared to twenty in 1693. Thus, in 1715, the correlation between social character and political complexion was unqualified: the Whigs did best in the wealthy inner wards, less well in the

14. Rogers, 'Popular Protest', p. 85.

15. 'Inner city' wards are Bassishaw, Billingsgate, Bishopsgate Within, Bread Street, Bridge, Broad Street, Candlewick, Cheap, Cordwainer, Cornhill, Langbourn and Walbrook; 'middle city' wards are Aldersgate Within, Aldgate, Castle Baynard, Coleman Street, Cripplegate Within, Dowgate, Farringdon Within, Lime Street, Queenhithe, Tower and Vintry; 'without walls' wards are Aldersgate Without, Bishopsgate Without, Cripplegate Without, Farringdon Without and Portsoken. The terminology and the data about London's electoral geography in the 1690s are derived from Professor Gary S. De Krey's study 'Trade, Religion, and Politics in London in the Reign of William III' (Ph.D., Princeton University, 1978). We would like to express our thanks for his generosity in making this material available to us.

other inner wards, and least well in the populous wards outside the walls.

The changing configuration of the City's electoral geography also has implications for national politics, attesting to that sea change undergone by the Whigs since the days of the first Earl of Shaftesbury, the Green Ribbon Club, and the Exclusion Crisis. From the early 1690s onwards, the Whigs had more and more become identified as the party of the Court and the established order. This transition can be detected in the club's attitude towards allowing 'unfreemen' the vote in Common Council elections. In 1692, it was the Whigs, with Major John Wildman (once a Leveller) in the lead, who pushed through the Common Council an act barring non-freemen from voting, at least partly on the grounds of preserving the traditional privileges of the freemen. But by 1715, the members of the club computed that a reversal of this act would, on balance, be to the Whigs' advantage, especially in the 'inner city' (**40**). Their reasoning is not spelled out in the minutes; they may have arrived at this conclusion out of a realisation that many of the well-to-do merchants and traders (men likely to support Whig candidates) were no longer troubling to become freemen. This, admittedly, is little more than a guess. What is clear is that the club was concentrating on strengthening the Whigs' position in the wards within the walls and that the members could see little to be gained by contesting most of the outer wards whether on a freeman franchise or upon some less exclusive one (**126** and ff.).[16]

The club's activities, coupled with the setbacks to its efforts in 1715 and again in 1716, also serve to underline the relatively insecure basis of the Whig ascendancy in the early years of George I's reign. Although the Whigs won a clear victory in the first general election of the reign, not least in the City where the Whig candidates polled nearly 55 per cent of all votes cast, the Tories retained a majority on the Common Council through the 1714, 1715 and 1716 elections. And as London was to remain a thorn in the side of the Whig ministry even after Walpole gained power, so the larger parliamentary boroughs (those with 1,000 voters or more) were at least as likely to return anti-ministerialists as they were supporters of Walpole or the Pelhams.

In conclusion, it may be useful to stress the uniqueness of the club's minutes. On the one hand, they reveal an unprecedented degree of partisan organisation, unknown at any other time in London during the later seventeenth and early eighteenth centuries, unknown, too, in any other constituency during this period. On the other hand, had not this record survived, it is unlikely that the activities of the club would have been discernible. Granted, contemporary accounts remark on the unusual 'endeavours' made by the City Whigs during the weeks before the election of December 1715 and also upon the involvement of some of the ministers in this campaign, yet these reports are endowed with much added meaning by a reading of the club's minutes.[17] Possibly, such an elaborate organisational effort could only have been mounted in London—thanks to the wealth and political sophistication of its elite and also to the City's traditional importance in ministerial eyes. But it is also possible that similar

---

16. This is not to say that the Whigs completely neglected the 'poorer sort': see **86**.
17. *Dawk's News Letter*, 20 Dec. 1715.

clubs or caucuses may have been active in Bristol, Norwich, or other major provincial towns where Whig–Tory animosities had long run high and that their records have either failed to survive or remain to be studied.[18]

Whether the London Whig club of 1714–17 was unique, the significance of its minutes is beyond doubt. Their chief usefulness is in furthering an understanding of the complex, and largely unwritten political history of the City; in addition, the club's linkage with the ministry and the continuing strength of the Tories within the City also cast light on the national political scene. It might be wished that the record was fuller and that the puzzles of the club's origin and apparent demise could be resolved. But within their limits, David Le Gros's orderly entries are quite clear.

Thus, in preparing this text for publication, it has not been necessary to adopt elaborate editorial conventions. Spelling, capitalisation and punctuation have been modernised, and the spelling of frequently recurring surnames has been standardised. Most abbreviations have been expanded, and all dates have been rendered in new style. Scribal corrections have been passed over in silence, while marginal notations have been incorporated in the text and printed in italic. Editorial interpolations have been placed within square brackets. In a few instances, material has been re-arranged for more economical presentation. The Index contains entries for persons, places and subjects.

18. The Loyal Society may have played a similar role on the Tory side in Bristol in the last years of Anne's reign, while from 1737 onwards the Steadfast Society was a major force in Tory affairs in that city: John Oldmixon, *The Bristol Riot* (London, 1714), p. 4; W. E. Minchinton (ed.), *Politics and the Port of Bristol in the Eighteenth Century* (Bristol Record Society Publications XXIII, Bristol 1963), p. xviii. Thanks for these references to Professor Nicholas Rogers.

MINUTES OF A WHIG CLUB 1714–1717
(Guildhall Library MS. 197)

1. (p. 1) Names of the members of a club. Richard Houblon esq.; Mr Henry Lyell, Broad Street Ward; Charles Cooke esq., Bishopsgate Without; John Eyles esq., Aldgate; Thomas Woodford esq., Broad Street; Mr Joshua Bagshaw, Lime Street; Col. John Shorey, Bassishaw; Mr Samuel Trench, Cordwainer; Mr John Younge, Cheap; Major Richard Lechmere, Tower; Mr John Daye, Cornhill; Robert Baylis esq., Bread Street; John London esq., Coleman Street; Mr Richard Blowen, Cripplegate Without; Major John Hatley, Farringdon Within; (p. 2) Mr James Fisher, Billingsgate Ward; Mr James Cooper, Vintry; Mr Gabriel Smythe, Langbourn; Samuel Perry esq., Portsoken; Mr John Warner [blank]; Mr Moses Raper, Dowgate; Mr John Thompson, Candlewick.

2. (p. 3) The names of the several wards and their representatives. Aldersgate Within [blank]; Aldersgate Without [blank]; Aldgate, Mr Eyles; Bassishaw, Col. Shorey; Billingsgate, Mr Fisher; Bishopsgate Within [blank]; Bishopsgate Without, Mr Cooke; Bread Street, Mr Baylis; Bridge [blank]; Broad Street, Mr Woodford, Mr Lyell; Candlewick, Mr Thompson; Castle Baynard [blank]; Cheap, Mr Younge; Coleman Street, Mr London; (p. 4) Cordwainer, Mr Trench; Cornhill, Mr Daye; Cripplegate Within [blank]; Cripplegate Without, Mr Blowen; Dowgate, Mr Raper; Farringdon Within, Major Hatley; Farringdon Without (Holborn Side) [blank]; Farringdon Without (Fleet Street Side), Mr Warner; Langbourn, Mr Smythe; Lime Street, Mr Bagshaw; Portsoken, Mr Perry; Queenhithe [blank]; Tower, Major Lechmere; Vintry, Mr Cooper; Walbrook [blank].
Vide Wards' and Precincts' names, page 55 [**63**].

3. (p. 5) Thursday, 20 May 1714. Present: Mr Woodford, Mr Cooke, Mr Lyell, Mr Houblon, Mr Bagshaw, Mr Trench, Mr Shorey, Mr Daye, Mr Younge.

It having been agreed upon the settling of this club that every member thereof at the first meeting after each Quarter Day shall pay to the Secretary one guinea towards defraying the ordinary and extraordinary charges of the year to be computed from Lady Day 1714.

Ordered, that the Secretary do prepare a list of the names of the members and their quarterly contributions and that the same be laid upon the table every time the club meets.

(p. 6) Every member of the club that has completed his ward book is desired to leave the same with the Secretary.

That the names of the liverymen therein contained may as soon as possible be posted into the books wherein are kept lists of the liveries of the several Companies in this City.

Ordered, that the Secretary do copy the lists of the liveries of the several Companies in so many several books as there are liveries, and that the same books be of the same size of paper and ruling as the specimen now agreed to.

Ordered, that the householders of the several wards be copied in books according (p. 7) to the precincts or divisions in each ward.

Ordered, that the names of the said householders be also copied in ward books, and that the same books be of the like paper and ruling with the specimen now agreed to.

Agreed, that the future meetings of this club be on every Thursday at seven of the clock in the evening.

Agreed, that every member of this club at the weekly meetings do pay two shillings to defray the expenses of the reckoning.

4. (p. 8) Thursday, 27 May 1714. Present: Mr Lyell, Mr Baylis, Mr Woodford, Mr Trench, Mr Younge, Mr Cooke, Mr Bagshawe, Mr Eyles.

The specimens for the livery books and the ward books brought in and approved.

5. Thursday, 10 June 1714. Present: Mr Cooke, Mr Woodford, Mr Lyell, Mr London, Mr Baylis, Major Lechmere, Mr Younge, Mr Daye.

Received of Mr Cooke the surplus of former reckonings: 8s. 6d.

Received by the surplus of the reckoning this night: 2s. 6d.

6. (p. 9) Thursday, 17 June 1714. Present: Mr Woodford, Mr Lyell, Mr Houblon, Mr Trench, Col. Shorey, Mr Bagshaw, Mr Daye, Mr Younge.

Received by the surplus of the reckoning this night: 1s. 6d.

7. Thursday, 24 June 1714. Midsummer Day. Present: Mr Cooke, Mr Woodford, Mr Lyell, Mr Baylis, Mr Bagshaw, Col. Shorey, Mr Daye, Mr Eyles.

Received of Mr Bagshaw the surplus of former reckonings: 14s.

Received by the surplus of the reckoning this night: 5s. 10d.

8. (p. 10) Thursday, 1 July 1714. Present: Mr Woodford, Mr Younge, Mr Lyell, Mr Cooke, Mr Daye, Major Lechmere, Mr Trench, Mr Baylis, Mr Bagshaw.

Received of all the gentlemen present (except Mr Bagshaw) one guinea apiece for their quarterage at Midsummer: £8 12s.

9. Thursday, 8 July 1714. Present: Mr Cooke, Mr Baylis, Mr Woodford, Col. Shorey, Mr Younge, Mr Lyell, Major Lechmere.

Persons recommended to be admitted members of the club: Billingsgate Ward, Mr James Fisher; Bridge, Mr Richard West; Candlewick, Mr Micklethwaite; (p. 11) Castle Baynard, Mr Awnsham Churchill or Mr Deacle; Cripplegate Within, Capt. Daniel Lock; Cripplegate Without, Mr Richard Blowen; Dowgate, Mr Gould or Mr Matthew Shepherd; Farringdon Within, Major John Hatley; Farringdon Without (Holborn

Side), Capt. Lewis, Mr Hibbert or Mr Dixon; Farringdon Without (Fleet Street Side), Col. Gower, Mr Goodwin or Mr Hasell; Langbourn, Mr Gabriel Smythe, Mr Hankey or Deputy Cooper; (p. 12) Portsoken, Mr Samuel Perry; Queenhithe, Capt. John Skey or Capt. Henry Langley; Vintry, Mr Deputy William Cooke; Walbrook, Mr Timbrell.

Received by the surplus of the reckoning this night: 6s. 6d.

10. (p. 13) Thursday, 15 July 1714. Present: Mr Daye, Mr Younge, Major Lechmere, Mr Bagshaw, Col. Shorey, Mr Trench, Mr Woodford.

Received by the surplus of the reckoning this night: 1s. 6d.

Mr Trench and Col. Shorey are desired to bring with them such gentlemen as they have engaged to become members of the club to the next meeting.

11. Thursday, 22 July 1714. Present: Mr Cooke, Mr Woodford, Mr Lyell, Mr Baylis, Mr Bagshaw, Mr Younge, Mr Daye, Major Lechmere, Mr Blowen.

Received by the surplus of the reckoning this night: 2s.

12. (p. 14) Thursday, 29 July 1714. Present: Mr Cooke, Mr Lyell, Major Lechmere, Col. Shorey, Mr Bagshaw, Mr Daye, Mr Trench.

Received by the surplus of the reckoning this night: 3s. 6d.

13. Thursday, 5 August 1714. Present: Mr Cooke, Mr Woodford, Mr. Baylis, Mr Lyell, Mr Eyles, Mr Trench, Mr Daye, Mr Younge, Col. Shorey, Major Lechmere.

Received by the surplus of the reckoning this night: 6d.

14. (p. 15) Thursday, 12 August 1714. Present: Mr Woodford, Mr Baylis, Mr Houblon, Mr Eyles, Mr Cooke, Mr Bagshaw, Major Lechmere, Mr Daye, Mr Younge.

Received of Mr Eyles and Mr Houblon for their quarterage due at Midsummer: £2 3s.

Received by the surplus of the reckoning this night: 6s. 10d.

15. Thursday, 19 August 1714. Present: Mr London, Mr Woodford, Mr Cooke, Mr Daye, Mr Younge, Mr Bagshaw, Col. Shorey, Major Hatley.

Received of Mr Bagshaw for his quarterage due at Midsummer: £1 1s. 6d.

Paid to make up the reckoning this night: 6s. 6d.

16. (p. 16) Thursday, 26 August 1714. Present: Mr Eyles, Mr Woodford, Mr Cooke, Mr Younge, Major Lechmere.

Received by the surplus of the reckoning this night: 2s. 6d.

17. Thursday, 2 September 1714. Present: Mr Daye, Mr Younge, Col. Shorey, Major Lechmere, Mr Bagshaw.

[No minute]

18. (p. 17) Thursday, 9 September 1714. Present: Mr Cooke, Mr Woodford, Mr Lyell, Mr Trench, Major Lechmere, Mr Daye, Mr Younge.
Paid to make up the reckoning this night: 8d.

19. Thursday, 16 September 1714. Present: Mr Daye, Major Lechmere, Mr Bagshaw, Mr Younge, Mr Cooke.
Received by the surplus of the reckoning this night: 1s.

20. (p. 18) Wednesday, 22 September 1714. Present: Mr Eyles, Mr Woodford, Mr Lyell, Mr Cooke, Mr Baylis, Mr Younge, Mr Bagshaw, Mr Blowen, Mr Fisher, Major Lechmere.
Received by the surplus of the reckoning this night: 8s. 9d.

21. Thursday, 30 September 1714. Present: Mr Daye, Col. Shorey, Major Hatley, Mr Younge, Mr Fisher, Mr Bagshaw.
[No minute]

22. (p. 19) Thursday, 7 October 1714. Present: Mr Woodford, Mr Cooke, Mr Lyell, Mr Baylis, Mr Houblon, Mr Eyles, Major Lechmere, Mr Daye, Mr Younge.
Received by the surplus of the reckoning this night: 2s. 6d.

23. Thursday, 14 October 1714. Present: Mr Younge, Mr Daye, Col. Shorey, Major Hatley, Mr Fisher, Major Lechmere.
[No minute]

24. (p. 20) Thursday, 21 October 1714. Present: Mr Woodford, Mr Cooke, Mr Lyell, Mr Daye, Mr Younge, Mr Fisher, Mr Bagshaw.
Received by the surplus of the reckoning this night: 6d.

25. Thursday, 4 November 1714. Present: Mr Fisher, Mr Bagshaw, Col. Shorey, Major Lechmere, Mr Younge, Mr Daye.
Paid to make up the reckoning this night: 6d.

26. (p. 21) Thursday, 11 November 1714. Present: Mr Cooke, Mr Woodford, Mr Eyles, Mr Baylis, Mr Lyell, Mr Daye, Mr Fisher, Major Lechmere.
Paid to make up the reckoning this night: 2s. 4d.

27. (p. 22) Thursday, 18 November 1714. Present: Mr Lyell, Mr Fisher, Mr Daye, Col. Shorey, Mr Blowen, Mr Eyles, Mr Perry, Mr Younge, Mr Cooke, Mr London, Mr Trench, Mr Baylis, Major Hatley, Mr Woodford, Major Lechmere, Mr Smythe, Mr Bagshaw.
Received by the surplus of the reckoning this night: 12s.

28. (p. 23) Thursday, 25 November 1714. Present: Mr Eyles, Mr Lyell, Major Hatley, Mr Younge, Mr Cooke, Col. Shorey.
Received by the surplus of the reckoning this night: 3s. 11d.

29. Thursday, 2 December 1714. Present: Col. Shorey, Major Hatley, Mr Bagshaw, Mr Younge, Mr Cooke, Mr Daye.
Received by the surplus of the reckoning this night: 10d.

30. (p. 24) Thursday, 16 December 1714. Present: Mr Trench, Mr Bagshaw, Mr Fisher, Major Lechmere, Mr Daye, Major Hatley, Mr Woodford, Mr Younge, Mr Cooper, Col. Shorey.
Persons inhabiting in Cornhill Ward who may be influenced at the next election of Common Councilmen: Nathaniel Halhead, by Sir Robert Furnese, Jeoffrey Staines, Mr Moses Berringer (memorandum, Mr Bagshaw to speak to Mr Staines); John Bulley, by Capt. Hyde, George Hatley (memorandum, Mr Woodford to speak to Capt. Hyde); John Akerman, by East India Company or Mr Ellwick; Charles Norris, by Mr Bagshaw; Samuel Manship, by the Lord Chancellor [Baron Cowper] or Mr Woodford; Edward Barber, by the same; [blank] Marshall, by the same; Joseph King, by Major Hatley.
(p. 25) Received by the surplus of the reckoning this night: 4s. 4d.

31. Thursday, 23 December 1714. Present: Mr Cooke, Mr Daye, Major Hatley, Mr Younge.
Paid to make up the reckoning this night: 4s. 10d.

32. Thursday, 6 January 1715. Present: Mr Fisher, Mr Bagshaw, Major Lechmere, Col. Shorey, Mr Younge, Major Hatley.
Paid to make up the reckoning this night: 7s. 6d.

33. (p. 26) Thursday, 20 January 1715. Present: Mr Cooke, Mr Woodford, Mr Bagshaw, Mr Smythe, Mr Blowen, Mr Trench, Mr Baylis, Mr London, Mr Younge, Mr Fisher, Major Lechmere, Mr Cooper, Mr Daye.
Memorandum, this night Mr Woodford treated the club with a bowl of punch.

34. Thursday, 3 February 1715. Present: Major Lechmere, Mr Bagshaw.
Paid for the reckoning this night: 5s.

35. (p. 27) Thursday, 10 February 1715. Present: Col. Shorey, Mr Blowen, Mr Younge, Mr Cooper, Mr Woodford, Mr Eyles, Mr Perry, Mr Fisher, Mr Cooke, Mr Baylis.
Memorandum, the Secretary to send to every member a list of the wards where members are wanting in order to fill up the number of the club with proper persons at the next meeting.
Received by the surplus of the reckoning this night: 5s. 6d.

36. Thursday, 17 February 1715. Present: Major Lechmere, Mr Daye, Mr Cooke, Mr Younge, Mr Fisher, Col. Shorey, Mr Bagshaw.
Paid to make up the reckoning this night: 1s.

37. (p. 28) Thursday, 24 February 1715. Present: Mr Woodford, Mr Perry, Col. Shorey, Mr Daye, Mr Younge, Mr Lyell, Mr Bagshaw, Mr Eyles, Mr Fisher, Major Lechmere.

Persons recommended for several wards to become members of the club. Aldersgate: Mr Sprint, bookseller, by Mr Lyell. Bishopsgate Within: Mr Alsop, against St Helen's, by Major Lechmere; Mr Partridge, brazier, in Gracechurch Street, by Mr Daye. Bridge: Mr Francis Hutchinson, in Gracechurch Street, by Mr Daye; Mr Henry Neale, soapmaker, in Thames Street, by Mr Fisher. Candlewick: Mr John Williams, woollen draper, by Deputy Sharpe, by Major Lechmere and Mr Fisher; Mr John Thompson, corn factor, by Mr Lyell and Mr Fisher. (p. 29) Castle Baynard: Mr John Halsey, cheesemonger, in Newgate Market, by Mr Fisher. Cripplegate Within: Mr Deputy Egleton, in Wood Street, by Col. Shorey and Mr Perry; Major Croshaw, by Mr Lyell. Dowgate: Mr Jacob Jacobsen, by Mr Woodford; Mr William Gould, by Col. Shorey. Farringdon Without (Holborn Side): Thomas Jordan, a turner, at the Rose and Crown on Snow Hill, by Mr Fisher; Mr Joseph Dawson, a cheesemonger, by Holborn Bridge, by Mr Fisher. Farringdon Without (Fleet Street Side): Mr Timothy Goodwin, bookseller, against St Dunstan's Church in Fleet Street, by Mr Fisher; (p. 30) Mr John Warner, a goldsmith, without Temple Bar, by Mr Eyles. Portsoken: memorandum, Mr Mayne, a woollen draper, without Aldgate, by Col. Shorey; memorandum, Mr Hawkins, a gunsmith in the Minories, by Major Lechmere. Queenhithe: Capt. Henry Langley, in Queenhithe, oilman, by Col. Shorey; Capt. Skey, in Thames Street, tobacconist, by Col. Shorey; Mr Steward, by Sir John Fryer. Walbrook: Mr Matthew Shepherd, by Mr Bagshaw; Mr Mark Warkman, wine merchant, in Cannon Street, by Mr Fisher and Major Lechmere; Mr Torriano, Spanish merchant.

Paid to make up the reckoning this night: 4s. 6d.

38. (p. 31) Thursday, 3 March 1715. Present: Mr Cooke, Mr Fisher, Col. Shorey, Major Lechmere, Mr Cooper, Mr Daye, Mr Woodford, Mr Eyles.

Received by the surplus of the reckoning: 1s. 6d.

39. Thursday, 10 March 1715. Present: Mr Woodford, Mr Eyles, Mr Cooke, Major Lechmere, Mr Warner.

Paid to make up the reckoning this night: 4s. 2d.

40. (p. 32) Thursday, 17 March 1715. Present: Mr Woodford, Mr London, Mr Smythe, Mr Cooper, Mr Fisher, Mr Baylis, Mr Younge, Mr Daye, Mr Warner, Major Hatley, Major Lechmere.

The club taking into consideration the act of Common Council made in 1692 which excludes unfreemen from voting in elections of Aldermen and Common Councilmen. And the question being put, that the bringing to trial that by law would be for the interest of [the] public in the several wards, the club gave their opinions following: Aldersgate Within, gain; Aldersgate Without, gain; Aldgate, gain; Bassishaw, gain; Billingsgate, gain; Bishopsgate Within, gain; Bishopsgate Without, gain; Bread Street, doubtful; Bridge, doubtful; Broad Street, gain; (p. 33) Candlewick, gain; Castle Baynard, lose; Cheap, gain; Coleman Street, doubtful; Cordwainer, gain; Cornhill, gain; Cripplegate Within, doubtful; Cripplegate Without, doubtful; Dowgate, doubtful; Farringdon Within, doubtful;

16

Farringdon Without, lose; Langbourn, gain; Lime Street, gain; Portsoken, doubtful; Queenhithe, doubtful; Tower, gain; Vintry, gain; Walbrook, gain.

Received by the surplus of the reckoning this night: 5s. 3d.

41. (p. 34) Thursday, 24 March 1715. Present: Mr Woodford, Mr Baylis, Major Lechmere, Major Hatley, Mr Smythe, Mr Cooper, Mr Fisher, Mr Younge, Mr Trench, Mr Warner, Mr Eyles, Mr Bagshaw, Mr Houblon.

Received by the surplus of the reckoning this night: 10s.

Mr Woodford is desired to give to Sir John Ward the list of names which the club have agreed upon to be part of the commissioners for the land tax.

42. Thursday, 31 March 1715. Present: Mr Cooke, Mr Perry, Mr Younge.

Paid to make up the reckoning this night: 2s.

Broke up at past eleven o'clock (memorandum, per Mr C[harles] C[ooke]).

43. (p. 35) Thursday, 7 April 1715. Present: Mr Fisher, Col. Shorey, Major Lechmere, Major Hatley, Mr Cooper, Mr Bagshaw.

Received by the surplus of the reckoning: 2s. 6d.

44. Thursday, 14 April 1715. Present: Mr Cooke, Mr Woodford, Mr Baylis, Mr Warner, Mr Younge, Mr Daye, Mr Lyell.

Mr Cooke, Mr Eyles, Mr Woodford, Mr Baylis and Mr Lyell are desired to attend the four members who serve in parliament for this City and request that the club may have the perusal of the list of the commissioners for the land tax, by them settled.

Paid to make up the reckoning this night: 1s.

45. (p. 36) Thursday, 21 April 1715. Present: Mr Eyles, Mr Woodford, Mr Daye, Major Lechmere, Mr Younge, Mr Fisher, Mr Bagshaw.

Paid to make up the reckoning this night: 3s. 6d.

46. Thursday, 28 April 1715. Present: Mr Cooke, Mr Fisher, Mr Daye, Mr Bagshaw, Major Lechmere.

Paid to Mr Daye his expenses for the club on Monday last and on this day: 7s. 6d.

Paid to make up the reckoning this night: 2s. 5d.

47. (p. 37) Thursday, 5 May 1715. Present: Major Lechmere, Mr Fisher, Col. Shorey, Major Hatley, Mr Bagshaw, Mr Younge, Mr Daye, Mr Eyles.

The Postmasters General [James, fourth Baron Cornwallis and James Craggs senior] having given leave to the club to recommend two persons out of each ward to be preferred to places in the General Post Office, the following persons were nominated for that purpose: Aldgate Ward, Philip Gage and Henry Smith, by Mr Eyles; Bassishaw, Henry Heath and William Henshaw, by Col. Shorey; Billingsgate, Henry Amey and John Gregory, by Mr James Fisher; Broad Street, Thomas Griffith and Andrew Parry, by Mr Woodford; Cheap, Sampson Coleclough and Thomas

Raymond, by Mr Younge; (p. 38) Cornhill, Benjamin Whitebread and Thomas Rawlins, by Mr Daye; Cripplegate Without, Andrew Vigners, by Mr Cooke; Farringdon Within, Richard Littleton and Charles Pickering, by Major Hatley; Langbourn, Thomas Petty, by Mr Eyles; Lime Street, Thomas Mayley and Nathaniel Bishop, by Mr Bagshaw; Tower, John Middleton and John Stevens, by Major Lechmere; Vintry, John Carey and John Feilder, by Mr Cooper; Southwark, Edmund Harris, by Mr Eyles.

(p. 39) Mr Eyles, Mr Cooke and Mr Woodford are desired to attend the Postmasters General with the recommendation of the aforesaid persons, subscribed by all the members of the club now present.

Paid to make up the reckoning this night: 2s. 10d.

48. Thursday, 12 May 1715. Present: Major Lechmere, Mr Fisher, Mr Cooke, Col. Shorey, Mr Eyles.

Memorandum, to speak to Mr Blowen about Andrew Vigners, recommended by Mr Cooke.

Memorandum, to speak to Mr Woodford for a list of the commissioners for the land tax as passed in the act of parliament.

Received by the surplus of the reckoning this night: 2s. 9d.

49. (p. 40) Thursday, 19 May 1715. Present: Major Lechmere, Mr Younge, Mr Daye.

Paid to make up the reckoning this night: 1s. 10d.

50. Thursday, 26 May 1715. Present: Mr Daye, Major Lechmere, Mr Younge.

A letter wrote by the members present to Mr Woodford about the meeting of the club.

Received by the surplus of the reckoning: 1s. 6d.

51. (p. 41) Thursday, 16 June 1715. Present: Mr Fisher, Mr Younge.
[No minute]

52. Thursday, 23 June 1715. Present: Mr Daye.

Memorandum, to write to such members of the club who have recommended persons to be preferred in the General Post Office that they meet at Garraway's Coffee House on Tuesday next between twelve and one to go with Mr Woodford to Mr Craggs for that purpose. To send also to Mr Woodford on Monday night to remind him of this, and the affair of Cheap Ward.

Paid to make up the reckoning this night: 6d.

53. (p. 42) Thursday, 30 June 1715. Present: Major Lechmere, Major Hatley.

Paid to make up the reckoning at the club this night: 6d.

54. Wednesday, 6 July 1715. Present: Mr Eyles, Mr London, Mr Lyell, Mr Cooke, Mr Woodford, Mr Baylis, Mr Bagshaw, Major Lechmere, Col. Shorey, Major Hatley, Mr Trench, Mr Daye, Mr Younge, Mr Blowen, Mr Fisher, Mr Smythe, Mr Perry, Mr Warner.

Mr Craggs acquainted the club that he had received the list of persons recommended by them to be preferred to places in the General Post Office, and that when any vacancies happened those persons should be taken care for.

Agreed, that the future meetings of this club be on the first Thursday in every month and that all the members be then summoned to attend and as often as anything extraordinary may happen.

Memorandum, this day Mr Craggs entertained the club at a dinner.

55. (p. 43) Wednesday, 27 July 1715. Present: Mr Cooke, Major Hatley, Col. Shorey, Major Lechmere, Mr Cooper, Mr Warner, Mr Eyles, Mr Younge, Mr Fisher, Mr Daye.

Col. Shorey acquainted the club that this meeting was to desire the members to give an account what houses there are in their respective wards who entertain persons disaffected to the government and non-jurors, in order to be searched by the officers of the Lieutenancy who are empowered for that purpose.

Received by the surplus of the reckoning this night: 4s. 10d.

56. Thursday, 4 August 1715. Present: Mr Smythe, Col. Shorey, Mr Trench, Major Hatley, Mr Fisher, Mr Cooper, Mr Bagshaw, Mr Daye.

List of suspected persons in Cornhill Ward.

*Nathaniel Crossly, barber, below the Exchange
*George Strahan, bookseller, against Exchange
*John Tart, pattern shop, near Swan and Hoop
 William Hyde, linendraper, at the Star
*[blank] Jones, a toy shop, at the Crown and Pearl
 (p. 44) Henry Wingfield, linendraper, at the Three Nuns
*John Bucannon, pattern shop, at the Black Boy
*William Murford, ditto, at the Royal Point
 Anthony Harrison, watchmaker, Birchin Lane
 Edward Warren, coffeeman, ditto
 Thomas Organ, barber, ditto
*James Brent, tallowchandler, ditto
*John Cooper, coffeeman, corner of Miles Alley
*at John Cooper's, a watchmaker, professed Papist
 The Rainbow Coffee House kept by a Papist woman and may entertain
    dangerous persons.
(The most dangerous marked thus, *)

57. List of suspected persons in Vintry Ward.
Edward White, pressmaker, in Thames Street near Elbow Lane
Thomas Hosier, at Fishermen's Hall
John Houghton, victualler, in Brick Hill Lane
(p. 45) John Boyce, cabinetmaker, Maiden Lane
Francis Zouch, snuff merchant, corner Garlick Hill, in Thames Street
Richard Yalding, victualler, Worcester Place
Edward Nurden, a non-juror, a dyer, in ditto
Thomas Rich, a non-juror, a dyer, in Black Swan Alley, Thames Street

William Daltry, ditto
George Whittle, dyer, in Sheppard's Alley
Thomas Shuttleworth, a Papist, exchange broker on Garlick Hill
Roger Penny, Black Swan Alley, Thames Street
Charles Badger, a Papist, in Sheppard's Alley in Thames Street
William Ward, grocer, lower end of Garlick Hill in Thames Street
Widow Fellows, on Garlick Hill, lets lodgings
William Kempster, a mason, Garlick Hill
Charles Drew, a mercer, in Bow Lane
John Parker, apothecary, in ditto
(p. 46) Randolph Fernley, a hot presser, Cloak Lane
Charles Mason, cabinetmaker, College Hill
Roger Lawrence, a non-juror, ditto
Thomas Mellan, bricklayer, ditto
John Brookes, carpenter, ditto
Henry Freeman, tailor, Queen Street
William Horton, tobacconist, ditto

58. List of suspected persons in Farringdon Without.
William Chesshire, mercer, the corner of the Old Bailey next Ludgate
Dr Browne, examiner, next behind him in the Old Bailey
Thomas Sowlter, glass seller, the corner of Fleet Street by Fleet Bridge
Cave Wiseman, hatter, ditto
Thomas Ketterick, upholder, ditto
Ambrose Rule, in Salisbury Court
(p. 47) George Parker, almanac maker, in Salisbury Court
[blank] Anson, goldsmith, turned Papist, in Fleet Street
Richard Keys, in New Street
[blank] Dunn, pewterer, ditto
Capt. Hide, ditto
Deputy John Tayler, ditto
William Kent, by the Ditch Side
Richard Norton, ditto
William Clarkson, ditto, upholder
Joseph Pluckrose, upholder, ditto
Thomas Robinson, City Smith, Bond's Stables
William Sparkes, Fetter Lane
John Stanton, ditto
William Almond, ditto
[blank] Humphreys, at Mr Kirkall's, a fanmaker, near Horn Tavern in
    Fleet Street
[blank] Dandridge, in Fetter Lane
William Howard, in Fleet Street
(p. 48) Thomas Parsons, in Fleet Street
Thomas Searle, in ditto
Samuel Keble, bookseller, in ditto
Robert Vincent, stationer, in ditto
Philip Overton, printseller, in ditto
Richard Peirson, goldsmith, Papist, in ditto

Robert Gosling, in ditto
Charles Lee, vintner, in ditto
John Child, ironmonger, by Bell Yard End in Fleet Street
Edward Cordwell, City Carpenter, by Bridewell
Thomas Newell, Ludgate Hill
[blank] Hatley, mercer, ditto
[blank] Halsey, apothecary, ditto
Humphrey Howes, barber, Bride Lane End in Fleet Street
[blank] Bristow, goldsmith, next door
[blank] Dolleigh, alehouse keeper, at the Twelve Bells next door
Daniel Hughes, an attorney, in Raquet Court in Fleet Street
(p. 49) [blank] Harker, a farrier's son, in Salisbury Court

59. Farringdon Without (Holborn Side).
Charles Price, a thread man, at the Sun near Shoe Lane End, Holborn
Henry Foster, bricklayer, in Scroop's Court in Holborn
(blank) Slaughter, grocer, near Leather Lane in Holborn
John Lawrence, pewterer, in King's Head Court in Holborn
(blank) Squire, hairseller, in Fulwood's Rents
William Eden, pewterer, in Bartlett's Court
John Eglesfield, victualler, at the Raven in Fetter Lane
William Sheldon, grocer, near the Pump, ditto
    Paid to make up the reckoning this night: 3d.

60. (p. 50) Thursday, 25 August 1715. Present: Mr Cooke, Mr Woodford, Mr Baylis, Mr Lyell, Mr Daye, Mr Younge, Mr Perry, Mr Smythe, Col. Shorey, Major Lechmere, Major Hatley, Mr Warner, Mr Fisher, Mr Bagshaw, Mr Blowen.
    This day Sir Gilbert Heathcote and Mr Craggs did the club the honour to dine with them.

61. List of suspected persons in Tower Ward.
Capt. Nicholas Batchellor, Tower Street
Henry Burlace, ditto
Richard Fabian, ditto
John Winsted, Mincing Lane
John Bamber, surgeon, ditto
John Johnson, ditto
Sir Samuel Ongley, ditto
Joseph Pigott, ditto
William Overy, ditto
Henry Williams, ditto
George Smith, ditto
Sir Samuel Clarke, ditto
(p. 51) Benjamin Gascoign, St Dunstan's Hill
Thomas Loveday, Tower Street
Robert Evans, plumber, ditto
Edward Bridgen, Portugal merchant, ditto
Benjamin Boyden, coffeeman, ditto

John Elderton, pewterer, ditto
Christopher Smith, ditto
Dod Brereton, Idle Lane
Robert Lord, cooper, Cross Lane
James Bedingfeld, Thames Street
Charles Townley, ditto
James Wyke
Ralph Rawlings, ditto
Charles White, ditto
John Coleman, cooper, ditto   *query dead*
Stephen Hudle, ditto
Robert Lekey, Tower Street
Martin Markland, ditto
Peter Bolton, ditto
(p. 52) Gostwick Cox, Tower Street
Thomas Brittle, ditto
Doctor Noy, Tower Hill
James Graves, ditto
Nicholas Hanbury, Seething Lane
John Davis, ditto
John Oliver, ditto
Samuel Nutt, ditto
Samuel Alcorne, ditto
John Lamb, ditto
Francis Hawkins, ditto
Charles Townley, Tower Hill
Samuel Percival, Muscovy Court
William Prescott, ditto
Robert Huckle, ditto
Sander Davis, Seething Lane
Mr Merrey, Mark Lane
Francis Vickers, ditto
Mr Sandiford, ditto
Stephen Bellaise, Hart Street
(p. 53) Edward Jasper, Hart Street
Charles Sergison esq., Navy Office
Dennis Lyddall esq., ditto
Henry Hyde, barber, Hart Street
Nicholas Williamson, Mark Lane
Nathaniel Lloyd, ditto
Joseph Taylor, ditto
Nathaniel Chamberlain, ditto
Edward Worgan, Tower Street
Richard Dart, ditto

62. Mr Woodford and Mr Lyell are desired to speak to Mr John Thompson of Candlewick Ward and Mr Raper of Dowgate Ward that they will become members of this club.

Mr Fisher is desired to speak to Mr Henry Neale of Bridge Ward that he will also become one of the club. Sir Gilbert Heathcote is desired to speak to Capt. Lewis that he will be one of the members for Holborn Side of Farringdon Without. (p. 54) Col. Shorey is desired to speak to Mr Henry Sherbrooke that he will be one of the members for Holborn Side of Farringdon Without. Mr Warner and Mr Daye are desired to speak to Mr Badcock that he will be one of the members for Fleet Street Side of Farringdon Without.

Agreed, that every member of this club do make a collection in his ward to carry on to trial the act of Common Council in 1692 about unfreemen, in the affair of Tower Ward, and pay the same to Mr Cooke who is desired to be treasurer, and he is to issue out the same as he thinks fit for the purpose aforesaid.

Received of Mr Woodford, Mr Baylis and Mr Fisher upon account of the reckoning: £3 4s. 6d.

Memorandum, Mr Trench, though absent, promised to pay his proportion.

63. (p. 55) A list of the several wards, with the divisions and precincts in each ward.

No. 1, Aldersgate Within, five precincts: St Leonard, St John Zachary, St Mary Staining, St Anne, St Martin le Grand.

No. 2, Aldersgate Without, four precincts: first, second, third, fourth.

No. 3, Aldgate, seven precincts: first, second, third, fourth, fifth, sixth, seventh.

(p. 56) No. 4, Bassishaw, two precincts: upper, lower.

No. 5, Billingsgate, six precincts: St Mary at Hill, St Botolph Billingsgate, St Andrew Hubbard, St George Botolph Lane, Pudding Lane, Rood.

No. 6, Bishopsgate Within, five precincts: All Hallows, St Peter Cornhill, St Martin Outwich, St Helen, St Ethelburga.

No. 7, Bishopsgate Without, four divisions: first, second, third, fourth.

(p. 57) No. 8, Bread Street, thirteen precincts: St Peter Cheap and St Mary Magdalen, All Hallows upper and lower, St Mildred upper and lower, St Margaret Moses upper and lower, St Augustine upper and lower, St Nicholas Cole Abbey upper and lower, St John Evangelist, St Matthew.

No. 9, Bridge, fourteen precincts: London Bridge first, second, third; Thames Street first, second, third; (p. 58) New Fish Street first, second, third; St Leonard East Cheap lower and upper; St Benet Gracechurch lower and upper; All Hallows Lombard Street.

No. 10, Broad Street, eight precincts: (upper division) St Mildred and Woolchurch, St Christopher, St Bartholomew Exchange, St Margaret Lothbury; (lower division) St Benet Fink, St Martin Outwich, St Peter le Poor, All Hallows on the Wall.

(p. 59) No. 11, Candlewick, seven precincts: St Mary Abchurch, St Lawrence Pountney, St Martin Orgar, St Clement East Cheap, St Leonard East Cheap, St Michael east and west.

No. 12, Castle Baynard, seven precincts: (first division) St Gregory east, west, south; St Mary Magdalen, St Faith; (second division) St Benet, St Andrew Wardrobe.

(p. 60) No. 13, Cheap, nine precincts: St Mary le Bow, All Hallows

Honey Lane, St Lawrence, Cateaton Street, St Martin Ironmonger Lane, St Mary Colechurch, St Mildred Poultry, St Stephen and St Benet, St Pancras Soper Lane.

No. 14, Coleman Street, six precincts: St Olave Jewry; St Margaret Lothbury; St Stephen Coleman Street first, second, third, fourth.

(p. 61) No. 15, Cordwainer, eight precincts: Aldermary upper and lower, All Hallows Bread Street, St Mary le Bow, St Antholin upper and lower, St Pancras [and] St Benet Sherehog and St John, St Thomas Apostle and Trinity.

No. 16, Cornhill, four precincts: first, second, third, fourth.

No. 17, Cripplegate Within, nine precincts: St Lawrence, St Mary Magdalen Milk Street, St Peter Cheap, St Michael Wood Street, St John Zachary, (p. 62) St Alban Wood Street, St Olave Silver Street, St Alphage, St Mary Aldermanbury.

No. 18, Cripplegate Without, four precincts: Fore Street, Grub Street, Red Cross Street, White Cross Street.

No. 19, Dowgate, eight precincts: (west division) first, second, third, eighth; (east division) fourth, fifth, sixth, seventh.

(p. 63) No. 20, Farringdon Within, seventeen precincts: St Peter Cheap, St Matthew, Goldsmiths Row, Saddlers Hall, Gutter Lane, St Augustine, St Michael le Querne north and south, Monkwell, St Faith Paternoster Row, St Faith Pauls Churchyard, St Martin Ludgate, Christ Church first and second, St Ewen, St Sepulchre, St Anne Blackfriars.

(p. 64) No. 21, Farringdon Without, fifteen precincts: (Holborn Side) St Andrew Holborn, St Bartholomew the Great, St Bartholomew the Less, Smithfield, Church, Old Bailey, Holborn Cross; (Fleet Street Side) St Dunstan West first and second divisions, Fleet, Salisbury Court, New Street, Whitefriars, Bridewell, St Martin Ludgate.

(p. 65) No. 22, Langbourn, twelve precincts: (east division) St Benet Gracechurch, St Dionis Backchurch north and south, St Gabriel Fenchurch, All Hallows Staining; (west division) St Mary Woolnoth north and south, St Nicholas Acon, Birchin Lane, Lombard Street, St Clement Lane, All Hallows Lombard Street.

No. 23, Lime Street, four precincts: first, second, third, fourth.

(p. 66) No. 24, Portsoken, five precincts: Houndsditch, High Street, Barrs, Tower Hill, Convent Garden.

No. 25, Queenhithe, nine precincts: St Michael first, second, third; St Mary Somerset fourth and fifth; St Peter, St Nicholas Cole Abbey and St Mary Mounthaw, St Nicholas Olave, Holy Trinity.

(p. 67) No. 26, Tower, twelve precincts: Dolphin, Mincing Lane, Salutation, Rood, Dice Quay, Ralph's Quay, Bear Quay, Petty Wales, Rose, Seething Lane, Mark Lane, Angel.

No. 27, Vintry, nine precincts: three precincts of St Martin, three precincts of St James Garlickhithe, three upper precincts.

(p. 68) No. 28, Walbrook, seven precincts: St Swithin first and second, St Mary Woolchurch, St Stephen Walbrook, St John Baptist, St Mary Bothaw, St Mary Abchurch.

Wards: 28. Precincts: 220

24

64. (p. 69) Thursday, 1 September 1715. Present: Mr Cooke, Mr Fisher, Mr Daye, Mr Bagshaw.

List of suspected persons in Broad Street Ward.

Christopher Toms, barber, against Stocks Market
Lawrence Andrews, linendraper, against ditto
James Woodward
John Ravis
Robert Cooper
Samuel Herbert
Thomas Ferrall
Thomas Dawson
John Fitch
Daniel Chandler
Edward Kitson
Percival Pott, attorney
William Wright
[blank] Prettyman
Adam Raw
John Taverner, scrivener, Threadneedle Street
Joshua Hoyland, Papist
(p. 70) Peter Olorenshaw, Papist
John Musson, lodger, Papist
[blank], Thornhill's clerk, Papist
George Simmonds
Abraham Vaughan
[blank] Bourn ⎫
[blank] Kelley ⎭ Papists, lodgers at Eaden's
[blank] Savage ⎫
[blank] Markallow ⎭ Papists, lodgers at Lucas's
John Eagle, clockmaker, Lothbury
Christopher Keen
John Long
[blank] Fitzgerald, Papist, at Robins's
John Andrews, attorney, Bartholomew Lane
John Kenyon
John White and lodger
Michael Cartwright
[blank] Stork ⎫
[blank] Keneday ⎭ lodgers at Mrs Hinton's
William Hacksbey
(p. 71) Major William Knight, plumber, Lothbury
Nicholas Swan, Papist
[blank] Coffeer, lodger
Thomas Thorowgood, baker, Lothbury
William Livingston ⎫
Gilbert Goudett ⎭ at Mr Drake's

65. The charge of the last dinner amounts to £12 3s. 7d., which amongst fifteen present comes to 16s. 6d. apiece.

25

Mr Cooke paid	16s. 6d.
Mr Woodford, ditto	16s. 6d.
Mr Baylis, ditto	16s. 6d.
Mr Fisher, ditto	16s. 6d.
Mr Daye, ditto	16s. 6d. ⎫
Mr Younge, ditto	16s. 6d. ⎬ for the cook's bill
Mr Bagshaw, ditto	16s. 6d. ⎭

£5 15s. 6d.

Received by the surplus of the reckoning: 6d.

66. (p. 72) Thursday, 8 September 1715. Present: Mr Daye, Mr Younge.

Ordered, that the club be summoned to meet this day sevennight, and that they have notice 'tis agreed to meet every Thursday till Christmas.

Paid to make up the reckoning this night: 2s. 6d.

67. Thursday, 15 September 1715. Present: Mr Cooke, Mr Warner, Mr Fisher, Major Hatley, Mr Blowen, Col. Shorey, Mr Younge, Mr Bagshaw, Mr Daye.

Mr Warner paid his proportion to the dinner on 5 [*recte* 25] August

	16s. 6d.
Mr Blowen, ditto	16s. 6d.
Major Hatley, ditto	16s. 6d.
Col. Shorey, ditto	16s. 6d.
Mr Perry, ditto	16s. 6d.

Memorandum, to bring a copy of return of Tower Ward Common Councilmen last year.

Paid to make up the reckoning: 1s. 4d.

68. (p. 73) Thursday, 22 September 1715. Present: Mr Cooke, Mr Fisher, Mr Cooper.

Received by the surplus of the reckoning this night: 10d.

69. Thursday, 29 September 1715. Present: Mr Trench, Mr Fisher.

Paid to make up the reckoning this night: 1s.

70. Tuesday, 4 October 1715.

This day Mr Baylis gave direction that the club should be summoned to meet tomorrow night, upon the affair of the land tax book for Bread Street Ward.

71. (p. 74) Wednesday, 5 October 1715. Present: Mr Woodford, Mr Baylis, Col. Shorey, Mr Daye, Mr Younge, Major Hatley, Mr Fisher, Mr Perry.

Agreed to proceed to make collections for the cause in Tower Ward.

The Secretary to go to the absent members and desire them to attend on Thursday sevennight, and give an account of their collections.

Mr Baylis acquainted the club with the difference between the commissioners and assessors in Bread Street Ward about the approbation of collectors of the land tax.

26

The members absent to be sent to, that they and their friends who are commissioners for the land tax do attend at Guildhall on Friday next.

Received by the surplus of the reckoning this night: 2s.

72. Thursday, 6 October 1715.
Received of Major Lechmere for his proportion of the dinner 5 [*recte* 25] August: 16s. 6d.

73. (p. 75) Thursday, 13 October 1715. Present: Major Lechmere, Mr Daye, Mr Cooke, Mr Trench, Mr Woodford, Mr Younge, Major Hatley, Mr Smythe, Mr Bagshaw, Mr Warner, Mr Fisher, Mr Cooper.

This day the club was especially summoned by the order of Mr Woodford to consider of recommending three persons to be admitted to be letter carriers in the General Post Office.

Received of Mr Gabriel Smythe his proportion of the charge of the dinner on 25 August: 16s. 6d.

Cordwainer Ward: Mr Trench recommends to be admitted to be letter carriers in the General Post Office the following persons, Thomas Gyde, a coffeeman in Bow Lane, and John Mathers.

Agreed, that Benjamin Whitebread of Cornhill Ward shall have the precedency of persons recommended for the General Post Office.

(p. 76) The several other wards being elected by way of ballot came up according to the following order: (1) Lime Street, (2) Tower, (3) Vintry, (4) Billingsgate, (5) Bassishaw, (6) Aldgate, (7) Cordwainer, (8) Cheap, (9) Langbourn, (10) Farringdon Within, (11) Broad Street, (12) Cripplegate. And ordered, that the persons nominated for the said wards be recommended according to the above mentioned order.

(p. 77) To the Right Honourable the Lord Cornwallis and James Craggs esq., Postmaster[s] General.

We whose names are hereunder written are of opinion that Benjamin Whitebread, Thomas Mayley and John Middleton are persons fit to be letter carriers for the Post Office. And as such we recommend them to Your Honours, hereby certifying that the persons recommended are honest, zealously affected for His Majesty King George, and citizens and freemen of London.

London, 13 October 1715. [Signed] Charles Cooke, Gabriel Smythe, Thomas Woodford, John Warner, John Hatley, John Younge, Samuel Trench, James Cooper, James Fisher, John Daye, Joshua Bagshaw, Richard Lechmere.

Received by the surplus of the reckoning: 7s.

74. (p. 78) Thursday, 27 October 1715. Present: Major Lechmere, Mr Fisher, Mr Daye.

Paid to make up the reckoning this night at the club: 2s. 6d.

75. Friday, 4 November 1715. Present: Sir Gilbert Heathcote, Sir Richard Houblon, Sir Gregory Page, Mr Craggs, Mr Eyles, Mr Warner, Mr Trench, Mr Younge, Mr London, Mr Cooper, Major Lechmere, Mr

Bagshaw, Mr Cooke, Mr Blowen, Mr Dawson, Mr Perry, Mr Fisher, Major Hatley, Mr Lyell, Col. Shorey, Mr Woodford, Mr Baylis, Mr Thompson.

This day the club were entertained by Mr Woodford at the Crown Tavern behind the Exchange, and Mr Moses Raper for Dowgate Ward and Mr John Thompson for Candlewick Ward were admitted members.

Received by surplus of the reckoning: 10s.

Saturday, 5 November 1715. This day Mr Younge gave directions that the club should be summoned to meet on Monday night next at Mr Bagshaw's about some affairs of importance.

76. (p. 79) Thursday, 10 November 1715. Present: Col. Shorey, Mr Trench, Mr Blowen, Mr Cooke, Mr Cooper, Mr Baylis, Mr Younge, Mr Bagshaw, Major Hatley, Major Lechmere, Mr Daye, Mr Raper, Mr Craggs, Mr Thompson, Mr Woodford, Mr Lloyd, Sir Gilbert Heathcote.

The club were summoned to meet this night by the particular direction of Mr Younge.

Agreed, that endeavours be used to procure the persons underwritten to be elected Common Councilmen on St Thomas's Day next: Aldersgate Within, Mr Thomas Gouge; Aldersgate Without, Mr Tranter (an innholder), Capt. William Smith, Mr Nicholson (a bookseller); Bassishaw, Col. Shorey, Deputy Eyer, Mr John Baker, Mr Samuel Ball; (p. 80) Bread Street, Mr Baylis, Mr Church, Mr Wormlayton, Mr Billers, Mr Marsh, Mr Knapp, Mr Proctor; Cripplegate Within, Deputy Egleton, Major Croshaw, Mr Lavarick, Mr Brookes; Cripplegate Without, Mr Harris, Deputy Blowen, Mr Tew; (p. 81) Tower, Sir Harcourt Masters, Mr Man (a cooper), Mr Thomas Clarke, Mr Beachcroft, Mr Britton, Sir Peter Eaton, Mr Godfrey, Major Lechmere, Mr Harris, Mr Francis Porten, Deputy Langton, Mr Samuel Tatam, Mr Stephen King.

The absent members of the club are desired to bring to the next meeting a list of such persons who will stand for Common Councilmen in their wards.

Agreed, that the validity of the act of Common Council about unfreemen's votes be tried after St Thomas's Day next.

(p. 82) Expedients to be used in the election of Common Councilmen: the Office of Ordnance (to be spoke to), the Navy, the Excise, the Custom House, the Victualling, the Bank, the East India Company, swearing the wards, an association, the unfreemen's votes to be supported, the Post Office, the Pay Office, list of artificers to the Court, Lord Mayor's influence [upon] alehouse keepers.

Memorandum, Mr Lloyd in Golden Lane.

Received by the surplus of the reckoning this night: 4d.

77. (p. 83) Monday, 14 November 1715.

Delivered out the following precinct books: Aldgate Ward to Mr Eyles; Bread Street to Mr Baylis; Candlewick to Mr Thompson; Cordwainer to Mr Trench; Cornhill to Mr Daye.

78. Thursday, 17 November 1715. Present: Mr Cooke, Mr Cooper, Col.

Shorey, Mr Raper, Mr Thompson, Major Lechmere, Mr Perry, Mr Fisher, Mr Eyles, Mr Younge.

Persons to be put in nomination for Common Councilmen in the several wards, and the sums requisite to carry on their interest.

Aldersgate Ward, £60: Christopher Parkinson, John Nicholson, John Whittaker, Thomas Gouge. (p. 84) Aldgate Ward, £100: persons not yet settled. Bassishaw, £30: settled last meeting. Billingsgate, £60: not yet settled. Bread Street, £100: not all settled. Bridge, £60: not yet settled. Broad Street, £40: not yet settled. Candlewick, £50: Mr Henshaw, Deputy Sharpe, Mr Masters, Mr Wilcocks, Mr Hayes, Mr Foster, Mr Hill, Mr David Cooke. (p. 85) Cheap, £40: the present Common Councilmen. Coleman Street, £50: not yet settled. Cordwainer [blank]: not yet settled. Cornhill, £40: not yet settled. Cripplegate Within, £50; not yet settled. Cripplegate Without, £40: not yet settled. Farringdon Within, £100: not yet settled. Langbourn, £20: not yet settled. (p. 86) Lime Street Ward, £20: not yet settled. Portsoken, £50: not yet settled. Queenhithe, £30: not yet settled. Tower, £200: settled last meeting. Vintry, £30: not yet settled. Walbrook, £30: [blank]. 21 wards. Sum total £1,200.

Paid to make up the reckoning at the club this night: 6d.

79. (p. 87) Monday, 21 November 1715.

This day Mr Craggs gave direction that the club be especially summoned to meet next Thursday night about the business of nominating commissioners to swear the inhabitants in the several wards.

80. Tuesday, 22 November 1715.

Delivered new precinct books for Billingsgate Ward to Mr Fisher.

81. (p. 88) Thursday, 24 November 1715. Present: Sir Gilbert Heathcote, Mr Craggs, Mr Woodford, Mr Cooke, Mr Younge, Mr Cooper, Major Hatley, Col. Shorey, Mr Fisher, Mr Thompson, Major Lechmere, Mr Perry, Mr Bagshaw, Mr London, Mr Daye, Mr Eyles, Mr Raper, Mr Baylis, Mr Lloyd.

Persons to be constituted by an Order of Council commissioners to administer the oaths to the inhabitants in the several wards.

Aldgate: Sir Randolph Knipe Kt., John Eyles, John Gore, William Clayton, John Carbonnel, Richard Holditch, John Ludlow, Francis Brown.

Bassishaw: Col. John Shorey, John Baker, Jeremiah Powell, Deputy John Eyer, Samuel Ball.

(p. 89) Billingsgate: Deputy William Jenkins, Joseph Chaplin esq., Charles Russell, Capt. Andrew Phillips, Edward Bellamy, Richard Ives, William Smith (orange merchant), Richard Maundrell.

Bishopsgate Within: Sir Joseph Lawrence Kt. (Alderman), Samuel Shepheard senior esq., Richard Partridge, John Lloyd, Edward Norman, Roger Atlee, Charles Burdett, Christopher Astley, Thomas Griffin, Thomas Hall of St Helen's, Edward Brown, John Shott.

(p. 90) Bishopsgate Without: Richard Chiswell, Charles Cooke, Samuel

Webb, Joseph Huntman, Joseph Eyles, Richard Hopkins of Devonshire Square, Henry Lovell, Capt. Jonathan Parker.

Bread Street: Robert Baylis, William Proctor, Jerome Knapp, James Church, John Wormlayton, Samuel Marsh, William Billers.

(p. 91) Bridge: Sir George Merttins Kt. (Alderman), Arthur Cutten, Henry Neale, Samuel Buck, Richard Savile, James Browne, Richard Clay, Richard Durnford.

Broad Street: Sir Gerard Conyers Kt. (Alderman), Deputy George Frye, John Townsend, David Heywood, Richard Turner, Thomas Cartwright, William Astell, John Dickenson, Robert Burchall, Henry Merttins, Henry Bedell, Richard Skynner.

(p. 92) Candlewick: Sir John Ward Kt. (Alderman and one of the sheriffs), Deputy Sutton Sharpe, Benjamin Henshaw, Edward Masters, Peter Foster, Robert Hayes, William Wilcocks, Thomas Hill, David Cooke, Nathaniel Micklethwaite, Matthew Brandon.

Cheap: Deputy Henry Colchester, John Younge, Samuel Spragg, John Moore, Robert Keynton, Robert Smithson, Benjamin Hill, Robert Norris, Henry Cornish esq., (p. 93) George Wilcocks, Christopher White, John Morgan.

Coleman Street: Deputy Simon Andrews, William Barnesley esq., Philip Constable, Robert Lovick, Daniel Garrett, James Nutcher, Thomas Gibson esq., John Newman.

Cordwainer: Deputy Samuel Hayward, George Morley, Henry King, Samuel Trench, Dr. Zachariah Gibson, Henry Clerke, Benjamin Hatley, Richard Froome.

(p. 94) Cornhill: Sir Thomas Scawen Kt. (Alderman), Deputy Richard Chauncy, John Ellwick, John Blunt, Robert Garbrand, John Wood, John Daye, Gabriel Glover, Joseph Goddard, John Smith, William Pate.

Cripplegate Within: Thomas Uvedale, Robert Mitchell, Thomas Warren, Edward Hulse, Michael Bovell, William Westfield, John Egleton, Robert Foyle, John Wade, (p. 95) Joseph King, Robert Croshaw, Samuel Lavarick, Zachariah Gisburne.

Farringdon Within: William Fawkener, Humphrey Thayer, Anthony Kingsley, William Birkes, John Edwards, Thomas Simpson, Daniel Midwinter, John Baskett, Samuel Ashurst of Paternoster Row, John Evans, Francis Musters, John Williams of Blackfriars, John Tayler of Blackfriars, Samuel Hoole, Major John Hatley, (p. 96) Joseph Beachcroft, Nicholas Toke, Thomas Rose, William Hulls of Newgate Street.

Langbourn: Sir Peter Delme Kt. (Alderman), Deputy John Cooper, Jonathan Miles esq., Lawrence Hatsell, Henry Herring, John Lloyd, Jeremiah Marlow, Henry Hankey, William Ingram, William Potter.

Lime Street: Deputy Lancelot Skynner, Joshua Bagshaw, Benjamin Ashwood, Henry Tombes, Jeoffery Staines.

(p. 97) Portsoken: Samuel Perry esq., William Brassey, John Dodson, Capt. John Hawkins, Capt. John Williams.

Tower: Sir Harcourt Masters, Deputy John Langton, Sir Peter Eaton, Charles Savage, Thomas Clarke, Samuel Beachcroft, John Britton, Peter Godfrey esq., Richard Harris, Richard Lechmere, Francis Porten, James

Paitfield, Stephen King, Richard Merriweather, Robert Jeffs, (p. 98) Robert Godfrey, John Bly, Joseph Windmills.

Vintry: Deputy William Cooke, John Samwaies, Henry Greenaway, Robert Smith, Joseph Wriglesworth, Bartholomew Clarke, Lieut. Col. Samuel Westal, Edmund Trench, John Cooper.

Walbrook: Sir Samuel Moyer, Deputy John West, Robert Stockdale, John Lane esq., Richard West, Samuel Keynton, Nathaniel Torriano, (p. 99) Matthew Shepherd, Francis Jackson.

82. A computation of the Whigs (marked A) and the Tories (marked B) which may be elected in the next Common Council.

	A	B		A	B
Aldgate	3	3	Cripplegate	2	10
Aldersgate	—	8	Dowgate	—	8
Bassishaw	4	—	(p. 100) Farringdon		
Billingsgate	6	4	Within	—	15
Bishopsgate	3	11	Farringdon Without	—	16
Bread Street	1	11	Langbourn	10	—
Bridge	4	11	Lime Street	3	1
Castle Baynard	1	9	Portsoken	5	—
Broad Street	10	—	Queenhithe	—	6
Cheap	12	—	Tower	6	6
Cornhill	6	—	Vintry	7	2
Cordwainer	8	—	Walbrook	6	2
Coleman Street	6	—			
Candlewick	8	—	Total	111	123

A computation of the charge to promote an interest in the several wards: Aldersgate, £60; Bassishaw, £30; Billingsgate, £60; Bread Street, £100; Bridge, £60; Broad Street, £20; Candlewick, £30; Cheap, £40; (p. 101) Coleman Street, £30; Cornhill, £40; Cripplegate Within, £50; Farringdon Within, £100; Langbourn, £20; Portsoken, £50; Tower, £200; Queenhithe, £20; Vintry, £20. Total, £930.

Ordered, that the club be especially summoned to meet on Monday night next to complete the list of commissioners for swearing the several wards.

Received by the surplus of the reckoning this night: 9s. 10d.

83. (p. 102) Monday, 28 November 1715. Present: Col. Shorey, Major Hatley, Mr Fisher, Mr Cooper, Mr Younge, Mr Thayer, Mr Sherbrooke, Mr Thompson, Mr Trench, Capt. Langley, Mr Daye, Mr Craggs, Mr Woodford, Mr Holditch, Mr Lant, Mr Cooke, Sir Harcourt Masters, Mr Lyell, Mr Warner, Mr Baskett, Mr Bagshaw.

Commissioners nominated for swearing the inhabitants in the several wards following.

Aldersgate Within: John Cartlitch, Thomas Gouge.

Aldersgate Without: Capt. William Smith, Capt. Christopher Parkinson, John Maud, John Whittaker, Francis Hole.

Cripplegate Without: Samuel Acton, John Harris, Thomas Catmore, Edward Buxton, Richard Farrington.

31

(p. 103) Dowgate: Sir Francis Forbes Kt. (Alderman), John Kendrick, John Harris, Abraham Foster, Josiah Nicholson, William Hughs, William Jolly.

Queenhithe: Sir John Fryer Bt. (Alderman and one of the sheriffs), Francis Foster, John Grant, Daniel Cockerill.

Ordered that the club be summoned to meet on Thursday next at six in the evening at the Crown Tavern behind the Exchange.

Q[uere] Liber Albus, modus eligendi commune concilium.[1]

Paid the reckoning of the club this night by order of Mr Craggs: £1 2s. 4d.

1. *Liber Albus: The White Book of the City of London*, trs. H. T. Riley (London, 1862), see pp. 397–99.

84. (p. 104) Tuesday, 29 November 1715.

Commissioners to be appointed to swear the inhabitants in the ward of Farringdon Without: Sir Robert Child Kt. (Alderman), John Nicholl, Nathaniel Rokeby, John Tayleur, Edward Edwards, Thomas Plasted, John Hibbert, John Darby, Richard Rider, Capt. John Lewis, Henry Sherbrooke, Nathaniel May, William Gardiner, Lieut. Col. Robert Gower, Timothy Goodwin, Capt. George Jenkins, Anthony Keck, James Seamer, (p. 105) Richard Hodgson, Herbert Herriott, Richard Badcock.

Castle Baynard: Dr George Paul, William Hayford, Ephraim Crow, Atkinson Bugby, William Territt, John Paitfield, John Rowland, John Peachy, Capt. Francis Horton, Awnsham Churchill, Thomas Walters, Timothy Childe, John Young.

85. Wednesday, 30 November 1715.

Delivered the list of commissioners for swearing the inhabitants in the several wards to the Lord Townshend by order of Mr Craggs. [Signed] D[avid] L[e] G[ros].

86. (p. 106) Thursday, 1 December 1715. Present: Sir Gregory Page, Mr Craggs, Mr Eyles, Mr Woodford, Mr Holditch, Sir Harcourt Masters, Major Lechmere, Mr Lyell, Mr Younge, Col. Shorey, Major Hatley, Mr Cooke, Mr Cooper, Mr Fisher, Mr Trench, Mr Warner, Mr Thomas Walker (Commissioner, Customs), Mr Brookes, Mr Nicholas, Mr Badcock, Capt. Jenkins, Mr Paitfield, Mr Gale (Commissioner, Excise), Deputy Egleton, Mr Lloyd, Mr Baskett, (p. 107) Mr Bagshaw, Mr Perry, Mr White, Mr London, Mr Morgan, Sir Gilbert Heathcote, Sir William Humfreys, Mr Nathaniel Herne, Mr Thompson, Mr George Wright, Sir John Fryer, Mr Staines, Mr Richard Harris, Mr Pitman, Mr Aislaby, Mr Edward Edwards.

(p. 106) Ordered, that a proper person be appointed in each ward to solicit the poorer sort of people in behalf of the A [Whig] candidates for Common Council.

Ordered, that lists of the candidates be given the solicitors for that purpose.

Paid to the reckoning this night by the order of Mr Craggs: £1 16s. 10d.

Ordered, that the association be engrossed upon twenty-six skins of parchment and sent to every ward to be subscribed upon St Thomas's Day next.

Ordered, that the club be again summoned to meet on Monday night next upon special affairs.

87. (p. 107) Friday, 2 December 1715.

This day sent the precinct books of Castle Baynard Ward to Mr Paitfield, a mercer, at the Black Moor's Head upon Ludgate Hill.

88. (p. 108) Monday, 5 December 1715. Present: Mr Thompson, Mr Daye, Mr Lloyd, Mr Gouge, Mr Fisher, Mr Cooper, Major Hatley, Mr Young (Castle Baynard), Mr Eyles, Mr Cooke, Sir Harcourt Masters, Mr Lyell, Mr Trench, Col. Shorey, Mr Craggs, Major Lechmere, Mr Paitfield, Mr Warner, Mr Bagshaw, Mr Woodford, Mr Raper, Mr Baskett, Mr Perry.

Alterations in the commissioners for swearing the wards.

Aldgate: to be added, Sir Benjamin Ayloffe, Robert Heysham, John Mayhew, David Petty, Henry Smith, Micajah Perry.

Cripplegate Without: to be left out, Samuel Acton, Capt. Thomas Catmore; to be added, Richard Blowen, Samuel Thayer.

(p. 109) Aldersgate Within: to be added, Isaac Grevil.

Castle Baynard Ward: to be allowed £50.

Aldersgate Ward: Mr Gouge and Mr Hole may be chosen Common Councilmen if Mr Cartlitch and Capt. Smith will join their interest with them, and Capt. Garrard to speak to his father.

Castle Baynard Ward: there are now two good, and the representatives hope to elect four more good.

Billingsgate Ward: they are not yet settled in their candidates.

Bridge Ward: they meet this night to consider of candidates to be put up.

Farringdon Within: have agreed upon most of their candidates.

Farringdon Without: to be allowed [blank].

(p. 110) Committee to issue money: Mr Thompson, Mr Daye, Mr Raper, Major Hatley, Mr Baskett, Mr Fisher, Major Lechmere, or three, to draw warrants upon D[avid] L[e] G[ros] for such sums as they shall think proper for the service of the several wards. And to be summoned to meet next Thursday at five.

Paid the reckoning by order of Mr Craggs: £1 3s. 6d.

Received of Mr Craggs to be paid as a quorum of the above named committee shall direct: £500.

89. Tuesday, 6 December 1715.

1. Castle Baynard Ward, paid to Mr Paitfield and Mr Young, as per warrant: £12 10s.

90. (p. 111) Thursday, 8 December 1715. Present: Mr Raper, Mr Daye, Major Lechmere, Major Hatley, Mr Eyles, Mr Woodford, Mr Cooper, Col. Shorey, Mr Trench, Deputy Egleton, Mr Gouge, Sir Harcourt Masters, Mr London, Mr Younge, Mr Lyell, Mr Fisher, Mr Lloyd, Sir Gilbert Heathcote, Mr Baskett, Mr Craggs.

2. Cornhill, paid to Mr Daye as per warrant: £10.

3. Farringdon Within, paid Major John Hatley as per warrant: £25.
4. Tower, paid Major Richard Lechmere as per warrant: £50.
5. Aldgate, paid Mr Eyles as per warrant: £30.
6. Bassishaw, paid Col. Shorey as per warrant: £7 10s.
7. Vintry, paid Mr Cooper as per warrant: £10.
8. Cripplegate Without, paid Mr John Lloyd as per warrant: £10.
9. Cheap, paid Mr John Daye, for Mr John Younge, as per warrant: £10.
(p. 112) 10. Queenhithe, paid Mr Cooper, for Capt. Langley, as per warrant: £15.
11. Bread Street, paid Mr Woodford as per warrant: £10.
12. Coleman Street, paid Mr London as per warrant: £7 10s.
Paid the reckoning this night by order of Mr Craggs: £1 2s. 4d.

91. Friday, 9 December 1715.
13. Paid Mr Baylis as per warrant for Bread Street Ward: £25.
14. Portsoken, paid Mr Perry as per warrant: £12 10s.

92. (p. 113) Saturday, 10 December 1715.
15. Castle Baynard, paid more to Mr Paitfield as per warrant: £12 10s.
Memorandum, the committee to be summoned to meet next Tuesday at six in the evening.

93. Tuesday, 13 December 1715.
16. Paid more to Major John Hatley as per warrant: £25.
17. Paid Mr Fisher as per warrant: £15.
Ordered, that the club be summoned to meet on Thursday next at six of the clock in the evening precisely upon extraordinary business.

94. Wednesday, 14 December 1715.
18. Paid more to Mr John Daye as per warrant: £10.
19. Paid more to ditto for Mr John Younge of Cheap as per warrant: £10.
(p. 114) Associations delivered to the several wards: Bassishaw, to Col. Shorey; Bread Street, to Mr Baylis; Castle Baynard, to Mr Young (Paul's Churchyard); Cheap, to Mr Younge (Cheapside); Cripplegate Within, to Deputy Egleton; Farringdon Within, to Major Hatley; Farringdon Without (Fleet Street Side), to Mr Badcock; Queenhithe, to Capt. Langley; Cordwainer, to Mr Trench.

95. (p. 115) Thursday, 15 December 1715. Present: Mr Cooke, Mr Trench, Deputy Egleton, Mr Raper, Capt. Langley, Major Lechmere, Mr Daye, Mr Badcock, Mr Cooper, Mr Woodford, Sir Harcourt Masters, Mr Lyell, Mr Younge, Mr Paitfield, Mr Fisher, Mr Young (Castle Baynard), Sir Theodore Janssen, Mr Holditch, Mr Perry, Mr Warner, Sir Gilbert Heathcote, Mr Craggs, Mr Bagshaw, Mr Baskett, Mr Baylis, Major Hatley, Mr Lloyd.
20. Farringdon Without, paid to Mr Warner as per warrant: £10.
21. Tower, paid more to Major Lechmere as per warrant: £50.

22. Aldersgate, paid to Mr James Cooper, for Mr Thomas Gouge, as per warrant: £15.

23. Cripplegate Within, paid Mr Deputy Egleton as per warrant: £5 7s. 6d.

24–6. Candlewick, paid Mr John Thompson as per three several warrants: £22 10s.

27. Queenhithe, paid more to Capt. Langley as per warrant: £10.

(p. 116) 28–9. Portsoken, paid Mr Samuel Perry more as per two warrants: £25.

Paid the reckoning of the club this night by order of Mr Craggs: 14s. 10d.

Received more of Mr Craggs to be paid as a quorum of the committee appointed the fifth instant shall direct: £500.

Associations delivered out this day to the several wards following: Aldersgate, to Mr Gouge; Aldgate, to Mr Eyles; Billingsgate, to Mr Fisher; Bishopsgate, to Mr Cooke; Bridge, to Mr Samuel Buck; Broad Street, to Capt. Cartwright; Candlewick, to Mr Thompson; Coleman Street, to Mr London; Cornhill, to Mr Daye; (p. 117) Cripplegate Without, to Mr Lloyd; Farringdon Without (for Holborn Side), to Mr Sherbrooke; Langbourn, to Mr Hankey; Lime Street, to Mr Bagshaw; Portsoken, to Mr Perry; Tower, to Sir Harcourt Masters; Vintry, to Mr James Cooper; Walbrook, to Mr John Lane.

96. Friday, 16 December 1715.
Dowgate association delivered to Mr Cooper.

30. Cripplegate Without, paid Mr Lloyd more as per warrant: £15.

31. Farringdon Within, paid Mr Baskett, for Major Hatley, more as per warrant: £25.

Bishopsgate Within association delivered to Mr Christopher Astley.

97. (p. 118) Saturday, 17 December 1715.
32. Cheap, paid more to Mr John Younge as per warrant: £10.

33. Cripplegate Within, paid more to Mr John Egleton as per warrant: £10 15s.

34–6. Langbourn, paid to Mr Hankey as per three warrants: £15.

98. Monday, 19 December 1715.
37. Castle Baynard, paid more to Mr John Paitfield as per warrant: £12 10s.

38–9. Bread Street, paid more to Robert Baylis esq. as per two warrants: £50.

40. Castle Baynard, paid more to Mr Paitfield as per warrant: £12 10s.

99. (p. 119) Tuesday, 20 December 1715.
41–2. Billingsgate, paid more to Mr Fisher as per two warrants: £30.

43. Cheap, paid more to Mr Younge as per warrant: £10.

44. Tower, paid more to Major Lechmere as per warrant: £50.

100. Saturday, 24 December 1715.
45. Cripplegate Without, paid more to Mr John Lloyd as per warrant: £50.

101. Tuesday, 27 December 1715.

46. Farringdon Within, paid more to Major John Hatley as per warrant: £25.

102. (p. 120) Thursday, 29 December 1715. Present: Mr Cooke, Mr Fisher, Col. Shorey, Mr Trench, Mr Younge, Mr Lloyd, Mr Eyles, Mr Daye, Mr Craggs, Mr Woodford, Mr Thompson.

Ordered, that the matter of choosing committees in Common Council be taken into consideration at the next meeting.

Ordered, that the committee lately appointed to make out dividend warrants be summoned to meet on Monday next at six in the evening.

47. Cornhill, paid more to Mr John Daye as per warrant: £5.

48. Cripplegate Without, paid more to Mr John Lloyd as per warrant: £6 9s.

Received by the surplus of the reckoning this night: 3s 10d.

103. (p. 121) Monday, 2 January 1716. Present: Col. Shorey, Major Hatley, Mr Daye, Mr Raper, Mr Fisher.

Letters to be sent to all the gentlemen who have had money that they are desired to be at the next meeting when the account is to be made up.

49. Bassishaw, paid more to Col. John Shorey as per warrant: £7 10s.

Paid to make up the reckoning this night: 3s.

104. (p. 122) Thursday, 5 January 1716. Present: Mr Perry, Mr Bagshaw, Col. Shorey, Mr Egleton, Capt. Langley, Mr Cooper, Mr Younge, Mr Fisher, Mr Eyles, Mr Lloyd, Mr Woodford, Major Lechmere.

Castle Baynard expenses: £49 19s.

Candlewick expenses: £27 1s. 2d.

Queenhithe expenses: £45 13s. 1d.

Billingsgate expenses: £26 17s. 7d. Ditto, more for copy of the poll: 10s.

50–1. Broad Street, paid more to Mr Woodford as per two warrants: £10.

Received by the surplus of the reckoning this night: 5s. 6d.

105. Tuesday, 10 January 1716.

Memorandum, Mr Woodford gave direction that the club be summoned to meet on Thursday next.

106. (p. 123) Thursday, 12 January 1716. Present: Col. Shorey, Mr Trench, Capt. Langley, Mr Daye, Mr Cooper, Mr Gouge, Mr Cooke, Mr Younge, Mr Fisher, Mr Egleton, Mr Eyles, Mr Craggs, Mr Thompson, Sir Gilbert Heathcote, Major Lechmere, Mr Bagshaw, Major Hatley, Mr Woodford.

Aldgate expenses: £51 13s. 6d.

Vintry expenses: £13 16s. 6d.

Langbourn expenses: £18 10s. 4d.

Members in the Common Council who may be influenced.

Aldersgate Within: Major John Smart, by Dr Fauquier and Sir Gilbert

Heathcote; Deputy Lawrence Coles, by the Lord Mayor [Sir Charles Peers]; Capt. Joseph Bird, by Sir Daniel Wray, and he by Lord Mayor.

Aldersgate Without: Capt. Wild, by Mr Vincent (Stationer to the Excise), by Mr Morris (the undertaker), and by Mr Sprint; Capt. William Smith, by Sir Randolph Knipe.

Aldgate: Deputy George Waylett, by Mr John Eyles.

Bassishaw: Deputy John Eyer, by Mr Nathaniel Herne; (p. 124) William Monck, by Col. John Shorey.

Billingsgate: Joseph Shepherd, by Mr James Fisher and Mr John Thompson; John Godden, by Sir William Humfreys and Mr Clay; Joseph Chaplin, by Lord Mayor and Mr Henry Hankey.

Bishopsgate Within: John Lloyd, by Mr John Daye; Henry Durley, by Commissioners of the Navy, Mr Samuel Shepheard, and Mr John Thompson.

Broad Street: Robert Burchall, by Sir John Ward.

Bridge: James Tallman, by Mr James Fisher and Mr Richard Clay; Richard Durnford, by ditto; James Brook, by Mr John Baskett.

Castle Baynard: Francis Mollineux, by Lord Falkland; Benjamin Tomlinson, by Mr Henry Cornish. [Both] *by Duke Kingston and Mr Thomas Gibson.*

(p. 125) Cornhill: John Ellwick, by Sir Gregory Page; John Blunt, by Mr Samuel Shepheard.

Cripplegate Within: Benjamin Russell (*dead*), by Col. Peter Lekeux.

Dowgate: Anthony Tournay Deputy, by Sir Gregory Page; William Tate, by Sir Gilbert Heathcote; Edward Lascells, by Mr John Dickenson, Capt. Nicholls, Mr Peter Foster, and Mr Stockdale.

Farringdon Within: Benjamin Bound, by Major Richard Lechmere, Mr Baskett, and Mr Simpson; Francis West, by South Sea Company and Mr Samuel Shepheard; Charles Wood, by Mr John London.

Farringdon Without: Robert Vincent, by Commissioners of the Excise; Paul Jarvis, King's Whipmaker.

(p. 126) Portsoken: Deputy Peter Monger, under prosecution.

Queenhithe: John Barber, under prosecution by the Secretary of State; Abraham Sewen, by Mr Lloyd of Cripplegate Without; Joseph Ayliffe, by Commissioners of Soap Duties.

Vintry: memorandum, Mr Gillam, master joiner at Greenwich Hospital, showed to the B's [Tories] a letter which directed him to vote for the A's [Whigs].

Query, what Common Councilmen have not taken the oaths at the sessions?

Received by the surplus of the reckoning this night: 7s.

107. (p. 127) Thursday, 19 January 1716. Present: Mr Eyles, Mr Bagshaw, Mr Cooper, Mr Fisher, Mr Raper, Sir Gilbert Heathcote, Mr Thayer, Mr Younge, Mr Lyell, Major Lechmere, Mr Craggs, Mr Woodford.

Aldersgate Within expenses: £15 19s. 5d.

Farringdon Within, to be influenced: Charles Wood, by Mr John London; Thomas Harris, by Mr Humphrey Thayer; Augustin Marriot, by Mr Toke.

52. Aldersgate Without, paid to Mr Tranter, per Mr Craggs, as per warrant: £5 7s. 6d.

53. Aldgate, paid to Mr John Eyles more as per warrant, £21 13s. 6d. Received by the surplus of the reckoning this night: 7s. 6d.

108. (p. 128) Thursday, 26 January 1716. Present: Mr Trench, Major Lechmere, Capt. Langley, Mr Fisher, Mr Lloyd, Mr Thompson, Mr Bagshaw.

54. Candlewick, paid more to Mr John Thompson as per warrant: £4 11s.

55. Vintry, paid more to Mr James Cooper as per warrant: £3 16s. 6d.

56. Langbourn, paid more to Mr Henry Hankey as per warrant: £3 10s. 4d.

109. (p. 129) Thursday, 2 February 1716. Present: Mr Trench, Mr Gough, Major Lechmere, Major Hatley, Capt. Langley, Mr Baylis, Mr Craggs, Mr Bagshaw.

B [Tory] Common Councilmen made good.

Aldersgate Within: Major John Smart, by Mr Gouge and Dr Fauquier; Mr John Cartlitch will be absent.

Aldersgate Without: Capt. John Wild, by Mr Sprint; Capt. William Smith [blank].

Aldgate: Deputy George Waylett, by Mr Eyles.

Bassishaw: Deputy John Eyer, by Mr Nathaniel Herne.

Castle Baynard: Mr Francis Mollineux will be absent.

Queenhithe: Abraham Sewen, by Mr Lloyd of Cripplegate Without.

Tower: Nicholas Hanbury [blank].

(p. 130) Committee of Common Council to address: [Aldermen] Sir Gilbert Heathcote, Sir John Ward; [Common Councilmen] Sir Harcourt Masters, Mr Richard Harris, Mr John Eyles, Major Lechmere, Sir Randolph Knipe, Richard Turner, William Astell, William Timms, Gabriel Smythe, Henry Hankey, Deputy Lancelot Skynner, Col. William Cooke.

Received by the surplus of the reckoning: 4s. 6d.

Memorandum, Mr Craggs gave direction that the club be summoned to meet next Thursday night upon particular business.

110. (p. 131) Friday, 3 February 1716.

57. Tower, paid more to Major Lechmere as per warrant: £50.

111. Thursday, 9 February 1716. Present: Mr Cooke, Major Lechmere, Mr Warner, Mr Fisher, Mr Daye, Mr Egleton, Mr Younge, Mr Craggs, Mr Baylis, Mr Perry, Capt. Langley, Mr Thompson, Mr Bagshaw.

Common Councilmen to be summoned to meet to consider of choosing committees: Sir Randolph Knipe, Mr John Eyles, Samuel Shepheard esq., Mr Robert Baylis, Richard Turner, Mr John Younge, Capt. John Heron, Mr Samuel Trench, Mr John Daye, Mr Gabriel Smythe, Mr Henry Hankey, Mr Lawrence Hatsell, Mr John Baker, (p. 132) Mr Deputy Samuel Hayward, Mr Benjamin Henshaw, Mr Joshua Bagshaw, Sir

Harcourt Masters, Major Lechmere, Mr Richard Harris, Sir Peter Eaton, Lt. Col. Cooke, Mr Robert Stockdale, Lt. Col. Westal, Mr Thomas Gibson.

The Aldermen Sir Gilbert Heathcote shall nominate to appoint the time when the above gentlemen shall be summoned to meet.

Memorandum, summoned to meet next Thursday by order of Sir Gilbert Heathcote.

Cripplegate Within expenses: £11 13s.

Received back from Mr Deputy Egleton of Cripplegate Within: £4 9s. 6d.

Received back from Mr John Warner of Farringdon Without: £4 8s.

Received by the surplus of the reckoning this night: 8s. 3d.

112. (p. 133) Thursday, 16 February 1716. Present: Sir Gilbert Heathcote, Sir William Humfreys, Sir Randolph Knipe, Sir Harcourt Masters, Mr John Eyles, Mr John Baker, Mr Baylis, Mr John Younge, Capt. Heron, Mr Thomas Gibson, Deputy Hayward, Mr Samuel Trench, Mr Daye, Mr Hatsell, Mr Bagshaw, Major Lechmere, Mr Richard Harris, Col. Westal, Mr Stockdale, Mr Woodford, Mr Fisher.

Committees agreed upon to be elected at the next Common Council.

Committee to address (four [Aldermen] and eight [Common Councilmen]): Sir Gilbert Heathcote, Sir William Stewart, Sir Thomas Scawen, Sir John Ward; Sir Randolph Knipe, Mr John Eyles, Mr William Astell [deleted and replaced by] Samuel Shepheard, Mr Thomas Gibson, Mr Deputy Lancelot Skynner, Sir Harcourt Masters, Lt. Col. Westal, Mr Robert Stockdale.

(p. 134) Committee City Lands: [Aldermen] to be continued, Sir Thomas Abney, Sir Samuel Stanier, Sir William Humfreys, Sir John Cass, Sir Gerard Conyers, Sir John Fryer; [Common Councilmen] to be continued, Mr George Ludlam, Mr Deputy Edmunds, Mr William Nutt; [new Common Councilmen] Mr Deputy Waylett, Lt. Col. Westal, Mr Richard Turner, Mr Lawrence Hatsell, Mr Henry Greenaway, Mr Joshua Bagshaw, Mr Richard Clay, Mr Deputy Chauncy [deleted and replaced by] George Wilcocks, Mr Benjamin Henshaw.

(p. 135) Memorandum, Sir Randolph Knipe to move that the order of Common Council, 1692, may be read, and to be seconded by Col. Westal.

Committee Irish Society: Sir Gilbert Heathcote (Vintner), Governor; Mr William Monck (Draper), Deputy Governor; [Aldermen] to be continued, Sir Samuel Garrard (Grocer), Sir Richard Hoare (Goldsmith), Sir James Bateman (Fishmonger), Sir John Cass (Skinner), Sir Francis Forbes (Haberdasher); [Common Councilmen] to be continued, Mr Thomas Harris (Merchant Taylor), Mr William Unett (Haberdasher), Mr John Becher (Salter), (p. 136) Mr Benjamin Wells (Ironmonger), Mr Thomas Preston (Vintner), Mr Braham Smith (Clothworker); [new Common Councilmen], Mr John Daye [deleted and replaced by] Richard Chauncy (Mercer), Mr John Ellwick (Mercer), Mr Gabriel Smythe (Grocer), Mr Thomas Gibson (Draper), Mr Robert Stockdale (Fishmonger), Mr Deputy Hayward (Goldsmith), Mr Charles Lloyd (Skinner),

Mr Benjamin Hill (Merchant Taylor), Mr Samuel Trench (Salter), Mr Robert Edwards (Ironmonger), Mr Richard Truby (Vintner), Sir Randolph Knipe (Clothworker).

The same gentlemen who were present this night to be summoned for Wednesday next.

Received by the surplus of the reckoning this night: 11s. 2d.

113. (p. 137) Wednesday, 22 February 1716. Present: Sir Gerard Conyers, Sir Harcourt Masters, Mr Samuel Shepheard, Col. Westal, Major Lechmere, Mr Younge, Mr Trench, Mr Baker, Mr Stockdale, Mr Gibson, Mr Fisher, Mr Bagshaw, Sir Gilbert Heathcote, Sir Randolph Knipe, Mr Baylis, Mr Woodford, Mr Eyles, Mr Daye.

Ordered, that Mr Samuel Shepheard be of the committee to draw up an address in the room of Mr William Astell.

Ordered, that a copy of the committees settled by this club be sent to every A [Whig] member of the Common Council, and that they be desired to attend punctually at the hour of summons.

The number of A [Whigs], B [Tories], and C [doubtful] in the Common Council, *anno* 1716.

	A	B	C		A	B	C
Aldersgate Within	—	2	2	Cornhill	6	—	—
Aldersgate Without	—	2	2	Cripplegate Within	1	7	—
Aldgate	3	1	2	Cripplegate Without	—	4	—
Bassishaw	2	—	2	Dowgate	—	7	1
[Billingsgate	2	6	2][1]	Farringdon Within	—	15	—
Bishopsgate Within	2	8	—	Farringdon Without	—	16	—
Bishopsgate Without	—	4	—	Langbourn	10	—	—
Bread Street	—	12	—	Lime Street	4	—	—
(p. 138) Bridge	2	11	2	Portsoken	—	4	1
Broad Street	10	—	—	Queenhithe	—	6	—
Candlewick	8	—	—	Tower	9	1	2
Castle Baynard	1	7	2	Vintry	8	1	—
Cheap	12	—	—	Walbrook	7	—	1
Coleman Street	6	—	—				
Cordwainer	7	—	1		100	114	20

(p. 139) Councilmen to be influenced and by whom: Major John Smart, by Dr Fauquier; Mr John Cartlitch, by ditto; Mr Deputy Robinson, by Capt. William Smith; Capt. William Smith, by Sir Randolph Knipe, Mr William Astell and Navy Office; Sir Benjamin Ayloffe, by Sir Randolph Knipe; Mr Deputy Eyer, by Mr London to keep away; Mr William Monck, by Col. Shorey; Mr Joseph Shepherd, by Mr Fisher; Mr Richard Maundrell, by ditto; Mr John Lloyd (B[ishopsgate Within]), by Mr Partridge; Mr James Tallman, by Mr Fisher; Mr Francis Mollineux, by Mr Thomas Gibson; Mr Christopher Bateman, by ditto and by Dr Mead; Mr John Farr, by Mr Samuel Trench; Mr Edward Lascells, by Mr Stockdale, Mr Peter Foster and Mr Samuel Trench; (p. 140) John Bridge, by Sir Randolph Knipe; Nicholas Hanbury, by Major Lechmere and Mr Francis Porten; Mr Deputy Langton, by Major Lechmere.

Paid to make up the reckoning of the club this night: 3s.

1. The secretary omitted Billingsgate; however, his totals include the ward and indicate the partisan distribution listed above.

114. Thursday, 1 March 1716. Present: Major Hatley.
Paid to the reckoning: 1s.

115. (p. 141) Thursday, 8 March 1716. Present: Major Lechmere, Major Hatley, Mr Bagshaw.
Paid to make up the reckoning of the club this night: 3s. 6d.

116. Friday, 9 March 1716.
58. Bread Street, paid more to Mr Baylis as per warrant: £25.

117. Friday, 16 March 1716.
Paid Mr Meere (the printer) for printing 300 lists of the Common Council in octavo: 12s.

118. Tuesday, 1 May 1716.
Paid a messenger for carrying out lists of the committees to several Common Councilmen: 1s. 6d.
Paid ditto for carrying out thirty-one summons to meet next Thursday: 2s. 6d.

119. (p. 142) Thursday, 3 May 1716. Present: Sir Randolph Knipe, Mr Turner, Deputy Chauncy, Major Lechmere, Mr Thompson, Mr Cooper, Col. Shorey, Deputy Egleton, Mr Clay, Mr Wilcocks, Mr Warner, Mr Eyles, Mr Holditch, Sir Harcourt Masters, Mr Cooke, Mr Younge, Mr Fisher, Mr Trench, Mr Gibson, Sir Gilbert Heathcote, Mr Woodford.
Mr Deputy Chauncy to be of the Committee Irish Society in the room of Mr Daye.
The lists formerly agreed to for committees to be presented at the next Common Council.
Persons to nominate committees in Common Council: Col. Cooke, Col. Shorey, Major Lechmere, Mr Younge, Sir Harcourt Masters, Mr Eyles, Sir Randolph Knipe, Mr Turner, Mr Hatsell, Col. Westal, Mr White, Mr Astell. And to meet next Tuesday night at seven in the evening.
Mr Wilcocks to be of the Committee City Lands in the room of Deputy Chauncy.
Memorandum, the committees City Lands and Irish Society to be first chosen in the Common Council.
Received by surplus of the reckoning: 7s. 6d.

120. (p. 143) Saturday, 5 May 1716.
Paid for carrying out twelve letters: 1s.

121. Tuesday, 8 May 1716. Present: Sir Gilbert Heathcote, Mr Woodford, Col. Cooke, Col. Shorey, Major Lechmere, Sir Randolph Knipe, Col. Westal, Mr Turner, Mr White, Mr Astell.

Adjourned to Thursday night next at seven, and the twelve managers to be summoned.

Paid to the reckoning: 5s. 10d.

122. Wednesday, 9 May 1716.
Paid with twelve letters to managers to choose committees: 1s.

123. (p. 144) Thursday, 10 May 1716. Present: Mr Woodford, Mr Younge, Major Lechmere, Mr White, Col. Westal, Mr Turner, Mr Hatsell, Sir Gilbert Heathcote.

Sir Gilbert Heathcote to move for an address if he thinks proper.

The three committees, for address, City Lands and Irish Society, distributed amongst the managers to nominate.

Received by surplus of reckoning: 1s. 2d.

124. Friday, 11 May 1716.
Paid messenger with letters: 6d.

125. Thursday, 23 August 1716.
Received back from Mr James Fisher of Billingsgate Ward: £25 13s. 6d.

126. (p. 145) Thursday, 15 November 1716. Present: Mr Baylis, Mr Warner, Mr Trench, Sir Gerard Conyers, Mr Younge, Mr Cooke, Mr Craggs, Mr Woodford, Mr Thompson, Sir Gilbert Heathcote, Sir William Humfreys, Sir Harcourt Masters, Sir Charles Peers, Mr Gibson, Mr Recorder [Sir William Thompson], Mr Fisher, Mr Lyell, Mr London.

This meeting was summoned to consider of the choice of a new Common Council, and in what wards it might be proper to make an interest.

In Cheap Ward, four of the old Common Council desire to decline that office for next year, viz.: Moore, Spragg, Smithson, and Norris. Mr Younge says they can choose the same Common Councilmen or others in their room.

Sir Harcourt Masters [Tower] says they can choose good men, but must have two new Common Councilmen in the room of Col. Porten and Major Lechmere. Mr Loveday was recommended by Sir Charles Peers and Mr Thompson to be re-elected, he having been disgusted by Sir Samuel Clarke.

Walbrook Ward: will elect good men.

Candlewick Ward: will do the like.

Coleman Street Ward: the same men will be elected again.

(p. 146) Bread Street Ward: Mr Baylis does not know whether that be practicable or not, but believes twelve gentlemen there may be prevailed upon to stand again if there can be any assurance that the Court of Aldermen will exert their power. The Aldermen are desired by this day sevennight to consider of this matter and give their opinion then to this club.

Cornhill Ward: is improved since last year.

Bassishaw Ward: the Aldermen desired to appoint a committee to examine how the rooms about Guildhall are disposed of.

Cordwainer: will again elect good men.

Bishopsgate: not to be attempted.
Castle Baynard Ward: judged practicable.
Dowgate Ward: Mr Nicholson and Mr Foster desired to stand for Common Council.
Aldersgate Ward: to be attempted.
Portsoken Ward: to be attempted.
(p. 147) Queenhithe Ward: to be attempted.
Farringdon Within: to be attempted.
Cripplegate Ward: to be attempted.
Billingsgate Ward: not practicable.
Sir Harcourt Masters will speak to Dr Penrice and Mr Hayford about Castle Baynard.
Mr Woodford will speak to Mr Foster about Dowgate.
Mr Perry to be summoned to attend next meeting.
Mr Bracey to meet Sir Harcourt Masters at the club, and to be summoned.
Capt. Langley to be summoned.
Bridge Ward: Mr Clay to be summoned.
Club to meet here again Wednesday night.
Cripplegate Without: Mr Lloyd to be summoned.
Memorandum, to go to Mr Gibson tomorrow night at eight of the clock.

127. (p. 148) Tuesday, 20 November 1716.
Precinct books sent out to the several persons following: Bassishaw Ward, to Mr John Baker; Coleman Street Ward, to Mr London; Broad Street Ward, to Mr Woodford; Cornhill Ward, to Deputy Chauncy; Cordwainer Ward, to Mr Trench; Vintry Ward, to Mr Cooper; Queenhithe Ward, to Capt. Langley; Bread Street Ward, to Mr Baylis; Farringdon Within, to Major Hatley; Cheap Ward, to Mr John Younge.

128. Wednesday, 21 November 1716.
Lime Street Ward, to Mr Bagshaw; Portsoken Ward, to Mr Perry; Tower Ward, to Sir Harcourt Masters; Langbourn Ward, to Deputy Hankey; Candlewick Ward, to Mr Thompson.

129. (p. 149) Wednesday, 21 November 1716. Present: Mr Younge, Mr London, Major Hatley, Mr Thayer, Mr Styles, Mr Cooper, Mr Perry, Major Jenkins, Deputy Egleton, Capt. Langley, Mr Baylis, Mr Troughton, Mr Cooke, Capt. Bell, Mr Smythe, Sir Harcourt Masters, Mr Trench, Sir John Eyles, Mr Baskett, Mr Bagshaw, Col. Westal, Mr Gibson, Mr Bracey, Mr Woodford, Mr Lyell, Mr Harris, Sir Gilbert Heathcote, Sir William Humfreys.
Joseph Goddard esq., woollen draper, near Pope's Head Alley in Cornhill, recommended to be a member for that ward.
Sir Gilbert Heathcote reported that the Aldermen will do all that lies in their power to determine the affair in Bread Street Ward, if there be any controversy this year.
Mr Perry believes that Portsoken Ward may this year be attempted with success, though they are not amended in general. Mr Bracey is of the con-

43

trary opinion. Resolved, either to compromise the matter or contend for the whole.

Deputy Egleton is of opinion there is no hopes of getting one man in the Ward of Cripplegate Within without the interest of the Alderman; otherwise, may gain two. He is desired to consult his friends against the next meeting of the club.

(p. 150) Sir John Eyles says if Sir Samuel Stanier can be prevailed upon to persuade his two nephews, [the] Mr Portens, to stand candidates they may be chosen. And Sir Gilbert Heathcote, Sir Charles Peers, and Sir John Eyles are desired to speak to Sir Samuel Stanier. And to speak to Mr Maximilian Western.

Mr Nicholas of Cornhill Ward to be summoned for next meeting.

Major Hatley of Farringdon Within believes they may get in two in the room of two dead.

Mr Thayer desired to speak to Mr Bugby of Castle Baynard Ward.

Col. Shorey to be summoned to be at the next meeting.

The club to be summoned to meet again on Tuesday next at seven of the clock.

130. (p. 151) Tuesday, 27 November 1716. Present: Mr Craggs, Sir William Humfreys, Mr Woodford, Mr Baylis, Mr Baskett, Mr Fisher, Mr Thompson, Deputy Egleton, Capt. Bell, Mr Sherbrooke, Mr Warner, Sir John Eyles, Col. Cooke, Mr Perry, Mr Trench, Mr Thayer, Mr Bugby, Mr Peachy, Capt. Langley, Mr Harris, Mr Younge, Major Hatley, Mr Cooke, Mr Lyell, Mr London, Sir Gilbert Heathcote.

Mr Fisher reports from Billingsgate Ward that the Tories will fling out the two Whigs that now are of the Common Council.

Mr Atkinson Bugby of Castle Baynard believes that ward is not to be attempted with success if they push for the whole, but otherwise may get in two.

Capt. Langley of Queenhithe believes they cannot get persons to stand for candidates on the Whigs' side, but the ward is something bettered in the inhabitants. To meet tomorrow night at seven at the Salutation near St Antholin's Church.

Mr Sherbrooke reports that in St Sepulchre's precinct in Farringdon Within there is no good to be done.

Mr Warner for Fleet Street Side says there is no hopes there.

Mr Perry for Portsoken believes two Whigs may be chosen there.

(p. 152) Aldersgate Ward: Capt. Bell believes Capt. Bird may be turned out and Mr Gouge elected.

Aldgate: Sir John Eyles spoke to Sir Samuel Stanier and the two Portens, and they cannot be prevailed on to stand candidates.

Vintry: Col. Cooke believes they may keep their ground.

Bassishaw: Mr London reports there will be a struggle for all four.

Bread Street and Bassishaw Wards depend upon the conduct of the Court of Aldermen.

Bread Street: Mr Baylis fears he cannot get twelve there to stand candidates; Mr Proctor having refused to stand, can oppose but nine.

Bridge: nothing to be done.

Cheap: is apprehended to be safe.

Coleman Street: left to Mr London.

Cripplegate Within: the Alderman to be spoken to tomorrow morning.

(p. 153) Dowgate: Mr Woodford reports Mr Foster is inclinable to stand a candidate there if Mr Nicholson will stand with him.

Tower: Mr Harris believes taking in Loveday, the election will go easily there.

Walbrook: the election will be good.

The club to be summoned to meet again tomorrow sevennight.

131. (p. 154) Wednesday, 5 December 1716. Present: Mr Craggs, Sir Harcourt Masters, Sir Peter Eaton, Sir Gregory Page, Mr Raper, Mr Herne, Mr Lyell, Mr Perry, Deputy Egleton, Mr Baylis, Mr Younge, Mr Thayer, Mr Baskett, Capt. Langley, Major Hatley, Mr London, Capt. Bell, Col. Shorey, Sir Randolph Knipe, Mr Baker, Mr Badcock, Major Jenkins, Mr Woodford, Mr Nicholas, Mr Bagshaw, Deputy Colchester, (p. 155) Mr Styles, Mr Cooper, Sir Thomas Abney, Sir William Humfreys, Sir Gilbert Heathcote, Sir Charles Peers, Sir William Stewart, Sir John Eyles, Mr Thompson, Mr Clay, Mr Gibson, Sir George Thorold, Mr Trench, Mr Richard Harris, Col. Westal, Sir Thomas Scawen.

(p. 154) Bassishaw: Col. Shorey says there are endeavours used there to turn out two A's [Whigs].

Bread Street: Mr Baylis says there can't be more than ten set up.

Cheap: Deputy Colchester reports that they have got four new candidates.

Coleman Street: Mr London says there will be some opposition.

Cornhill: Mr Nicholas says there wants one candidate in the room of Mr Daye.

Bridge: Mr Clay says that ward is not to be attempted.

Club to be summoned to meet next Friday, and the several members to bring with them lists of the candidates they intend to set up in the several wards.

132. (p. 156) Friday, 7 December 1716. Present: Sir Harcourt Masters, Col. Shorey, Deputy Egleton, Deputy Hankey, Capt. Langley, Deputy Colchester, Capt. Skey, Capt. Bell, Mr Younge, Sir Gilbert Heathcote, Mr Baylis, Mr Woodford, Mr Benson, Mr Craggs, Mr Nicholas, Mr Thompson, Mr Perry, Major Hatley, Mr Baskett, Mr Bagshaw.

Queenhithe: Mr George Moult will stand candidate.

Money to be allowed the wards: Bassishaw Ward, £20; Bread Street, £100; Broad Street, £10; Candlewick, £25; Cheap, £40; Coleman Street [blank]; Cornhill, £40; Langbourn, £20; Queenhithe, £100; Tower, £50. [Total] £405.

(p. 157) Portsoken Ward adjourned till next meeting on Monday night.

133. Saturday, 8 December 1716.

Received of the honourable James Craggs esq., for which I gave a note to be accountable: £500. [Signed] D[avid] L[e] G[ros].

45

134. Ditto *die*.

1. Queenhithe Ward, paid to Capt. Henry Langley by Capt. Joseph Bell, for which Bell is to bring me a receipt: £100.

Received the receipt the tenth. [Signed] D[avid] L[e] G[ros].

135. (p. 158) 10 December 1716.

2. Paid to Capt. Joseph Bell for Bread Street and Queenhithe Wards, per order of Mr Craggs: £20.

136. Monday, 10 December 1716. Present: Mr Craggs, Mr Woodford, Sir Peter Eaton, Col. Shorey, Mr Thompson, Mr London, Mr Cooper, Mr Gibson, Capt. Bell.

Money to the wards following: Coleman Street, £10; Vintry, £10.

Lists of the candidates for these wards following to be made out: Bread Street, Bassishaw, Cornhill, Queenhithe, Tower.

Club to be summoned to meet next Friday night at seven o'clock.

137. (p. 159) Wednesday, 12 December 1716.

3. Cheap Ward, paid to Mr John Younge as per receipt: £40.

138. Thursday, 13 December 1716.

4. Cornhill Ward, paid to Mr John Nicholas as per receipt: £40.

5. Bassishaw Ward, paid to Mr John Baker as per receipt: £20.

6. Langbourn Ward, paid to Mr Henry Hankey as per receipt: £20.

139. (p. 160) Friday, 14 December 1716. Present: Mr Craggs, Mr Warner, Mr Baker, Mr Bagshaw, Sir Gilbert Heathcote, Mr Thompson, Mr Baylis, Sir William Humfreys, Mr Nicholas, Deputy Egleton, Mr Cooper, Capt. Bell, Deputy Colchester, Mr Woodford, Mr Gibson, Mr Trench, Col. Westal, Mr Troughton.

Ordered, that Vintry Ward be paid the further sum of £10.

7. Bread Street Ward, paid to Robert Baylis esq. as per receipt: £100.

8. Candlewick Ward, paid to Mr John Thompson as per receipt: £25.

Club to be summoned to meet again next Wednesday night at seven a clock.

9. Vintry Ward, paid to Mr James Cooper as per receipt: £20.

Ordered, that Sir Harcourt Masters be paid for the arrears of his expenses the last year the further sum of £150.

140. (p. 161) Saturday, 15 December 1716.

Received of the honourable James Craggs esq., for which I gave the like note as on the eighth instant: £200. [Signed] D[avid L[e] G[ros].

141. (p. 162) Wednesday, 19 December 1716. Present: Mr Sheriff Cooke, Sir Harcourt Masters, Deputy Egleton, Mr Clay, Sir William Humfreys, Deputy Colchester, Mr. Trench, Mr Troughton, Mr Craggs, Mr Woodford, Mr Lyell, Mr Thompson, Major Hatley, Col. Shorey, Capt. Bell, Mr Fisher, Mr Bagshaw, Capt. Heron, Mr Smythe, Mr Perry, Mr Baskett, Mr Baker, Mr Styles, Mr Josia Gee, (p. 163) Sir Gilbert Heathcote, Mr Gibson, Mr Cooper.

46

(p. 162) Cheap Ward: Mr Davis, partner to Sir Joshua Sharp, serves the Customs and votes contra; Mr Hind and Mr Lyddell will vote right at the instance of Excise.

Queenhithe: the electors are in a good method and the A's [Whigs] reckon they have a majority of twenty.

Tower: there are only three B [Tory] candidates set up, and the A's hope they are in no danger.

Vintry: the proper influences are sent out and they hope to turn out one A [*sic*].

Bread Street: the A candidates meet this night and everything is done there that can be done.

(p. 163) Coleman Street: there is an opposition there.

Farringdon Within: Mr Baskett to be allowed £15.

Bread Street and Queenhithe: Capt. Bell to be paid more, £10.

142. Thursday, 20 December 1716.

10. Paid to Capt. Joseph Bell as per receipt: £10.

11. Cheap Ward, paid to Mr John Younge, by order of Mr Woodford, as per receipt: £20.

143. (p. 164) Thursday, 27 December 1716.

12. Broad Street Ward, paid to Thomas Woodford esq. as per receipt: £8 12s.

144. Monday, 31 December 1716.

13. Tower Ward, paid to Sir Harcourt Masters Kt. as per receipt: £200.

145. Wednesday, 2 January 1717.

14. Farringdon Ward Within, paid to Mr John Baskett as per receipt: £15.

APPENDIX

THE POLITICAL INCLINATIONS OF COMMON COUNCIL, 1716

The list of common councilmen printed below appeared in *The Post Boy* for 19–21 April 1716 (No. 4170) on the occasion of the installation of the Common Council elected the previous December. The list was organised by wards, with 132 names (those of the Tories) printed in roman, 95 names (those of the Whigs) in italic, and seven names (those of the doubtful) in a combination of roman and italic. In addition, newly-elected members' names were distinguished with an asterisk. Here, the asterisk has been retained to indicate new members, and the designations 'Tory', 'Whig' and 'doubtful' have been employed for the sake of clarity in place of the printing distinctions of the original.

146.   *Aldersgate Within*
Major John Smart (Tory)   John Cartlitch (Tory)
Deputy Lawrence Coles (Tory)   Capt. Joseph Bird (Tory)

Aldersgate Without

William Harrison (Tory)
Capt. John Wild (Tory)

Lieut. Col. Samuel Robinson,
   Deputy (Tory)
Capt. William Smith (doubtful)

Aldgate

Sir Benjamin Ayloffe Bt. (Tory)
Sir Randolph Knipe (Whig)
Deputy George Waylett (doubtful)

William Nutt (Tory)
Thomas Parry (Tory)
*John Eyles (Whig)

Bassishaw

Deputy John Eyer (Tory)
William Monck (Tory)

Lieut. Col. John Shorey (Whig)
*John Baker (Whig)

Billingsgate

Deputy William Jenkins (doubtful)
Braham Smith (Tory)
Richard Deane (Tory)
*Joseph Shepherd (Tory)
Richard Maundrell (Tory)

John Godden (Tory)
Samuel Bennet (Tory)
Roger Lynch (Tory)
William Lea (Tory)
*Joseph Chaplin (Whig)

Bishopsgate Within

John Hamers (Tory)
James Dansie (Tory)
Richard Partridge (Tory)
John Lloyd (Tory)
Samuel Shepheard (Whig)

Deputy Samuel Edwards (Tory)
Henry Durley (Tory)
Richard Stert (Tory)
Thomas Woolhead (Tory)
*Edward Parrott (Tory)

Bishopsgate Without

Deputy Henry Burton (Tory)
Nicholas Cripps (Tory)

Edward Becher (Tory)
William Nockells (Tory)

Bread Street

Deputy Jeremy Gough (Tory)
Capt. James Lund (Tory)
Richard Brocas (Tory)
*George Mills (Tory)
George Ludlam (Tory)
William Yerbury (Tory)

*James Carey (Tory)
John Becher (Tory)
Robert Carey (Tory)
Robert Aston (Tory)
Benjamin Wells (Tory)
John Barwick (Tory)

Bridge

Deputy William Parrott (Tory)
James Brook (Whig)
James Tallman (Tory)
Richard Durnford (Tory)
William Tyson (Tory)
Richard Symons (Tory)
*James Pitts (Tory)
Thomas Preston (Tory)

Noy Willey (Tory)
Richard Cambridge (Tory)
Capt. Henry Daniel (Tory)
*Richard Clay (Whig)
John Colt (Tory)
Thomas Abbis (Tory)
William Mingay (Tory)

Broad Street

Deputy George Frye (Whig)
David Heywood (Whig)
Capt. Thomas Cartwright (Whig)
Richard Turner (Whig)
John Dickenson (Whig)

William Astell (Whig)
*William Nash (Whig)
*Robert Burchall (Whig)
*Henry Merttins (Whig)
John Townsend (Whig)

147. *Candlewick*

Capt. Sutton Sharpe, Deputy (Whig)
Benjamin Henshaw (Whig)
Robert Hayes (Whig)
*Peter Foster (Whig)

*Thomas Hill (Whig)
William Wilcocks (Whig)
*David Cooke (Whig)
Edward Masters (Whig)

Castle Baynard

Deputy Benjamin Tomlinson (Tory)
*John Cordon (Tory)
*Richard Davenport (Tory)
*John Bateman (Tory)
Richard Truby (Tory)

Francis Mollineux (Tory)
William Hayford (Whig)
Thomas Daniel (Tory)
Richard Ladbrooke (Tory)
Christopher Bateman (Tory)

Cheap

Deputy Henry Colchester (Whig)
*Capt. John Heron (Whig)
John Younge (Whig)
Samuel Spragg (Whig)
John Moore (Whig)
Robert Keynton (Whig)

Robert Smithson (Whig)
Benjamin Hill (Whig)
Robert Norris (Whig)
George Wilcocks (Whig)
Christopher White (Whig)
John Morgan (Whig)

Coleman Street

Deputy Simon Andrews (Whig)
Philip Constable (Whig)
Daniel Garrett (Whig)

James Nutcher (Whig)
Thomas Gibson (Whig)
John Newman (Whig)

Cordwainer

Deputy Samuel Hayward (Whig)
Henry King (Whig)
Samuel Trench (Whig)
Samuel Hatton (Whig)

John Farr (Tory)
John Caseberd (Whig)
John Browne (Whig)
George Morley (Whig)

Cornhill

Deputy Richard Chauncy (Whig)
John Ellwick (Whig)
John Blunt (Whig)

Robert Garbrand (Whig)
John Wood (Whig)
John Daye (Whig)

Cripplegate Within

Deputy Thomas Foxall (Tory)
William Patten (Tory)
Robert Haddock (Tory)
*William Timms (Tory)

Henry Bull (Tory)
*Joshua Redshaw (Tory)
*Charles Hartley (Tory)
John Prankard (Tory)

Cripplegate Without

Deputy William Edmunds (Tory)   Edmund Joyner (Tory)
Felix Feast (Tory)   *Capt. Thomas Catmore (Tory)

Dowgate

Deputy Anthony Tournay (Tory)   George Monke (Tory)
William Mason (Tory)   *Edward Lascells (Whig)
*John Norwood (Whig)   Thomas Gilbert (Tory)
William Tate (Tory)   Robert Edwards (Tory)

Farringdon Within

Charles Lloyd (Tory)   Robert Knaplock (Tory)
Charles Wood (Tory)   Henry Sisson (Tory)
Deputy John Everet (Tory)   Joseph Sandwell (Tory)
Francis West (Tory)   Augustin Marriot (Tory)
William Unett (Tory)   John Sherman (Tory)
Benjamin Bound (Tory)   William Clinch (Tory)
Needler Webb (Tory)   Thomas Harris (Tory)
John Wheatley (Tory)

148.   *Farringdon Without*
Paul Jarvis (doubtful)   Cave Wiseman (Tory)
*Gregory Shepherd (Tory)   Thomas Sowlter (Tory)
John Murdock (Tory)   Thomas Ketterick (Tory)
Deputy Simon Beckley (Tory)   Deputy Nathaniel Turner (Tory)
Samuel Mawhood (Tory)   Charles Gretton (Tory)
Capt. James Guillam (Tory)   Robert Vincent (Tory)
John Chellingworth (Tory)   Benjamin Rogers (Tory)
*John Shaw (Tory)   Charles Thatcher (Tory)

Langbourn

Deputy John Cooper (Whig)   Lawrence Hatsell (Whig)
Gabriel Smythe (Whig)   Henry Hankey (Whig)
*Stephen Ram (Whig)   William Ingram (Whig)
John Lloyd (Whig)   *John Henry Boock (Whig)
Jeremiah Marlow (Whig)   William Potter (Whig)

Lime Street

Deputy Lancelot Skynner (doubtful)   Benjamin Ashwood (Whig)
Joshua Bagshaw (Whig)   Henry Tombes (Whig)

Portsoken

Deputy Peter Monger (Tory)   *Roger Foster (Tory)
*James Rochester (Tory)   *Valentine Brewis (Tory)
John Bridge (Tory)

Queenhithe

*Deputy Augustin Meadows (Tory)   John Barber (Tory)
Robert Alsop (Tory)   Abraham Sewen (Tory)
Simon Roberts (Tory)   Joseph Ayliffe (Tory)

Tower

Deputy John Langton (doubtful)
Nicholas Hanbury (Tory)
Joseph Taylor (Tory)
*Francis Porten (Whig)
*Thomas Clarke (Whig)
*Robert Jeffs (Whig)

*Samuel Beachcroft (Whig)
*Robert [John] Britton (Whig)
Sir Peter Eaton (Whig)
*Sir Harcourt Masters (Whig)
*Major Richard Lechmere (Whig)
*Richard Harris (Whig)

Vintry

Lieut. Col. William Cooke, Deputy (Whig)
John Samwaies (Whig)
Henry Greenaway (Whig)
Robert Smith (Tory)

*John Yerbury (Whig)
*Philip Pinchis (Whig)
Lieut. Col. Samuel Westal (Whig)
John Cooper (Whig)
Edmund Trench (Whig)

Walbrook

Deputy John West (doubtful)
William Drake (Tory)
Richard West (Whig)
Samuel Keynton (Whig)

Robert Stockdale (Whig)
*Nicholas Jackman (Whig)
Matthew Shepherd (Whig)
Launder Smith (Tory)

INDEX

All references are to serial numbers in the text, not to pages. To indicate individuals' service as Common Councilmen, those serving during the club's recorded life are designated 'CC', those who served before 1714 but not between 1714 and 1716 are designated 'CCp', and those elected only after 1716 are designated 'CCf'. Service as an Alderman (Ald) or as an MP is indicated in the same way. In recording the presence of individuals at the club's meetings, only the total number of attendances has been given for those present at seven or more meetings; this total is given together with a reference to the first and last meetings attended (e.g., attended seven times, 7–27). London street and tenement names have not been indexed. The names of trades and occupations have been grouped together under the heading 'Trades and occupations'.

Abbis, Thomas (CC), 146
Abney, Sir Thomas (Ald), 112; attended, 131
Acton, Samuel, 83, 88
Aislaby, ——, attended, 86
Akerman, John, 30
Alcorne, Samuel, 61
Aldermen, Court of, 126 (ter), 129
Aldersgate Ward, 37, 78, 82 (bis), 88, 95 (bis), 126, 130; Within, 2, 40, 63, 76, 83, 88, 106, 107, 109, 113, 146; Without, 2, 40, 63, 76, 83, 106, 107, 109, 113, 146
Aldgate Ward, 1, 2, 40, 47, 63, 73, 77, 78, 81, 82, 88, 90, 95, 106 (bis), 107, 109, 113, 130, 146
Almond, William, 58
Alsop
  ——, 37
  Robert (CC), 148
Amey, Henry, 47
Andrews
  John, 64
  Lawrence, 64
  Deputy Simon (CC), 81, 147
Anson, ——, goldsmith, 58
Ashurst, Samuel, 81
Ashwood, Benjamin (CC), 81, 148
Association, of loyalty, 76, 86, 94–6
Astell, William (CC), 81, 109, 112, 113 (bis), 119, 146; attended, 121
Astley, Christopher (CCp), 81, 96
Aston, Robert (CC), 146
Atlee, Roger (CCp), 81
Ayliffe, Joseph (CC), 106, 148
Ayloffe, Sir Benjamin, 4th bt. (CC), 88, 113, 146

Badcock, Richard, 62, 84, 94; attended, 86, 95, 131

Badger, Charles, 57
Bagshaw, Joshua (CC), 1, 2, 7, 8, 15, 30 (bis), 37, 47, 65, 73, 75, 81, 95, 111, 112, 128, 148; attended fifty-six times, 3–141
Baker, John (CC), 76, 81, 111, 127, 138, 146; attended, 112, 113, 131, 139, 141
Ball, Samuel (CCf), 76, 81
Bamber, John (CCf), 61
Bank of England, 76
Barber
  Edward, 30
  John (CC), 106, 148
Barnesley, William, 81
Barwick, John (CC), 146
Baskett, John, 81, 88, 96, 106 (bis), 141, 142, 145; attended ten times, 83–141
Bassishaw Ward, 1, 2, 40, 47, 63, 73, 76, 78, 81, 82 (bis), 90, 94, 103, 106, 109, 113, 126, 127, 130 (bis), 131, 132, 136, 138, 146
Batchellor, Nicholas (CCf), 61
Bateman
  Christopher (CC), 113, 147
  Sir James (Ald), 112
  John (CC), 147
Baylis, Robert (CCp, Aldf, MPp), 1, 2, 44, 62, 65, 70, 71, 76, 77, 81, 90, 94, 98, 111, 116, 126, 127, 130, 131, 139; attended thirty-four times, 4–141
Beachcroft
  Joseph, 81
  Samuel (CC), 76, 81, 148
Becher
  Edward (CC), 146
  John (CC), 112, 146
Beckley, Deputy Simon (CC), 148
Bedell, Henry (CC), 81
Bedingfeld, James, 61
Bell, Capt. Joseph, 130, 134, 135, 141, 142;

52

55

57

58

Steward, ——, 37
Stewart, Sir William (Ald), 112; attended, 131
Stockdale, Robert (CC), 81, 106, 111, 112 (bis), 113, 148; attended, 112, 113
Stork, ——, 64
Strahan, George, 56
Styles, ——, attended, 129, 131, 141
Swan, Nicholas, 64
Symons, Richard (CC), 146

Tallman, James (CC), 106, 113, 146
Tart, John, 56
Tatam, Samuel (CCf), 76
Tate, William (CC), 106, 147
Taverner, John, 64
Tayler
  John, of Blackfriars, 81
  John (CC, Farringdon Within), 58
Tayleur, John, 84
Taylor, Joseph (CC), 61, 148
Territt, William, 84
Tew, ——, 76
Thatcher, Charles (CC), 148
Thayer
  ——, 129; attended, 83, 107, 129, 130, 131
  Humphrey, 81, 107
  Samuel (CCp), 88
Thompson
  John (CCp, Aldf), 1, 2, 37, 62, 75, 77, 88, 95 (bis), 106 (bis), 108, 126, 128, 139; attended nineteen times, 75–141
  Sir William (Recorder, MP), attended, 126
Thornhill, ——, clerk of, 64
Thorold, Sir George, 1st bt. (Ald), attended, 131
Thorowgood, Thomas, 64
Timbrell, ——, 9
Timms, William (CC), 109, 147
Toke, Nicholas, 81, 107
Tombes, Henry (CC), 81, 148
Tomlinson, Deputy Benjamin (CC), 106, 147
Toms, Christopher (CCp), 64
Torriano, Nathaniel, 37, 81
Tournay, Deputy Anthony (CC), 106, 147
Tower Ward, 1, 2, 40, 47, 61–3, 67, 71, 73, 76, 78, 81, 82 (bis), 90, 95 (bis), 99, 109, 110, 113, 126, 128, 130, 132, 136, 141, 144, 148
Townley, Charles, 61
Townsend
  Charles, 1st Viscount, 85
  John (CC), 81, 146
Trades and occupations: alehouse keeper, 58, 76; almanac maker, 58; apothecary, 57, 58; attorney, 58, 64 (bis); baker, 64; barber, 56 (bis), 58, 61, 64;

bookseller, 37 (bis), 56, 58, 76; brazier, 37; bricklayer, 57, 59; cabinetmaker, 57 (bis); carpenter, 57; cheesemonger, 37 (bis); clockmaker, 64; coffeeman, 56 (bis), 61, 73; cooper, 61 (bis), 76; corn factor, 37; dyer, 57 (passim); exchange broker, 57; fanmaker, 58; farrier, 58; glass seller, 58; goldsmith, 37, 58 (ter); grocer, 57, 59 (bis); gunsmith, 37; hairseller, 59; hatter, 58; hot presser, 57; innholder, 76; ironmonger, 58; linendraper, 56 (bis), 64; lodging house keeper, 57, 64 (passim); mason, 57; medical examiner, 58; mercer, 57, 58 (bis), 87; merchant, 37 (bis), 57, 61, 81; oilman, 37; orange merchant, 81; pattern shop, 56 (ter); pewterer, 58, 59 (bis), 61; plumber, 61, 64; Portugal merchant, 61; pressmaker, 57; printseller, 58; scrivener, 64; snuff merchant, 57; soapmaker, 37; Spanish merchant, 37; stationer, 58; surgeon, 61; tailor, 57; tallowchandler, 56; thread man, 59; tobacconist, 37, 57; turner, 37; upholder, 58 (ter); victualler, 57 (bis), 59; vintner, 58; watchmaker, 56 (bis); wine merchant, 37; woollen draper, 37 (bis), 129
Tranter, ——, innholder, 76, 107
Trench
  Edmund (CC), 81, 148
  Samuel (CC), 1, 2, 10, 62, 73 (bis), 81, 94, 111, 112, 113 (bis), 127, 147; attended thirty-six times, 3–141
Troughton, ——, attended, 129, 139, 141
Truby, Richard (CC), 112, 147
Turner
  Deputy Nathaniel (CC), 148
  Richard (CC), 81, 109, 111, 112, 119, 146; attended, 119, 121, 123
Tyson, William (CC), 146

Unett, William (CC), 112, 147
Uvedale, Thomas, 81

Vaughan, Abraham, 64
Vickers, Francis, 61
Victualling department, 76
Vigners, Andrew, 47, 48
Vincent
  ——, Stationer to the Excise, 106
  Robert (CC), 58, 106, 148
Vintry Ward, 1, 2, 9, 40, 47, 57, 63, 73, 78, 81, 82 (bis), 90, 95, 106 (bis), 108, 113, 127, 130, 136, 139 (bis), 141, 148

Wade, John, 81

LONDON POLLBOOKS, 1713

INTRODUCTION

A list of those who voted in the general election of 1713 for London is printed with the minutes of the Whig club for two reasons. First, it is the nearest available list to the period during which the minutes were compiled, for although the 1715 election was hotly contested, no pollbook is known to have been produced. Secondly, and more importantly, the list is unique in its own right. Although several pollbooks for London have survived from the eighteenth century, until recently the 1713 contest was not known to have been fully documented. Lists of those who polled for one set of candidates, Peter Godfrey, Robert Heysham, Thomas Scawen and John Ward, were known to scholars; but the existence of a corresponding list of those who polled for the other set, Sir John Cass, Sir Richard Hoare, Sir George Newland and Sir William Withers, was unrecorded until Dr Jeremy Mitchell purchased a copy in 1974. We wish here to thank him both for drawing our attention to it, and for allowing us to publish an edition of it.

Cass, Hoare, Newland and Withers were Tories who had represented London in the previous parliament. Their four rivals stood again in 1715, when they were all regarded as Whigs. To justify calling them all Whigs in 1713, however, needs some explanation, for one of them, Robert Heysham, had previously been described as a Tory. What the opposition to the Tory government was trying to do in 1713, at least in London, was to promote parliamentary candidates not so much as Whigs as opponents of a commercial treaty with France, the defeat of which in June had been the biggest setback to the ministry since its formation in 1710. It had been accomplished by a combination of Whigs and dissident Tories, and by getting one of the latter to stand against ministerial candidates in London, opposition elements in the City were trying to keep up this alliance during the general election. The main objection to the treaty had been that it would jeopardise English trade and thereby the livelihoods of merchants, and the four opposition candidates stressed that they were 'eminent merchants and great traders . . . who will never give up your trade to France, to the impoverishment of your own nation', unlike, by implication, their Tory rivals.[1]

This ploy was resisted by their opponents, however, who described all four opposition candidates indiscriminately as Whigs throughout the contest. Dyer's Tory newsletter, for instance, reported the day's polling on

1. See for example the *Daily Courant*, 13 October 1713. For newspaper references from the Burney Collection in the British Library we are indebted to Dr Eveline Cruickshanks.

19 October with the comment that 'the Whigs brought down a great mob of weavers and such people at Guildhall who made a disturbance and caused much fighting and quarrelling in the street, but the poll went on notwithstanding the rabble to the great advantage of the Church party'.[2] When the poll ended on 24 October the equally Tory *Post Boy* proclaimed the victory of Hoare and his colleagues, exulting 'that to the inexpressible joy of all true friends to the Church and Queen the four old members got the . . . majority, which considering the last efforts of the Whigs, atheists, deists, Quakers and Republicans of all distinctions to hinder them, is very great'.

The reported outcome of the election was: Hoare, 3,842; Newland, 3,826; Cass, 3,802; Withers, 3,763; Ward, 3,730; Heysham, 3,688; Godfrey, 3,657; and Scawen, 3,625. This close result led the defeated candidates to demand a scrutiny, which began on 31 October. On 2 November the Whig candidates published the list of those who had polled for the four Tories, asking the citizens of London to peruse it, and 'if you observe your friends or selves to be polled by others, or those polled which are dead, or have no right, you are desired (with what speed you can) to bring or send accounts thereof to Lawrance's Coffee-house, Freeman Yard in Cornhill, from 9 to 12, and from 1 to 6, and to furnish what necessary evidence can be obtained for the proof of your observations'.[3] The Tory sheriffs, however, brought the scrutiny to a close before the end of November, insisting that it should end when the time for the writ for the election ran out.

Despite their defeat in both the poll and the scrutiny the Whigs prepared to petition parliament, to which end they were 'industriously busy in collecting objectors to the pollers' for the Tories. This led the scrutineers and friends of the Tory candidates to retaliate by publishing in February 1714 a list of those who had polled for their opponents. As they stated in their prefatory remarks, 'if therein you observe that your selves, or any persons else, have been personated by others, or those persons dead, or having no right to poll, were falsely polled, we entreat you to bring, or send an account thereof with the necessary proofs of your observations, to the London Coffee-House, in Ship Yard, in Bartholomew Lane, behind the Royal Exchange, any day (Sundays only excepted) between the hours of ten in the forenoon and six in the evening; at which time and place there will be attendance to receive them'.[4]

The two pollbooks, therefore, were published quite separately, at least three months apart, being in fact produced by the rivals of the candidates whose votes they purported to record. They were compiled for a decidedly partisan purpose. In both lists the names of the voters were recorded in rough alphabetical order under their respective livery companies. Where no information other than the name of the voter was recorded, the entries indicated that those named had polled for all four candidates on the relevant list. When they exercised their option of polling for fewer than four,

---

2. British Library MSS Loan 29/18.
3. *A List of the Poll for . . . Hoare . . . Withers . . . Cass . . . Newland* (1713). A list of those allegedly disqualified was published in the *Daily Courant*, 3 December 1713.
4. *A List of the poll for . . . Ward . . . Scawen . . . Heysham . . . Godfrey* (1714), p. 2.

or of 'splitting their tickets' in the convenient American phrase, the initial letters of the candidates for whom they polled were entered against their names. Thus John Allen, a glass-seller, voted for Godfrey, Hoare, Scawen and Ward. He therefore appears on the list of Whig voters as Allen John, *W. S. G.*, and on the list of Tory voters as Allen John, *H.*

In editing the two pollbooks for publication in a single alphabetical list, the following conventions have been employed. Surnames and christian names have been transcribed precisely as they appear in the original lists. The terms esquire (esq), junior (jun), senior (sen) and the younger (yr) were occasionally used by the compilers of the lists. Baronets and knights have been distinguished by the abbreviations 'bt' and 'kt'. The name of the voter is followed by an abbreviated reference to his membership of one of the livery companies; a list of these abbreviations follows this Introduction. The vast majority of voters (6,787) appear on only one list and voted for all four Whig or Tory candidates. If a voter supported all four Whigs, the letter A has been placed at the end of his entry; if all four Tories, the letter B has been used. To indicate those who cast fewer than four votes, or who split tickets, the candidates have been identified individually by numbers, thus

A1 Ward	B5 Withers
A2 Heysham	B6 Hoare
A3 Godfrey	B7 Newland
A4 Scawen	B8 Cass

Consequently, John Allen, the glass-seller, who appears in both lists, here has the single entry Allen, John, gls A134B6. 615 individuals have been identified as appearing in both lists. In some cases the spelling of their names differed. Most of these differences were trivial and the choice of spelling has been made silently. However, where the difference was significant, the variant spelling has been placed in brackets after the name chosen and a cross-reference inserted.

64

LIVERY COMPANY MEMBERSHIP: ABBREVIATIONS

apo	apothecary	glz	glazier
arm	armourer	gol	goldsmith
bak	baker	gro	grocer
bar	barber surgeon	hab	haberdasher
bla	blacksmith	inn	innholder
bow	bowyer	iro	ironmonger
bre	brewer	joi	joiner
bri	bricklayer	lea	leatherseller
bro	broderer	lor	loriner
but	butcher	mas	mason
car	carpenter	mer	mercer
clo	clothworker	mus	musician
ck	cook	nee	needlemaker
coa	coachmaker	pai	painterstainer
cor	cordwainer	pew	pewterer
cp	cooper	pla	plasterer
cur	currier	plu	plumber
cut	cutler	pou	poulter
dis	distiller	sad	saddler
dra	draper	sal	salter
dye	dyer	scr	scrivener
far	farrier	ski	skinner
fis	fishmonger	sta	stationer
fle	fletcher	tai	merchant taylor
fou	founder	tal	tallowchandler
fra	framework knitter	tur	turner
fru	fruiterer	uph	upholder
gir	girdler	vin	vintner
glo	glover	wax	waxchandler
gls	glass-seller	wea	weaver

ALPHABETICAL LIST OF VOTERS

Abbey, William, car B
Abbis, Thomas, tai B
Abbot, Edward, pai A
Abbot, Thomas, cut A
Abbott, Robert, bak B
Abbott, William, joi A
Abel, Richard, hab A
Abell, John, lea A
Abney, Thomas kt, fis A
Abraham, James, cut B
Abraham, John, pai B
Abraham, Samuel, wea A
Abraham, Williams, fis B
Ackhurst, Alexander, clo A
Ackland, William, uph B
Acton, Edward, gol B
Acton, Samuel, gro B
Acton, Thomas, pai A
Acton, Walter, gol B
Adam, Henry, cor A
Adam, Robert kt, dra B
Adams, Benjamine, dis B
Adams, Edward, cor A
Adams, Henry, pew A
Adams, James, cp A
Adams, Job, lor B
Adams, John, gro A
Adams, Joseph, tai B
Adams, Nathaniel, clo A
Adams, Nathaniel, pew A
Adams, Paul, dis B
Adams, Robert, glz B
Adams, Robert, sal A
Adams, Seth, far B
Adamson, Char, apo B
Addington, William, cp B
Addison, John, bla A
Addley, Thomas, inn B
Addy, John, gro B578
Adland, Andrew, wea A
Adley, John, bla B
Agar, Edward, gro B
Aking, John, glo A
Albin, James, apo A
Alcroft, Thomas, cut A
Alder, Jos, tai A
Alders, James, cor A
Aldersy, Samuel, tai B
Aldridge, Abel, cur A124B6
Aldridge, Timothy, but A34B58
Aldworth, Thomas, bak B
Alexander, Nich, lea A

Alexander, Thomas, tai B
Alexander, William, cp A2B678
Alford, Joseph, dra A
Alland, Samuel, bre B
Allatt, Thomas, coa B
Allay, Matthew, vin B
Allbritton, Samuel, glo A
Allbury, William, cut A
Allcock, Joseph, sal B
Allen, Austin, pla B
Allen, David, coa B
Allen, Edward, wea A
Allen, George, dye A
Allen, Henry, bla A
Allen, Henry, tai A
Allen, James, ski A
Allen, John, gls A134B6
Allen, John, nee B
Allen, John, tai A
Allen, Josiah, wea A
Allen, Richard, dra B
Allen, Salathael, cur A
Allen, Theophilus, mas B
Allen, Thomas, hab A
Allen, William, bak A4B578
Allen, Zachariah, apo A
Allett, John, joi A
Allin, Thomas, sal B
Allingham, Samuel, glz A
Allison, Edward, pew B
Allison, John, tai B
Allison, Robert, gol B
Allwright, Loveday, wea B
Almond, Daniel, but B
Almond, Edward, but B
Almond, William, glo B
Alpha, James, cor A
Alridge, Thomas, car A
Alsop, Richard, vin B
Alsoph, Robert, hab B
Alstane, Richard, fou B
Alstone, George, inn B
Alwell, William, gol B
Ambler, John, lor A
Amblin, John, fra A
Ambrose, Tho, bre A
Amery, John, sta B
Amos, William, inn A2B568
Amy, John, tai B
Anbury, Robert, bar A
Anderson, Daniel *see* Andrew, Daniel
Anderson, Henry, gro A

66

Anderson, Thomas, inn B
Andrew (Anderson), Daniel, sad A12B78
Andrew, Matthew, dye B
Andrew, Richard, gol B
Andrew, William, gol B
Andrews, Christopher, tai B
Andrews, Daniel, far A
Andrews, John, but A
Andrews, John, glo A
Andrews, John, pla A
Andrews, Oliver, mer B
Andrews, Richard, gir A
Andrews, Richard sen, cur B
Andrews, Robert, car A
Andrews, Robert, sal B
Andrews, Robert, sta B
Andrews, Simon, apo A
Andrews, Thomas, coa A
Andrews, William, clo B
Andrews, William, dye B
Andrews, William, fou B
Andrews, William, tal A
Angeband, Charles, apo A
Ansell (Anselin), James, pai A123B5
Ansty, Christopher, bre B
Anthony, Edward, dra A
Antrim, Samuel, glz A
Antrobus, Benjamin, dra A
Appleby, Gabriel, joi B578
Appleby, John, arm A
Appleby, Thomas, bre B
Appleford, Richard, pou B
Applegath, Edward, dye A
Appleton, John, nee B
Apthorp, John, fou A
Apthorp, Simon, wea B
Arbunott, Jacob, lor A
Archer, Andrew, gol B
Archer, John, gls B
Archer, John, gol A
Archer, John, sal A
Archer, Thomas, mer A
Archibold, Francis, gol B
Arden, John, clo B
Ariatt, Theophilus, lor B
Aris, John, joi B
Arkesdon, William, pai A12B67
Arlidge, Abraham, car A
Armstead, Michael, apo B
Armstrong, Hen, vin, B
Arn, Jo, tai B
Arne, Thomas jun, uph B
Arne, Thomas sen, uph B
Arnell, Thomas, car B
Arnock, James, lea A
Arnold, John, car B
Arnold, John, dis B
Arnold, Nathaniel, ski B
Arnold, Samuel, uph A
Arnold, William, fis A14B56

Arnold, William, glz B
Arnott, John, cur A
Aron, Samuel, clo B
Arrowsmith, Anthony, clo A4B678
Arundell, James, dye A234B5
Ash, Isaac, fis A
Ashbey, Stephen, hab B
Ashburne, Robert, joi B
Ashby, Thomas, bri A134B6
Ashman, William, tal A124B6
Ashton, Anth, car A
Ashton, James, fru A4B578
Ashton, Nicholas, tai A
Ashurst, Benjamin, fis A
Ashurst, Robert, sal A
Ashurst, Samuel, sta B
Ashurst, Samuel, tai A
Ashurst, William, tai A
Ashwood, Benjamin, clo A
Ashworth, Daniel, but A
Ashworth, Edward, but A
Askew, Roger, pai B
Askue, John, fru A
Asly, Francis, gro B
Aspenall, Zachariah, but A
Aspley, Fluellin, gls B
Aspley, Thomas, clo B
Asplin, Jacob, hab A
Assgell, Edward, pai A
Astile, William, joi B
Astill, Thomas, tur A
Astom, Thomas, bri B
Aston, John, cp A
Aston, Robert, fis B
Atkins, Abraham, bla A
Atkins, Francis, fis B
Atkins, Francis, fis B
Atkins, John, dye A
Atkins, Maurice, sta B
Atkins, Robert, mer A
Atkinson, Farries, wea B
Atkinson, Joseph, bar A124B8
Atkinson, William, bla B
Atkinson, William, bro B
Atkinstall, Richard, ski B
Attley, Roger, tai A
Atton, Roger, but A
Attwell, William, gol A123
Atwood, Matthew, wea A4B568
Atwood, Robert, cor A
Atwood, Robert, dra A
Atwood, Samuel, arm B
Atwyck, Daniel, fou B
Audlaby, Edmund, gir B
Audley, Benjamin, scr B
Augar, Henry, glz B
Aunger, Samuel, tai B
Austin, George, cp B
Austin, John, gol B
Austin, Michael, tai B

67

Austin, Thomas, tur B
Aven, Richard, cut A134B8
Avery, Edward, glz B
Avery, Joseph, ski A12
Avery, William, bak B
Avery, William, far A
Ayliff, Robert, tal B
Ayliffe, Isaac, wea A
Aylloffe, Benjamin bt, clo A3B678
Aylofe, Thomas, tur B
Ayloff, John, uph B
Aylworth, George, mer A2B568
Ayre, Robert, gro A
Ayres, John, gir B
Ayres, Richard, ck B

Babington, Richard, bar A
Bachelor, Nicholas, cp B
Backshell, William, vin A
Backshill, Samuel, tal A
Bacon, Thomas, joi A
Badcott, William, wax B
Baden, Robert, mer B
Badger, Daniel, tal B
Badham, Richard, but A
Bagley, Mathew, lor B
Bagnal, Gibbons, vin B
Bagnall, John, sal A
Bagnall, Samuel, sal B
Bagshaw, Joshua, wea A
Bagwell, James, fis A
Bagwell, Samuel, dye A
Bailey, Benjamin, fis A
Bailey, Daniel, joi A
Bailey, Daniel, sal A
Baily, James, dye A
Baine, Henry, bla B
Bains, Richard *see* Barnes, Richard
Baker, Bartholomew, sta B
Baker, Beresford, lea B
Baker, Edmond, bri A
Baker, Edward, apo A
Baker, Edward, mas A
Baker, Edward, tai A
Baker, George, dis A
Baker, George, gol A
Baker, George sen, dis A
Baker, James, joi A24B56
Baker, John, bak A124B7
Baker, John, mer A1B567
Baker, John, uph A
Baker, John, wea A
Baker, Joshua, gro A
Baker, Richard, bri A
Baker, Richard, plu A2B67
Baker, Richard, ski A
Baker, Robert, bar A
Baker, Sam, sad B
Baker, Samuel, dis A
Baker, Thomas, dye A

Baker, Thomas, wax A
Baker, Thomas, wea B
Baker, William, bak A1B567
Baker, William, dra A
Baker, William, glo B
Baker, William, ski A
Baldwin, John, cp A
Baldwin, Peter, cp A
Baldwin, Thomas, cp A
Baldwin, Thomas, vin B
Baldwin, William, dis B
Bale, Gratian, bar B
Bale, Robert, tai B
Bales, Daniel, vin B
Baley, James, bow B
Ball, Anthony, cut B
Ball, Charles, bar B
Ball, Charles, plu A
Ball, James, tai A
Ball, John, vin A2B578
Ball, Levi, apo A
Ball, Nathaniel, ck A
Ball, Samuel, joi B
Ball, Samuel, pou A
Ball, Samuel, sal A
Ball, Samuel, wax A
Ball, William, bre A
Ball, William, hab B
Ball, William, tai B
Ballard, James, dra A
Ballard, John, tai A123B6
Ballard, Joseph, arm B
Ballard, Samuel, sta B
Bally, Thomas, dye B
Bamber, John, sal B
Bamford, Joseph, bla A
Baniel, Richard, but B
Banister, Gilbert, bro B
Bankes, Benjamin, bar B
Bankes, Jonathan, joi B
Banks, Adam, gir B
Banks, Allen, lea A
Banks, Benjamin, clo A2B678
Banks, John, hab A
Banks, Matthew, mas A
Banks, Thomas, tai B
Bannier, Edmund, clo B
Bannister, George, mer B
Bannister, William, glo A
Baptistshorer, John, bro A
Baradale, John, mer B
Baratt, Jonas, tai B
Barber, Edward, wea B
Barber, John, sta B
Barber, John, wea A
Barber, Michael, joi A
Barcaber, John, bar B
Barclay, John, vin B
Bardoe, James, tai B
Barewell, Jonathan, ck B

68

Barford, Arthur, clo B
Bargrave, Andrew, sad B
Barker, Edward, apo B
Barker, John, cur A
Barker, John, inn B
Barker, Joseph, dra A
Barker, Richard, tai A
Barker, Thomas, hab A1B567
Barkley, John, hab B
Barksdale, William, plu B
Barley, George, joi A
Barlow, Benj, car A
Barnaby, Henry, bar B
Barnadisten, Nathaniel, gro A
Barnard, Charles, lea A124B5
Barnard, Samuel, mer A
Barnard, Thomas, dra A
Barne, Henry, lea B
Barnes, Edward, tai B
Barnes, Francis, plu A
Barnes, Gilbert, pou B
Barnes, Martin, inn B
Barnes (Bains), Richard, clo A12B56
Barnes, Thomas, hab A
Barnes, Thomas, sal B
Barnesley, William, clo A
Barnett, William, but B
Barney, John, bar A
Barnfeild, Francis, bla A
Barns, John, wea A
Barnwell, Richard, joi B
Barr, George, wea A
Barras, Joshua, mer A
Barret, Nicholas, wax B
Barrett, Edward, fru A
Barrett, Phil, sta B
Barrett, William, but B
Barron (Parran), John, dis A134B6
Barrow, William, but B
Barrow, William, ck B
Barsham, Edward, gol A134B6
Barson, Thomas, iro B
Bartholomew, John, tur A
Bartlett, Roger, arm A
Barton, Henry, gro A
Barton, John, cor B
Barton, Nathaniel, wax A
Bartram, Christopher, fru A3B567
Barwell, Matthew, tal B
Barwell, Richard, iro A
Barwell, William, arm B
Barwell, William, iro A
Baskett, John, sta B
Baslett, John, sal A
Bass, William, mer B
Bass, William, vin A4B578
Bat, Timothy, gol A
Batchelor, Giles, bro A24B58
Bateman, Chr, sta B
Bateman, John, lea B

Bateman, John, tai A3B568
Bateman, Joseph, sal A
Bateman, Richard, bar A
Bateman, Richard, sal A
Bateman, William, mer B
Bates, Edward, bro B
Bates, John, bri B
Bates, Thomas, bri A
Bates, Thomas, cp A
Bathrust, Edmond, dis B
Baton, William, gir B
Batsford, Thomas, tai B
Batt, George, inn B
Battinson, John, lor B
Bauks, Benjamin, dis B
Bawick, John, clo B
Baxter, Daniel, apo B
Baxter, John, vin B
Baxter, Robert, clo A
Baxter, Thomas, but B
Bayes, John, dra A
Bayley, Calamy, cor A
Bayley, Christopher, fou A
Bayley, Edmund, cor A
Bayley, Edward, plu B
Bayley, John, cut A
Bayley, Richard, bro A
Bayley, Richard, gol B
Baylis, John, bla A12B58
Baylis, Robert, gro A
Baylis, William, lea B
Bayly, Daniel, dis B
Bayly, John, arm A
Bayly, Capt. John, arm A
Bayly, John, dye B
Bayly, John, dye B
Bayly, John, gol A
Bayly, Joseph, gol B
Bayly, Richard, pai A23B58
Baytes, Mark, tur B
Beach, George, cur A
Beachcroft, Jos, hab A
Beachcroft, Samuel, clo A
Beacher, Edward, dra B
Beacher, Francis, iro B
Beacher, John, sal B
Beacher, William, gro B6
Beachey, William, cur B
Beadle, Henry, scr A12B78
Beadle, Robert, vin B
Beadle, Thomas, inn B
Beadle, William, joi B
Beal, John, tal B
Beal, Richard, ck A23
Beale, Henry, pla B
Beale, John, cor A14B68
Beane, Elisha, tai A
Bearcroft, Stephen, sal A24
Beard, Benjamin, cut A
Beard, Edward, bri B

69

Beard, Sampson, pew A
Beardleys, Richard, fou B
Bearfoot, John, bak A
Bears, Thomas, joi A124
Bearsly, Job, pew A
Beasley, Allison, pew B
Beasly, John, dis B
Beastow, Joseph, dye B
Beaucham, Ephraim, mas A3B678
Beaumont, William, coa B
Beaver, Thomas, sta B
Beazley, Samuel, lea A
Beck, Peter, but A
Becke, Peter, but B
Becket, John, gol B
Beckley, Simon, joi B
Bedbury, Abraham, arm A
Beddington, John, gol B
Bedford, Benjamin, uph B
Bedford, Thomas, bow B
Bedhurst, Thomas, bro B
Bedingfield, Edmund, tai B
Bedwell, John, tal A
Bee, Edward, pai B
Beedle, Thomas, pai B
Beekeley, John, dis A
Beendsley, Job, lea B
Beeson, John, pai A
Beiston, James, cor B
Belamy, Thomas, clo A
Belch, John, joi B
Belitha, Edward, hab A
Bell, Adam, lor A
Bell, Benjamin, glo A
Bell, Christopher, cor A
Bell, Humphry, cor A123B7
Bell, Humphry, inn A
Bell, Jacob, hab B
Bell, John, bla B
Bell, John, hab A
Bell, John, pou B
Bell, Joseph, gol A
Bell, Leonard, wax B
Bell, Richard, cp A123B8
Bell, William, wea B
Bellamy, Edward, fis A12B78
Bellamy, Humphry, cut B
Bellamy, John, fis A124B7
Bellamy, Robert, fis A
Bellamy, Samuel, arm A
Bellis, John, pou A23B56
Beltch, Joseph, glo A
Benne, John, gir A
Bennet, James, sal B
Bennet, James, ski A
Bennet, Joseph, hab A
Bennet, Samuel, cp B
Bennet, Thomas, bla B
Bennet, Thomas, lor A3B578
Bennett, Thomas, cur B

Benning, Stephen, fou B
Benskin, Thomas, sta B
Benson, Charles, tal A12B78
Benson, John, gir B
Bentall, John, wea A
Bently, Benjamin, gol A
Bently, Elisha, wea A
Bently, Jonathan, sad A
Benwick, James, sta B
Berdsley, Benjamin, tai A
Berisford, John, sta B
Bernard, Joseph, coa A
Bernard, Robert, dis A
Bernardiston, John, vin B
Berret, Richard, inn B
Berrey, William, wea B
Berroby, John, hab B
Berry, Edward, fru A
Berry, Ralph, coa B
Berry, Robert, vin B
Berry, William, bri B
Bescoutts, James, tai B
Best, Anthony, but B
Best, John, bar A3B678
Best, Thomas, fru B
Best, William, bar B
Bestman, Gabriel, wea B
Bestoe, Wm, pou B
Bethel, William, vin B
Betsworth, Thomas, dra A
Betteress, Samuel, cur B
Betterton, Robert, fis B
Bettesworth, Arthur, sta B
Betton, Timothy, iro B
Bettres, William, dye B
Betts, Edmond, bla B
Betts, Francis, fra B
Betts, Luking, coa A
Betts, Thomas, bar A
Bevoice, John, lea A
Bew, George, apo B
Bey, Thomas, joi B
Beyfeild, William, tai A
Bezard, Francis, bri A
Bibb, Thomas, cut B
Bickerton, John, ck B
Biddle, Joseph, tur B
Biddle, Thomas, inn A
Bigg, Henry, car A134
Biggs, Thomas, bla B
Biggsby, William, inn B
Bignal, James, iro B
Bignall, James, cor A
Bignall, William, bar B
Bigsby, Nicholas, ski B
Bill, William, dye A
Billers, Joseph, gir B
Billers, William, hab A
Billing, Nath, vin B
Billinghurst, Richard, bla B

70

Bilson, William, bak A
Bincks, Charles, dye A
Bindon, John, hab B
Bingley, George, ski B
Bingley, William, dra A
Birch, John, dye A
Bird, Daniel, dye A
Bird, Daniel, glz B
Bird, Jeremy, joi B
Bird, John, ck B
Bird, Joseph, bre B
Bird, Matthew, cor B
Bird, Nathaniel, bla A
Bird, Robert, but A
Bird, Robert, dye B
Bird, Robert, mer A
Bird, Thomas, cp A
Bird, Thomas, cur A124
Bird, William, sal A
Biscoe, Joseph, apo A
Biscoe, Thomas, iro A
Bishop, Benjamin, ck B
Bishop, George, dis A
Bishop, John, but B
Bishop, Joseph, bar A
Bishop, Thomas, gro A
Bishop, Thomas, hab A
Bishop, William, sal A
Bisk, Edmond, wax B
Bissell, James, sta B
Bissell, James, sta B
Bissell, John, pou B
Bithell, Robert, bak A2B578
Blackburn, Abraham, hab A134B6
Blackden, Thomas, joi A
Blackett, Robert, bla B
Blackhall, John, clo B
Blackhall, Thomas, hab B
Blackhorne, Thomas, gir A
Blackland, Samuel, gir B
Blackley, Griffin, bla A
Blackman, Robert, tur A
Blackmore, Arthur, pai B
Blackmore, Charles, mus B
Blackmore, John, tal B
Blackmore, Thomas, mer B
Blackston, Charles, bow B
Blackstone, Charles, bow B
Blackstone, John, apo B
Blackstone, Richard, bar B
Blackwell, Charles, gro A
Blackwell, James, clo A
Blackwell, John, lor A
Bladley, Roger, bro B
Blagrave, Richard, tai B
Blake, Benjamin, dye B
Blake, Daniel esq., vin A
Blake, John, bla B
Blake, John, cp A2B5
Blake, Thomas, bar B

Blakesley, John, cut B
Blakesly, Nathanael, cur B
Blakesly, Samuel, cur B
Blakeway, William, dra B
Bland, John, fis B
Bland, Nath, glo A13
Bland, Robert, but A
Bland, Thomas, tai A
Blandford, William, bar A123B6
Blanford, John, dra A123B7
Bleatz, Thomas, vin B
Blettsoe, Thomas, cp A
Blewitt, Samuel kt, ski A
Bley, John, dis A
Blincoe, John, pla B
Blinghorne, John, inn B
Bliss, Edward, dye A
Blizard, James, dye A124B5
Blockford, Anthony, gol B
Bloodworth, George, dye B
Bloodworth, George, wea B
Bloodworth, John, wea B
Blowen, Thomas, hab A
Blowing, Richard, wea A
Bluck, John, clo B
Blundell, Edmund, cur A
Blundell, James, bla B
Blundell, Richard, bar A
Blunkett, Edmond, fis A
Blunt, Edward, wea A
Bly, Christopher, fou A
Bly, Robert, tal B
Blye, Thomas, bar A123B6
Blythe, John, fou B
Board, John, tai B
Bockett, John, tur B
Boddicoat, Thomas, cp A3B678
Boddington, George, clo A
Boddington, Henry, clo A
Boddington, James, clo A
Boddington, Mark, sta B
Boddington, Nicholas, sta B
Boddington, Richard, but A
Boddington, Thomas, clo A
Boddington, Walter, bro A
Boddle, Thomas, car A
Boden, Adam, gro A
Bodham, Philip, tai A
Bodington, Edward, cor B
Bodington, Isaac, clo A
Bodington, Thomas, lea B
Bodington *see also* Doddington
Bodwell, William, bak B
Body, John, lor A
Bohomi, Morris, gol B
Boldery, John, but B
Bolton, Amos, dye A
Bolton, Job, gro A
Bolton, Samuel, gro A
Bond, Anthony, bre B58

71

Bond, Thomas, pai B
Bond, William, bar A4B678
Bonfield, William, bar B
Bonfoy, Hugh, fis A4B568
Bonwick, William, plu B
Booker, James, far A
Booker, Richard, dra A
Boon, Charles, inn B
Boon, Richard, tur B
Boon, Stephen, tur B
Boone, Henry, bar B
Booth, Christopher, hab A
Booth, James, gro A
Booth, Joseph, bak A
Booth, Richard, inn B
Boreman, Henry, mer B
Bosley, John, joi B
Bosley, Richard, mer B
Boston, Thomas, bla B
Bostwick, John, gir B
Bosvill, Alexander, sta A1B567
Boswell, Gervase, cut A
Boswell, John, hab B
Bosworth, Joseph, cp A3B678
Bosworth, Richard, clo B
Bosworth, Thomas, lor A
Botham, William, sta A
Bothwright, Samuel, dis B
Botley, Thomas, bak B
Bott, Walter, joi B
Bott, William, bla B
Boucher, John, wea A
Bouchrett, David, apo A
Boughey, Theophilus, bak B
Boughton, Richard, cp A
Boughton, Stephen jun, iro B
Boulter, Jonathan, dis A
Boulton, Benjamin, vin B
Boulton, Samuel, pai A
Bound, John, arm A
Bounde, Moses, hab A
Bourn, Thomas, bla B
Bourne, Benjamin, glo A24B67
Bourne, Samuel, dra A3B567
Bouton, Samuel, car A
Bowater, Henry, mer B
Bowater, Richard, mer A
Bowcher, Edward, car B
Bowcher, Tho, car A
Bowcher, Thomas sen, car A
Bowden, Joseph, pew B
Bowden, Nich, bar B
Bowden, William, hab A
Bowell, Nicholas, iro A
Bowen, Humphry, lea A
Bowen, Peter, cor A
Bowes, Richard, tai B
Bowes, Samuel, tai A
Bowler, Joseph, fou A1
Bowler, Samuel, but B

Bowles, James, ski A
Bowles, Nathaniel, gol A
Bowles, Richard, cp A
Bowles, Thomas, joi B
Bowles, Thomas sen, joi B
Bowley, Samuel, vin A
Bowlin, Bernard, tai A
Bowmer, John, vin B
Bows, Thomas, tur A
Bowtell, Francis, gro B
Bowton, Stephen, iro A
Bowyer, Jonah, sta B
Bowyer, Thomas, uph A
Bowyer, William, sta B
Boyce, John, vin A
Boyfeild, Richard, tai A
Boylston, George, but B
Boyse, John, joi B
Boyse, Richard, joi B
Brabben, John, joi B
Brace, James, pou A
Bracey, John, gol A
Bracey, William, hab A
Brackley, Samuel, gol B
Bradborne, Joseph, ski A
Bradbury, John, glo B
Bradford, George, glz A
Bradford, Henry, lor B
Bradford, John, iro B
Bradford, John, joi B
Bradford, Thomas, glz A
Bradley, Benjamin, tai A
Bradley, James, tai A
Bradley, John, dye A
Bradley, John, far A
Bradley, Joseph, bar B
Bradley, Joseph, joi B
Bradley, Thomas, tai B
Bradley, William, far B
Bradly, Thomas, bak A123B7
Bradshaw, Francis, sad B568
Bradshaw, John, sta A3B678
Bradstock, William, ski B
Bradyl, Thomas, sta A
Brail, John, bow B
Brailesford, Henry, glz A
Brain, James, joi A
Braine, Benjamin, glo A
Braine, Thomas, gro B
Braithwait, Benjamin, bla B
Braithwaite, William, uph B
Brampton, John, vin B
Brand, Benjamin, pai B
Brand, Jonathan, tur A
Brand, Joseph, plu A
Brand, Thomas, fis B
Brand, Thomas, joi B
Brandon, Charles, pai A
Brandon, Edward, joi B
Brandon, Joseph, gol B

72

Brandrake, Thomas, fra B
Branson, Henry, joi B
Branson, William, tai A
Brasher, William, ck B
Brasier, George, sal A
Brassey, Williams, cor B
Bray, Henry jun, glz B
Bray, Henry sen, glz B
Bray, William, hab B
Braynan, Christopher, inn B
Brazier, William, hab B
Breardcliffe, Thomas, bar B
Bredon, Robert, bre A
Breercliff, Mark, pou B
Breivicks, Jacob, clo B
Brenard, John, cor A
Brent, Humphrey, scr B
Brent, Jacob, iro B
Brent, Michael, uph A
Brereton, Dod, clo B
Bretland, Benjamin, gls B
Brett, William, pai B
Brewer, Timothy, dis A
Brewis, Valentine, dis B
Brewood, Benjamin, gol A
Brewster, Samuel esq., gro A124B6
Briane, Daniel, clo A
Brice, Joshua, sal A
Brice, Robert, bla B
Brich, William, gro B
Brickland, William, ck B
Brickley, William, glz A
Bricknell, William, inn B
Bricquett, Thomas, gro B
Briddon, Ambrose, fis B
Briden, Jeremiah, car A
Bridgen, Edward, cut B
Bridges, Edward, fou A
Bridges, John, bak B
Bridges, John, bak A
Bridges, John, clo B
Bridges, Joseph, tur A
Bridges, Richard, mer B
Bridges, Stephen, pew A
Bridges, Thomas, bar A
Bridgman, Richard, mer A234B5
Bridgman, Thomas, tur B
Bridgman, William, sal A
Bridgwater, Edward, dye B
Briggs, Ebenezer, arm A
Brigham, Philip, coa A
Bright, Charles, dis A2B678
Bright, Jeremiah, lea A124B6
Bright, John, cp B
Brightred, Samuel, arm A
Brightwell, Peter, bla A
Brightwell, Peter, vin B
Brigs, Thomas, wea B
Brikes, William, tai A
Brind, William, pai A

Briscoe, John, apo A
Briscoe, John, fis A
Briscoe, Robert, gro B
Briscoe, Stafford, gol A
Briscow, Henry, cp B
Briscow, Samuel, sta B
Briscow, Thomas, hab A4B578
Bristoe, William, vin A
Bristow, Richard, gol B
Bristow, Thomas, gro B
Brittain, James, car B
Brittain, John, clo A
Brittain, Richard, dye A
Brittell, Thomas, glz B
Britton, William, but B
Broadbank, Thomas, tal A
Broadhurst, John, hab A
Broadwell, Richard, wea B
Brocast, Richard, gro B
Brock, Thomas, tai B
Brock, William, bar B
Brockden, Benjamin, mer B
Brockden, James, wea B
Brockelesby, Charles, inn B
Brockly, Richard, vin B
Bromfield, Thomas, hab B
Bromfield, William, ski B
Brook, John, sta A
Brook, Joseph, tai A
Brook, Robert, hab A
Brook, William, bar B
Brooke, Edward, dye A234B8
Brooke, Samuel, wea B
Brooke, Thomas, vin A
Brooke, Walter, dye A
Brookes, Christopher, bar B
Brookes, Thomas, bro A
Brookes, William, inn B
Brookman, John, joi A
Brookman, William, joi A
Brooks, Henry, pai B
Brooks, John, fou A
Brooks, William, inn B
Brooksbank, John, hab A
Brooksbank, Joseph, hab A
Broomer, John, bri B
Brough, George, iro A
Broughton, John, apo A
Broughton, William, tai A
Broutherton, William, arm A
Brown, Abraham, bri B
Brown, Andrew, arm B
Brown, Benjamin, hab B
Brown, Benjamin, sta B
Brown, Christopher, sta B
Brown, Edmond, iro A
Brown, Edward, dra B
Brown, Francis, cp A234B8
Brown, James, bak B
Brown, John, bar B

73

Brown, John, but B
Brown, John, glo A
Brown, John, inn A
Brown, John William, vin B
Brown, Philip, dye B
Brown, Philip, fle A23B58
Brown, Richard, mas B
Brown, Samuel, coa B
Brown, Samuel, cp A
Brown, Thomas, bar A
Brown, Thomas, but B
Brown, Thomas, cor A
Brown, Thomas, dis B
Brown, Thomas, dye A
Brown, Thomas, pou B
Brown, Thomas, ski B
Brown, Thomas, sta A123
Brown, William, far A
Brown, William, inn B
Brown, William, lea A134B5
Brown, William, tur B
Browne, Benjamin, sta B
Browne, Benjamin, sta B
Browne, George, bar A1B567
Browne, John, bri A34B67
Browne, Joseph, bak A123B7
Browne, Matthew, scr B
Browne, Nath, arm A
Browne, Richard, pla B
Browne, William, bar A
Browne, William, tai A34B67
Browne, William, uph A
Brownscombe, James, wea A
Brownshith, John, fle B
Brownsword, Ellis, fis A
Broxell, William, bak A
Bruges, Richard, sta A
Brumfield, Thomas, gro B
Brumford, William, lea B
Brunskill, George, ck B
Bryan, Augustine, hab A
Bryan, John, pla B
Bryan, Thomas, but A
Bryan, William, bak B
Bryan, William, far A3B567
Bryant, William, bre A
Buchanan, John, sta B
Buck, Henry, fis A4B568
Buck, Samuel, sal A
Buckby, Vere, iro A4B568
Buckett, Joseph, cur B
Buckham, John, gir A
Buckingham, Edward, mas A
Buckingham, Jeremy, mas A
Buckingham, Joseph, lea A134B5
Buckland, James, car A
Buckly, George, vin B
Bucknall, Will, bre A
Bucksher, John, gir A
Buckstone, Edward, dis A

Budworth, Timothy, coa A
Bugbey, Atkinson, joi A
Buirchmore, William, joi A
Bulkly, Richard, sad B
Bull, Edward, fis A23B57
Bull, George, joi A
Bull, Henry, bar B
Bull, John, clo A123B6
Bull, Richard, gro B
Bull, Richard, gro A234
Bull, William, but A
Bull, Young, but A
Bulley, John, cut A
Bullock, Adam, bak A
Bullock, Francis, wax B
Bullock, James, wea A
Bulphin, Edward, dis A
Bunce, John, pla A
Bunch, James, cur A
Bunn, Henry, ck B
Bunney, William, tai A
Burbage, George, vin B
Burbidge, Thomas, uph A
Burbroe, John, tal A
Burch, Benjamin, pla B
Burch, John, glo A
Burch, Samuel, apo B
Burchall, Robert, clo A13B56
Burchell, Thomas, scr B
Burchmore, William, joi A
Burd, Edward, pai B
Burden, Thomas, joi A
Burdett, Charles, sta A
Burdett, Thomas, tal B
Burdg, Thomas, tal B
Burding, William, cut B
Burford, Edward, fru A
Burges, Edward, tal A
Burges, Nathaniel, but A
Burges, Robert, gol A
Burgess, John, wea A
Burgess, Thomas, inn A
Burgin, Samuel, car A
Burgis, Charles, sal A
Burgis, Edward, clo B
Burgis, Richard, pla A
Burgis, Thomas, coa A
Burgoin, John, lea A23
Burkhead, Edward, cur A
Burless, Henry, cp B
Burley, George, vin A
Burnet, Nicholas, hab B
Burnet, Obediah, gir A
Burr, Edward, cp A
Burr, Francis, bak B
Burreau, Thomas, bro A
Burren, Anthony, mer B
Burridge, John, sal A
Burrough, Thomas, cut B
Burroughs, Roger, iro B

74

Burroughs, Samuel, wea A
Burrow, Abraham, ck B
Burrow, John, fis B
Burrow, Thomas, bri B
Burrow, Thomas, sta A
Burrows, Humphrey, wea A
Burrows, Jos, joi A
Burrows, Thomas, bar A
Burt, Jeremiah, lea B
Burt, John, joi B
Burton, Edward, bar A
Burton, Henry, bak B7
Burton, John, joi B
Burton, Jonathan, glo B
Burton, Joseph, wea A
Burton, Richard, fis B
Burton, Richard, wea A14B67
Burton, Robert, dye B
Burton, Robert, fis B
Burton, Robert, fou B
Busfeild, John, bar A
Bush, William, pou A
Bushnel, Thomas, joi B
Bushnell, Robert, mas A
Buskin, James, vin B
Buss, Edward, pou B
Buston, William, nee A
Butcher, Robert, cor B
Butcher, William, bla A
Butler, Crispin, pew B
Butler, John, bak B
Butler, John, bak A123
Butler, John, but B
Butler, John, clo B
Butler, John, glz A
Butler, William, dye B
Butler, William, pla B
Butler, William, tur B
Butterfield, Richard, sta A
Butterfield, Thomas, gro B
Buttler, Samuel, cor B
Byard, John, cut B
Byeland, George, glz B
Byercy, Henry, dye B
Byfield, Josiah, clo A
Byrond, Nathaniel, fou A
Bywater, Charles, cut B

Cable, John, hab A
Caddey, John, tal B
Cadwell, John, bla A
Cager, Robert, bak B
Calcutt, Richard, but A
Calcutt, Will, but A
Cale, John, tai B
Callaway, Robert, pou A
Callcot, John, tal B
Calpin, Richard, tai B
Calverly, Bewick John, gro B
Calverly, Thomas, gro B

Calvert, Thomas, joi B
Cam, Joseph, hab B
Cam, William, tai A2B578
Cambell, Jonathan, vin B
Cambridge, Richard, mer B
Camfield, Francis, lea A
Camfield, Nathaniel sen, dra A
Campfield, Richard, uph B
Campiere, George, bak B
Cann, Richard, tur B
Cannon, John, vin B
Cannon, Thomas, vin B
Carbonell, Delillers, dye A
Carbonell, John, dye A
Carbonell, Michael, dye A
Carbonell, Thomas, dye A
Carew, Thomas, iro A
Carey, James, sal B
Carey, Thomas, sal B
Carington, Richard, wea B
Carles, Robert, hab B
Carleton, Bostock, mer A
Carleton, Edward, mer A
Carleton, Harden, mer A
Carne, Francis, dis B
Carpenter, Joseph, hab B
Carpenter, Nathaniel, dra B
Carpenter, Thomas, hab A
Carpenter, Thomas, hab A
Carpenter, Thomas, pai B
Carpenter, William, arm B
Carpenter, William, cur A
Carpenter, William, hab B
Carr, Edward, glz A
Carr, James, bro A
Carr, John, joi B
Carr, Robert, clo B
Carr, Thomas, scr B
Carr, William, joi B
Carrell, Joseph, fis A
Carrington, Edmund, dye A
Carrington, Henry, dye A
Carroll, William, tai A
Cars, Moses, bar B
Cart, Richard, but A
Carter, George, uph A
Carter, Humfry, bak B
Carter, John, bla B
Carter, John, ski A134B5
Carter, John, tal A
Carter, Martin, tai B
Carter, Nathaniel, gol B
Carter, Samuel, sad B
Carter, Thomas, glo A
Carter, William, cur B
Carterell, Robert, apo B
Cartlich, John, gol B
Cartright, Ralph, bak A
Cartwright, Francis, dye B
Cartwright, Jonathan, ck A

75

Cartwright, Peter, hab A
Cartwright, Thomas, mas A
Carus, John, glo A
Casamire, Josiah, uph A
Casbeard, Richard, wax B
Casbeard, Richard, wax A14
Case, Thomas, tal A
Case, William, bri A
Casebeard, John, cp A
Caseby, Humphrey, sal B
Cass, John kt, car A2B567
Castell, Robert, hab B
Castor, Alexander, hab A
Catesby, John, lea A
Cather, John, dra A124B7
Catmore, Thomas, dis B
Caulcott, Thomas, lea A
Caunell, John, tal B
Cave, Francis, dra B
Cave, Thomas, bak A134B7
Cave, Thomas jun, bak A
Cawcutt, Obediah, lor A
Cawsey, James, bro B
Cawsins, John, bow B
Cecill, James, dye A
Chad, Richard, tur B
Chadey, Jeremiah, pou B
Chadsey, John, tai A
Chadwell, John, gol B
Chadwick, John, tai A
Challener, John, apo B
Chaloner, John, tai B
Chamberlain, Joseph, bla A
Chamberlain, Richard, ski B
Chamberlain, Richard, wea A
Chamberlain, Thomas, arm A
Chamberlin, George, car A
Chamberlin, John, car A
Chambers, Chadwick, ski A
Chambers, Jeremiah, cut B
Chambers, John, bar A234B5
Chambers, Richard, uph B
Chambers, Robert, far B
Chambers, Thomas, wax A
Chambers, William, lea A
Chamflower, Thomas, iro A
Champion, John, vin B
Chancey, William, iro B
Chancy, Richard, mer A
Chancy, William, mer A
Chandler, Henry, sad A
Chandler, Joseph, sad A
Chandler, Nathaniel, tal B
Chandler, Percivall, fis B
Chandler, Robert, bar A
Chandler, William, bak B
Chandler, William, fis A
Chandler, William, tal A34B68
Channing, John, apo A
Chantree, John, cor B

Chaplin, Joseph, cp A
Chaplyn, Sampson, fis A
Chapman, Daniel, glo A
Chapman, Francis, dye A
Chapman, John, arm A
Chapman, John, inn B
Chapman, John, wea B
Chapman, Joseph, arm A
Chapman, Lewis, gir B
Chapman, Nicholas, arm A
Chapman, Richard, apo A123B6
Chapman, Richard, cut A
Chapman, Robert, arm A
Chapman, Samuel, apo A134B6
Chapman, Thomas, dis A
Chapman, William, bla A
Charles, Henry, inn B
Charles, Thomas, inn B
Charles, William, bar B
Charley, Hen, gls A
Charlton, Michael, cut B
Charton, William, bar B
Chase, Emmaliel, gir A
Chase, Richard, iro B
Chase, William, iro A134B5
Chatfield, Bernard, apo B
Chauncy, Charles, wax A
Chauncy, Richard, clo B
Chellingworth, John, pai B
Chelton, Andrew, tur A
Cheney, William, cp A
Cheret, Thomas, wea A
Cheshire, John, nee A
Cheshire, Peter, tal B
Cheshire, Richard, coa A12B78
Cheshire, William, tal B
Chester, Gamaliel, mer B
Chester, Granado, tal B
Chester, Thomas, mer B
Cheswall, Richard, dra B
Chewter, Thomas, tal A
Chicham, Edward, wea A
Chide, John, inn A
Child, Daniel, tal B
Child, Francis, gol B568
Child, Henry, bro B
Child, John, bak B
Child, John, iro B
Child, John, tal A
Child, John, tal A
Child, John jun, tal A
Child, Lawrence, pew A
Child, Robert esq., gol B
Child, Stephen, gol B
Child, Thomas, pou B
Child, Timothy, sta A
Child, William, but B
Child, William, ck B
Child, William, cut B
Child, William, hab A

76

Child, William, lea B
Chinn, Daniel, dye A123B5
Chiselton, William, bar A
Chiswell, Richard, mer A
Chitham, Edward, wea A
Chittle, John, lea A
Chitty, Joseph, car B
Chitty, Josiah, bre A
Cholmley, William, fis A
Christian, Daniel, bro B
Christmas, Michael, joi A
Christopher, William, hab B
Church, Bower, bre A
Church, Gabriel, lor A
Church, James, ski A123B6
Church, Randall, bar B
Churcher, Thomas, lea B
Churchill, Awnsham, sta A
Churchill, John, car B
Churchill, Richard, plu B
Churchill, Robert, hab B
Claris, Peter, hab A
Clark, Bartholomew, cp A23B78
Clark, Christopher, lea B
Clark, Daniel, tai A
Clark, Edward, tai A
Clark, Henry, uph B
Clark, Henry, vin A
Clark (Cluck), John, bak A1B568
Clark, John, cp A14B67
Clark, John, dis B
Clark, John, dis B
Clark, John, ski B
Clark, John, tal A
Clark. Nicholas, uph A
Clark, Richard, bre B
Clark, Samuel, cp A
Clark, Samuel, sta A
Clark, Thomas, cur B
Clark, Thomas, pou B
Clark, Thomas, sta A
Clark, Thomas, tai A
Clark, William, hab B
Clarke, Anthony, bak A24B78
Clarke, Edmund, gir A
Clarke, Francis, dra B578
Clarke, George, tai B
Clarke, George, tai B
Clarke, George, vin B
Clarke, Henry, bro B
Clarke, Henry, clo B
Clarke, Henry, clo A2
Clarke, Henry, wax A
Clarke, Humphry, bro B
Clarke, Isaac, vin A
Clarke, James, cor B
Clarke, James, dis A
Clarke, Jeremy, but A23B67
Clarke, John, bla B
Clarke, John, bla A

Clarke, John, bre A
Clarke, John, gol B568
Clarke, John, sal A
Clarke, Jonathan, gls A
Clarke, Jos, bro A
Clarke, Joseph, hab B
Clarke, Joshua, sal A
Clarke, Lancelot, dis A
Clarke, Lancelot, ski A
Clarke, Philip, gro B
Clarke, Richard, pla A
Clarke, Samuel, bak B
Clarke, Samuel, mer A
Clarke, Stephen, gir A
Clarke, Thomas, dra A
Clarke, Thomas, fou A
Clarke, Thomas, pew A
Clarke, Thomas, scr A
Clarke, Thomas, tal B
Clarke, William, fra A
Clarkson, Daniel, tai A134
Clarkson, William, dye B
Clarkson, William, ski B
Clay, Richard, dra A
Clayter, William, bak A
Clayton, David, tai A
Clayton, John, fou A1B567
Clayton, Thomas, tur A
Cleave, Alexander, pew B
Cleave, Isaac, sta B
Cleaver, John, bla A
Cleeleh, Francis, bow B
Cleer, James, glo B
Cleever, William, but A
Cleggot, Richard, dra B
Clemens, Robert, gol B
Clement, John, fis B
Clement, Jos, tai A
Clement, Phillip, bro A
Clement, Samuel, ski A
Clements, Henry, sta B
Clemmon, Edward, bro B
Clerk, Samuel kt, ski B
Clerk, William, pla B
Cletherow, Michael, bri A
Cliff, Nathaniel, sta A
Clifford, William, gir A
Cliffton, Henry, clo A
Clifton, Francis, bak A
Clifton, William, bla A
Clinch, William, wea B
Clinton, William but B
Clogie, Thomas, hab A
Clowes, Robert, gro B
Clowse, Robert, hab A13B57
Cluck, John, *see* Clark, John
Coartman, Thomas, pai B
Coates, Henry, dye A
Coatsworth, William, bar A
Cobb, Thomas, bla A

Cobett, Joseph, dis A
Cock, John, plu B
Cock, Richard, plu A
Cock, Robert, bow B
Cockain, John, cor A
Cockbill, Richard, glo A
Cockerill, Daniel, iro A
Cocking, William, gro A
Cocks, Isaac, tai B
Cockshut, Thomas, tai A
Codd, Thomas, hab B
Coggs, John, gol A
Coggs, Richard, wax A2B568
Coish, Elisha, mer A
Coke, Thomas, joi B
Colchester, Henry, gro A
Colcutt *see* Coleat
Cole, Benjamin, ck B
Cole, Benjamin, dra A
Cole, Benjamin, dye A
Cole, Edward, scr A12B67
Cole, Edward, ski B
Cole, Francis, bre A
Cole, George, dye A
Cole, Henry, bak A
Cole, Henry, glz B
Cole, Humphry, but A
Cole, John, cp A
Cole, Lawrence, gol B
Cole, Robert, vin B578
Cole, Samuel, inn A4B8
Cole, Stephen, hab A
Cole, Thomas, bre A
Cole, Thomas, bre A
Cole, Thomas, ck B
Cole, William, bar A
Coleat (Colcutt), Daniel, lea A23B58
Colebath, Benjamin, tai A3B568
Colebeck, Edward, bar A
Colebran, Thomas, fle A
Colebrook, John, tai A124B8
Colebrooke, James, mer A
Coleclough, Sampson, fra A
Coleman, Abraham, glo A
Coleman, Francis, sal B
Coleman, Henry, bla A
Coleman, Henry, tai A
Coleman, Isaac, sal B
Coleman, John, dye A
Coleman, Robert, hab A
Coleman, Samuel, glo A
Coleman, Thomas, glz A134
Coleman, Thomas, sal B
Coleman, William, glo A
Colemer, Thomas, but B
Coles, Benjamin, dye A
Coles, George, ski A
Coles, Richard, pou B
Coles, Thomas, dis A
Coles, William, bri A

Coles, William kt, fis A34B58
Collet, Christopher, bro A
Collet, William, wea A
Collett, Benjamin, iro A
Collett, Elias, cp A
Collett, John, cp A
Collett, Matthew, dra A
Collett, Richard, vin A
Collett, Thomas, vin B
Collewis, George, wea A
Collier, Benjamin, gro A
Collier, Henry, cor A
Collier, John, but B
Collier, Jonathan, mer A
Collier, Joseph, lea A
Collier, Joseph, mer A
Collier, Richard, tal A
Collier, William, joi B
Collier, William, tal A123B8
Collier, William, tal A
Collings, Richard, bak B
Collingwood, George, far A
Collins, Christopher, gol B
Collins, Henry, vin B
Collins, John, dye B
Collins, Joseph, bar B
Collins, Joseph, mer A
Collins, Richard, bar A
Collins, William, inn A
Colly, John, wea B
Collyer, Nicholas, fou B
Collyer, Samuel, inn A
Colson, Edward, mer B
Colson, Richard, tai A
Colt, Edward, wea B
Colt, John, dra B
Colton, George, bla B
Colvill, John, bro A
Combs, Thomas, but B
Comer, George, inn A
Comes, Oliver, nee A
Comes, Thomas, pla A
Commins, William, pai A
Compear, George, bak A1
Compeire, Leonard, lea B
Compiers, Thomas, apo B
Compton, John, bak A
Compton, Water, gol B
Conant, Robert, fis B
Condee, Francis, apo A134B6
Coner, Michael, bar B
Coney, Thomas, plu B
Congrave, Peter, fou A
Conningsby, Christopher, sta B
Constable, Henry, ck B
Constable, Philip, tal A
Constable, Thomas, bri B
Constantine, Samuel, tur B
Conyers, Gerrard esq., sal A
Conyers, Samuel, pla A

78

Cook, Ezekiel, joi B
Cook, George, bar A
Cook, Jacob, dra A
Cook, John, glz B
Cook, Thomas, joi A
Cook, Thomas, uph B
Cook, William ck B
Cook, William, fru A
Cooke, Charles, mer A
Cooke, David, inn A
Cooke, Edward, vin B
Cooke, James, fis B
Cooke, John, glz A
Cooke, John, iro B
Cooke, Richard, car B
Cooke, Thomas, clo A23B67
Cooke, Thomas, clo A134B6
Cookes, John, mer A13B56
Coombes, William, bro B
Coop, Peter, plu B
Coop, Richard, sal A
Cooper, Benjamin, pew A123B6
Cooper, Charles, cp B
Cooper, Charles, pla A
Cooper, Daniel, uph A
Cooper, Edmund, bow B
Cooper, Francis, cp A
Cooper, Isaac, vin B
Cooper, James, bar A
Cooper, John, clo A
Cooper, John, cor B
Cooper, John, cur A
Cooper, John, far B
Cooper, John, fis B
Cooper, John, glo A
Cooper, John, glz A
Cooper, John, gol B
Cooper, John, hab B
Cooper, John, joi A
Cooper, John, mas A
Cooper, John, tai A
Cooper, Joseph, glz A
Cooper, Matthew, gol B
Cooper, Nathaniel, hab B
Cooper, Richard, coa A2B578
Cooper, Richard, gro B
Cooper, Robert, gol B
Cooper, Robert, lea B
Cooper, Rowland, tur B
Cooper, Thomas, glz B
Cooper, Thomas, sal A
Cooper, Thomas, tai A
Cooper, William, glo A14B56
Cooper, William, joi A
Cooper, William, tai A12B67
Cooper, William, tai A
Cooter, Matth, bar B
Cope, Walter, fis B
Copeland, John, glo A
Coplestone, Lancelot, bar B

Copperwhite, John, inn B
Coppin, Stephen, lea A
Coppindale, Daniel, dis A
Corbet, Thomas, cut B
Corbett, John, pai B
Corbison, John, pla B
Cordwell, Edward, car B
Cordwell, John, fra B
Corey, Samuel, car A
Corker, George, pla B
Corner, Charles, glz B
Corner, John, dye A
Corner, Thomas, dye A
Corner, William, wea B
Cornhill, John, tai A4
Cornish, Henry, hab A
Correvus, James, bak B7
Cort, Benjamin, tai A
Corthorpe, Bryan, sta B
Cory, Thomas, joi B
Coster, William, fra B
Cotchet, Nicholas, vin B
Cotchett, Thomas, tai B
Cotten, Charles, far A
Cotterel, Bernard, mer B
Cottis, Thomas, but B
Cotton, James, hab A2B578
Cotton, John, sal A
Cotton, Jonathan, pew A
Cotton, Richard, pla B
Cottrell, Bazil, scr B
Couch, Nicholas, mus A4B567
Coulston, Stephen, plu A
Coulter, James, tai A
Coursey, William, bla B
Court, Richard, bla B
Court, William, cut B
Court, William, cut A23
Courthope, William, uph B
Courthorpe, Peter, joi B
Courtris, Jacob, bro A
Couser, Abraham, wax A
Coventry, Thomas, gro A
Cowdrey, Richard, bla A
Cowell, George, glo A
Cowell, John, coa B
Cowley, John, tai A123B6
Cowley, William, dis A
Cowley, William, pew A
Cowley, William, pew A
Cowper, Thomas, tai B
Cowsey, John, gol A
Cox, Ambross, gro B
Cox, Charles kt, bre A34B57
Cox, Edmund, dra B
Cox, George, bro A
Cox, Gostwick, plu B
Cox, Isaac, tai A13
Cox, Isaac, tal A
Cox, John, cur A

79

Cox, John, iro B
Cox, John, tur B
Cox, Jonathan, pla B
Cox, Robert, bla B
Cox, Thomas, clo A
Cox, Thomas, cut B
Cox, Thomas, joi A234B5
Cox, Thomas, mus A
Cox, Thomas, sad B
Cox, Thomas, tai A12B67
Cox, Thomas, vin A123B6
Cox, William, iro B
Coxey, Richard, joi B
Coxhead, John (Tho), joi A2B567
Coxhead, Robert, dye A
Coxson, John, gro B
Cozens, Oliver, wea A
Craawell, William, bak B678
Craddock, Matthew, hab A
Cradock, John, hab A23B58
Craggs, Jos, inn A
Craige, John, bro A
Crainer, Samuel, wea A
Crane, Charles, dye A
Crane, James, gir A
Crane, Richard, uph B
Crane, William, bak A13B78
Cranstone, Robert, far A
Cranwell, Jonathan, scr A
Cranwell, William, tal A
Craven, Thomas, mas A
Crawley, John, glz A
Crawley, Thomas, lea A
Craycer, Joseph, mer B
Crayle, John esq., clo B
Creagh, Stephen, lea B
Creamer, Charles, fis B
Cresner, Edward, bro A
Cressiner, George, gro A
Cretchlow, Samuel, dra A
Crey, Richard, cor A
Cripple, William, joi A
Cripps, Nichol, dra B678
Crips, George, bar A
Crisp, John, pla A
Crisp, Pheasant, ski A
Crisp, Thomas, gls A
Crockford, Fam, lor B
Crockson, John, dra B578
Crodwell, George, plu A
Croft, Richard, vin B567
Crofts, William, gol A
Crome, Thomas, tai A
Crompton, John, lea B
Cromwell, Henry, pla A
Cropwell, William, lea A
Crose, George, wea B
Crosley, Naham, wea B
Crosley, Nathanael, bar B
Cross, Andrew, bre B

Cross, John, far A
Cross, Peter, gir A
Cross, Stephen, gir A
Cross, Stephen, glo A
Cross, William, wea A12B67
Crothley, John, dye A
Crouch, Edward, pou B
Crouch, John, bak A
Crouch, John, uph A
Crouch, Samuel, sta A
Crouch, Thomas, pou B
Crouch, Zarobabel, cut A
Croutch, John, bak A3B8
Crow, Ephram, gol B
Crow, Patrick, apo A
Crowder, Edward, wea A
Crowder, George, but A
Crowshaw, Robert, gls A
Crudge, Alexander, vin B
Crutcher, Richard, mas A123B7
Cruttenden, Joss, apo A
Crynes, Jonathan, lea A
Culley, John, gol B
Culliford, William, tal A
Cullin, Thomas, bak B
Cullum, Lawrence, ski A
Cumberland, John, dis A
Cumberlidge, John, gol B
Cumbers, James, dra A
Cuney, Lewis, gol A
Curd, Richard, ck B
Curle, Edmund, cor A134B6
Curry, Thomas, joi A
Curthope, Edward, gol B
Curtis, John, bak A124
Curtis, Robert, pou A
Curwin, William, apo B
Cushy, Thomas, lea A
Cutbeard, Matthew, gol A
Cutbert, William, gol B
Cuthbert, John, gol A13B67
Cutler, John, joi B
Cutting, Arthur, iro A
Cutting, John, dra A
Cutts, Charles, hab A

Dabbs, Arthur, gol B
Dacres, Philip, gro B
Dagley, Giles, cur A
Daintry, William, wea A
Daking, Abraham, clo A12B67
Dakins, Charles, bar B
Daldron, William, ski B
Dale, William, bar B
Dale, William, uph A
Dalton, Andrew, bro A
Dalton, Thomas, apo A
Dalton, Thomas, plu B
Dalton, Thomas, scr B
Dalton, Thomas, sta B

80

Dam, John, joi B
Damon, Michael, inn A
Dampney, Jos, fou A3B578
Dance, Giles, tai B
Dance, Nicholas, bri B
Dance, Thomas, pla A
Dandridge, John, pai B
Dandridge, Joseph, tai A
Dane, John, pai B
Dane, Richard, ski B
Dane, William, fru B
Dangerfield, Stephen, cor B
Daniel, Henry, hab B
Daniel, Jonathan, joi A3B567
Daniel, Joseph, inn B
Daniel, Stephen, hab A
Daniel, Thomas, inn B
Dann, John, scr A2B568
Dansey, James, bar B
Danter, William, joi B
Danvas, John, dra B
Darby, John, sta A
Darby, Roger, clo A
Dare, Matthew, dis B
Darrack, Enock, nee A
Darret, John, fis B
Darrington, Thomas, bri B
Dash, Joseph, gro A
Dashwood, John, joi A
Dashwood, Thomas, vin A
Daulting, Benjamin, ski B
Davall, John, bla B
Davenish, Joseph, uph A
Davinish, Joshua, glz B
Davis, Belvier, apo A
Davis, Daniel, ck B
Davis, Ed, bla B
Davis, Edward, dye B
Davis, Edward, wea A
Davis, Evan, glz A
Davis, Henry, wax A
Davis, John, car B
Davis, John, car A
Davis, John, ck A
Davis, John, coa B
Davis, John, dye B
Davis, John, fou A
Davis, John, lor B
Davis, John, lor A
Davis, John, lor A
Davis, John, vin B
Davis, Joshua, wea B
Davis, Philip, fou A2B578
Davis, Richard, bre B
Davis, Richard, dye A
Davis, Richard, hab A
Davis, Richard, vin B
Davis, Richard, wea B
Davis, Roger, wax A
Davis, Thomas, bla A

Davis, Thomas, but A14B68
Davis, Thomas, car B
Davis, Thomas, ck A34B5
Davis, Thomas, joi B
Davis, Thomas, mas B
Davis, William, bla A
Davis, William, tai B
Davis, William, tai A1B568
Davise, William, lea B
Davison, John, but B
Davison, William, pew B
Davyes, George, clo B
Daw, John, glz B
Dawes, William, cur B
Dawks, Ichabod, sta A14B58
Dawling, Andrew, hab B
Daws, Samuel, fis A
Dawson, Anthony, bla A
Dawson, Edward, inn B
Dawson, John, tai B
Dawson, John, tai A
Dawson, Joseph, tai A
Dawson, Newcome, gro A
Dawson, Robert, gro A
Dawson, Robert, vin B
Dawson, Thomas, car B
Dawson, Thomas, fra A
Dawson, Thomas, uph A
Dawson, William, tai A
Dawson, William, wea A
Day, James, uph A
Day, John, bak A
Day, John, cor A
Day, John, hab B
Day, John, mer A
Day, Josiah, pou A14B56
Day, Robert, tai A
Day, Stephen, pou A
Day, Valentine, bar A
Deacle, John, dra A
Deacon, Thomas, wea B
Dean, Matthew, car B
Dean, Thomas, but B
Deane, John, cut B
Deane, John, gls A
Deane, Robert, fou B
Decaux, Mich, bro A
Dee, William, bak B
Dee, William, bak A13
Degrave, John, hab A
Delanoy, Peter, dye A
Deleau, Elias, mer B
Delight, Peter, tal A
Dell, Francis, pai A2B568
Dell, Henry, glo A
Dell, Humphry, gol B
Dell, William, cut B
Dell, William, joi B
Delmee, Peter esq., fis A
Deloane, Noah, fou B

81

Denew, Isaac, dye A
Denew, John, dye A
Denham, James, joi A14B67
Denne, Alud, bre A
Dennee, Edward, wea A
Dennet, Robert, bar B
Dennett, Tho, car A
Denning, George, sal B
Denning, Philip, inn A
Denning, Thomas, sal B
Dennis, David, wea A
Dennison, Hugh, cor B
Dennison, John, inn A
Dent, George, glo B
Dent, John, wea A
Dent, Marmaduke, bro A
Dent, Thomas, sad B
Dent, Thomas, sad A
Denton, Richard, bla B
Dequestor, Jacob, vin B
Desbouvery, Christ kt, mer B
Desbouvery, Jacob, mer B
Devinck, Benjamin, gir A
Dew, Edward, dye B
Dewdney, Richard, bak B
Dewe, Thomas, inn A
Dewick, William, bla A
Diamond, Richard, lor A
Diamond, Robert, lea A
Dickenson, Ambrose, bar B
Dickenson, William, bar A
Dickins, Robert, fra A
Dickinson, John, gro A
Dickinson, Rivers, bre A
Dickinson, Robert, far A
Dickinson, William, tur B
Dickonson, John, mer A
Dickson, Ralph, gro A
Dickson, Richard, hab B
Dickson, Richard, hab B
Dickson, Thomas, uph A
Diffeld, John, glo A
Dighton, Henry, hab B
Dighton, Samuel, bak A134B7
Dillham, Joseph, joi B
Dillingham, Theophilus, tai A
Dillingham, William, mer A
Dimmock, Thomas, far B
Dimmock, Thomas, far B
Diston, Richard, joi B
Diston, Thomas, ck A
Diston, William, dis B
Divett, Thomas, lea A
Dixon, Michael, vin B
Dixon, Richard, tai A
Dixson, Michael, vin A
Dobbins, John, fru A
Dobbins, Joseph, bla B
Dobbs, Wills, pou B
Dobins, John, bar B

Dobinson, Henry, gir B
Dobson, John, inn A
Doby, John, gol A
Dockwra, William, arm A
Dodd, James, hab A
Dodd, John, sal B
Dodd, Robert, fis B
Dodd, Thomas, hab A
Doddington (Bodington), James, lea
A12B78
Dodge, Thomas, joi A
Dodridge, Daniel, wax A
Dodsworth, Christopher, mer A
Dolbey, Andrew, but A124
Dolby, Andrew, but B
Doldarn, William, ski A
Doldron, George, glz A134B6
Dolen, John, but B
Donn, Joseph, gol B
Donne, John, pew B
Donne, Obad, bla B56
Dormond, William, cor A
Dorrell, Edward, sta A
Dorrell, John, uph B
Dottin, George, bar B
Dottin, George, bar A4
Doubledee, Francis, cut A
Doughty, Edmond, ski B
Dove, John, pew B
Dove, Matthew, fis A14B58
Dove, Robert, mer A
Dovey, James, bla A
Dovey, Joseph, tai B
Dovey, William, hab B
Dowdesell, Edward, gol A
Dowdeswell, Thomas, tal A
Dowell, Thomas, cp A
Dowley, Hugh, gro B
Dowley, Robert, tai A
Downer, Peter, hab A
Downer, William, hab A
Downes, Phillip, fis A4B567
Downes, Richard, fou A
Downing, Joseph, sta B6
Dowse, Francis, bar A
Dowse, Thomas, joi B
Doyley, Robert, mer B
Drafgate, Richard, gir B
Drage, Theodorus, hab A
Drake, Humphry, bla B
Drake, Thomas, hab B
Drake, William, sal B
Drake, William, tai A
Draper, Richard, gir B
Drayton, Joseph, gro A
Drayton, Joshua, dye A
Drayton, Thomas, vin A
Drew, Benjamin, sal A13B68
Drew, Cornelius, tai A
Drew, Richard, tai A

82

Dring, Thomas, arm B
Drinkell, John, pou A
Drinkwater, Francis, glo B
Drinkwater, Robert, sal B
Drought, Thomas, clo B
Drury, John, inn B
Drury, Jos, fou A
Drury, Richard, bak A
Drury, Walter, apo A
Dry, Augustine, ski B
Dry, Henry, ski A
Drybutter, Peter, hab B
Dubert, William, sal B
Dubois, Samuel, fis A
Duboise, Ralphell, wea A
Duck, John, gol A
Dudley, James, glz A
Dudley, Samuel, clo B
Dudley, Will, but A
Duffield, Edward, tai A
Dufremey, Samuel, glz A
Dugdale, Abraham, gls B
Duhamel, Jacob, bro A2B567
Duke, Edward, bar A
Duke, Edward, bar A
Dukson, Zachary, tal B
Duncalfe, Simon, cut A4B578
Duncomb, Preston, bow B
Duncomb, Thomas, bow B
Duncomb, Thomas, clo B
Dundridge, Fran, apo B
Dunham, Geo, apo B
Dunkley, Robert, glo B
Dunkley, Robert kt, hab B
Dunklin, Samuel, scr B
Dunn, John, but A12B78
Dunn, Thomas, mas A14B78
Dunning, Richard, fis A
Dunton, John, sta A
Duprie, John, hab A12B67
Durand, John, pew B
Durban, Henry, tal A
Durham, John, hab A
Durvill, Thomas, bri A134B5
Durvill, William, bla A
Dutch, Cornelius, wea A
Dutton, Adam, bla B
Dye, Jonas, fou A
Dyer, Benjamin, cut A
Dyer, Doyley, vin B
Dyer, Edward, pla A
Dyer, John, pew A134
Dyer, Lawrence, pew A134
Dyer, William, bri A
Dyerson, Thomas, bak A12B78
Dyos, Thomas, mer B
Dyson, Richard, plu A
Dyton, Samuel, bak A

Eades, Thomas, inn B

Eades, Thomas, wea A
Eady, Charles, sad B
Eales, Isaac, arm B
Eales, John, pla A
Eales, Thomas, pai B
Earle, John, fou A
Earle, Joshua, wea B
Earle, William, tai A
East, James, cut B
East, John, gol B
East, Thomas, sad A
East, William, sad B
Eastman, Nehemiah, sal A
Easton, John, inn B
Easton, Richard, dra A
Eaton, Barrington, mer A
Eaton, Edward, clo A
Eaton, James, lea A
Eaton, Josiah, hab A12B78
Eaton, Peter, cp A
Eaton, William, fis A4B578
Eaton, William, pew B
Ebbitt, Edward, dye A
Ebbitt, Edward jun, dye A
Ebbut, Edmund, vin A
Ecclestone, Theodore, gro A234B6
Edden, John, car B
Eddowes, John, fle B
Eden, John, bri B
Eden, Nathaniel, glo B
Eden, Ralph, cp B
Edge, Jacob, hab A
Edgley, Arthur, apo B
Edgley, Benjamin, fra B
Edlin, Samuel, gol B
Edmonds, Giles, tur B
Edmonds, John, coa B
Edmonds, Joseph, dra A
Edmondson, John, pla A4B578
Edmund, Richard, tai A14B56
Edmunds, William, wea B
Edward, Samuel, hab B
Edward, Thomas, tai B
Edward, William, cp B
Edwards, Edward, mas B
Edwards, Eliazer, tai A
Edwards, George, wea A
Edwards, John, but A
Edwards, John, cor B
Edwards, John, far B
Edwards, John, mer B
Edwards, John, mer A
Edwards, Robert, iro B
Edwards, Thomas, but B
Edwards, Thomas, ck B
Edy, John, bri A
Eeles, Charles, ck B
Eeles, Thomas, hab A
Eels, Jacob, gls A
Eels, Markham, gls A

83

Effington, Thomas, bar B
Eggerton, Thomas, but B
Eglesfield, John, bak B
Egleston, Organ, cur A
Egleston, William, wax B
Egleton, Francis, hab A
Egleton, John, gol A
Ekins, Robert, tal B
Elderton, John, pew B
Eldridge, Richard, bak A2B578
Elford, George, tai B
Elford, Richard, tai B
Elford, Thomas, bri B578
Elgar, Jeremy, mer A
Ellcie, Henry, pai B
Ellerick, Edward, sal B
Ellice, James, tal B
Ellingham, William, tai A13B58
Elliot, Edward, cor A
Elliot, Richard, cur B
Elliot, William, but B
Elliott, Thomas, dis B
Ellis, David, pla B
Ellis, George, wax B
Ellis, James, pla B
Ellis, John, dra A
Ellis, John, hab B
Ellis, Patrick, glo A
Ellis, Richard, wea B
Ellis, Robert, ck B
Ellis, Simon, hab A
Ellis, Thomas, mer A
Ellison, John, bro A
Ellison, John, dra A
Ellison, John, tai A234B7
Ellitt, Richard, bow A14B58
Ellord, Robert, wea B
Ellwood, William, pew A
Elman, William, gro B
Elmes, Edward, gol B
Elmes, Robert, sta B
Elsdon, William, joi B
Elsey, Rupert, pla B
Elsworth, Samuel, clo A
Elton, John, cut A
Elton, Thomas, hab B
Elwick, Edrion, vin B
Elwick, John, mer A
Emerton, John, gro A
Emett, Henry, pai A
Emley, Henry, but A3B578
Emmerson, Marmaduke, lor A
Emms, John, gol B
England, Thomas, but B
English, John, sal B
Ennis, William, but B
Enns, John, but B578
Enoch, George, joi B7
Erdswicke, Isaac, tur A
Esson, Joseph, nee A

Esthop, Jacob, glo B
Estwick, Usher, fis B
Estwick, William, dis B
Eswick, Edrion, vin B
Ethery, Hugh, apo B
Ethridge, James, gro B
Eubank, Michael, tai A
Eubendon, John, joi B
Evance, William, pai B
Evans, Alexander, plu B
Evans, Arthur, dra B
Evans, Asgill, pai B
Evans, John, clo A123B7
Evans, Jos, tai B
Evans, Richard, pai B
Evans, Robert, plu B
Evans, Thomas, bla B
Evans, Thomas, lea B
Evans, William, bar B
Evans, William, bri B
Everard, John, bar B
Everard, William, joi A
Everden, Anthony, cut B
Everet, John, bro B
Evin, Thomas, joi A234
Evins, Jonathan, but B
Ewer, Daniel, mer A
Ewer, John, tal A
Ewer, Nathaniel, ski A
Ewin, Nathaniel, fis A
Ewin, Thomas, joi B
Exelby, Thomas, wea A
Exell, Henry, cor B
Exton, John, glo A
Eyles, Francis esq., hab A
Eyles, Henry, bak A
Eyles, John, hab A
Eyles, Jos, hab A
Eyles, Peter, inn B
Eyles, Richard, pew A
Eyles, Robert, pew B
Eyloe, John, ck B
Eyme, Solomon, tai A
Eynes, William, ski B
Eyre, Edward, plu B
Eyre, John, tal A
Eyre, Samuel, fis A24B56

Facer, John, glo A
Faickney, David, ski A
Fairchild, Charles, coa A
Fairclough, John, dra A
Faire, John, apo A
Fairman, Robert, bre A
Faithful, Francis, plu B
Falkingham, Thomas, gol A4B678
Faltrop (Folhop), Samuel, car A12B78
Fandry, John, gol B
Fane, Mildmay, ski A
Far, Thomas, fru B

Farey, Robert, gro B
Farlam, Christopher, bla A
Farlow, Richard, but B
Farmborough, Thomas, bak A
Farmer, Edward, bri A
Farmer, January, bar A
Farmer, John, ski B
Farmer, Rich, clo B
Farmer, Richard, clo A234
Farmer, Richard, vin B
Farmer, William, clo A
Farr, John, sal B
Farr, Robert, fou B
Farr, William, mer B
Farrin, Jonathan, coa A
Farrington, Edmond, hab A
Farrington, Edmond jun, hab A
Farrington, John, hab A
Farrington, Richard, dis B
Farrow, William, cur B
Farum, John, bak B
Fashion, William, scr B
Fashions, Lawrence, fis A34B67
Faulkner, Benjamin, tur B
Faulkner, Thomas, cor B
Faushaw, Edward, uph B
Favill, Joseph, bar B
Fawcett, Richard, apo A
Fawdon, Henry, cut B
Fawdrey, William, gol B
Fawkner, George, car A13B68
Fawkner, William, mer A
Fawson, Stephen, inn B58
Faxoll, Thomas, gol B
Fazakerly, Edward, dye B
Feast, Felix, bre B
Feast, William, wax A
Feifield, Richard, arm A
Fell, James, plu B
Fell, John, vin A
Fell, Roger, far B
Fellow, Thomas, bre A
Fellows, Thomas, uph A
Feltham, Charles, bre B
Fenn, Sampson, dis A
Fenwick, Edward, fis A
Fenwick, Lambert, vin B
Fern, Amos, vin B
Ferne, James, bar A
Fernham, James, uph B
Fernley, Randall, dye A
Ferrour, William, lea B
Fery, Joshua, tai A
Fevin, John, ski A
Fidoe, Thomas, uph A
Field, Jacob, lea B
Field, John, dis B
Field, Nathaniel, tal A
Field, Nicholas, bar B
Field, Richard, tal B

Fielding, Edward, ski B
Fielding, Samuel, glz B
Figgs, Henry, wax B
Fildes, James, gls A
Filp, Thomas, tal B
Filzar, Thomas, bla B
Finall, William, gol B
Finch, John, cut A12B58
Finch, Michael, tai A
Finch, Robert, bre B
Finch, Thomas, clo B
Finch, William, apo B
Finch, William, lea A
Finney, Richard, gro A
Firebras, Bazil kt, vin B
Fish, Samuel, tal A
Fish, Thomas, fle B
Fish, William, gol B
Fisher, Edward, mer B
Fisher, George, bar B
Fisher, George, bar B
Fisher, Henry, vin B
Fisher, James, fis A234B7
Fisher, John, cut A
Fisher, John, hab A
Fisher, John, ski A
Fisher, Joseph, dra A
Fisher, Robert, joi B
Fisher, Samuel, lea B
Fisher, Thomas, tur A
Fisher, William, bla A
Fisher, William, joi A2B578
Fisher, William, vin B
Fitch, Samuel, tal A
Fitzer, Jesse, sad B
Fitzgarrard, James, vin B
Fitzhugh, John, bar A4B568
Fitzhugh, Leonard, arm B
Fitzhugh, Thomas, wea A12B78
Fitzwilliams, John, gro A
Flagott, Henry, but B
Flanders, Thomas, bla B
Fleckney, John, wea A
Fleet, Ralph, gol B
Fleming, Benjamin, clo B
Fleming, Edw, cut B678
Fleming, William, gol B
Fletcher, James, bak B
Fletcher, John, bak A2B578
Fletcher, John, bri B
Fletcher, John, cp A12B78
Fletcher, Ornabar, tai A34B56
Fletcher, Robert, coa B
Fletcher, Thomas, gir A
Fletcher, Thomas, glz B
Fletcher, William, fis B
Flower, Adam, gir B
Flower, Francis, far B
Flower, John, dye B
Flower, Richard, bro B

Flower, William, bro B
Fludyer, Samuel, bri A
Fly, John, dis A
Fly, Richard, pla B
Fly, Timothy, pew A
Foard, John, tai A
Fogarly, John, bre B
Folhop *see* Faltrop
Folker, George, inn B
Folwell, John, wea A
Foot, George, iro A
Ford, Christopher, plu A
Ford, Henry, car B58
Ford, Henry, car B
Ford, Henry, joi B
Ford, Henry, joi A
Ford, Jeremy, inn A
Ford, John, pew B
Ford, John, pou A
Ford, John, tal A
Ford, Nathaniel, tur A3B568
Ford, Robert, bro A
Ford, Thomas, tai A
Ford, William, tai A
Fordham, William, wax B
Forefeite, Thomas, tai A
Foreman, John, tai A13B68
Foreman, Luke, dis B
Forrest, John, far A
Forster, Nathaniel, lea B
Forster, Peter, gro A
Forster, Thomas, dye A
Forster, William, pou A
Forth, Hugh, gir B
Forty, Anthony, hab A
Forward, Jonathan, wea A4B678
Forward, Jonathan, wea A
Foscue, Thomas, arm B
Fosley, Joseph, sal A
Fosque, Thomas, far A
Foster, Abraham, gro A
Foster, Anthony, fis A
Foster, Francis, glo A
Foster, Henry, bri B
Foster, Michael, tai B
Foster, Ralph, apo A
Foster, Thomas, iro A
Foster, William, fis A
Foston, Stephen, inn B
Fotherby, John, sal B
Fotherby, Robert, sal B
Fothergill, Thomas, vin A4B678
Fothingsby, Francis, but B
Foulk, Samuel, hab B
Fountain, Rich, bro A
Fowell, William, tai A
Fowler, Charles, apo A1B67
Fowler, Edward, fis A
Fowler, Hepathadithus, tai A
Fowler, John, dye B

Fowler, John, dye A
Fowler, Matthias, vin B
Fowler, Richard, nee B
Fowler, Richard, nee A1
Fowler, Robert, cor A
Fowler, Samuel, bri B
Fowler, Thomas, gro A
Fox, Daniel, gir B
Fox, Joseph, sta A
Fox, Josiah, bow B
Fox, Thomas, apo A
Fox, William, tai A
Foxcroft, William, inn B
Foxley, Thomas, dra A
Foyle, Robert, mer B
Frachard, Phillip, wax A
Fraddin, Francis, bar A
Fradin, Daniel, bar A
Frame, Robert, gro B
Francis, Simon, vin B
Francis, William, gol A1B567
Franckling, George, bak A
Francks, William, bla A
Frank, Edward, gro B
Franklin, Joshua, bar A
Franklin, Joshua, bar A
Franklin, Nathaniel, cut B
Franklin, Richard, joi A2B578
Franklin, Theo, but B
Franklin, Thomas, cut B
Frankling, Richard, bla B
Franklyn, George, bak A12B78
Franklyn, Richard, pew A134B7
Franklyn, William, bro B
Franks, John, sta B
Fray, Henry, far B
Frazier, Hugh, tai A
Freak, John, lea A
Frearson, Samuel, wax B
Frearson, Samuel, wax A4
Freebody, Elisha, dra A
Freebody, Samuel jun, ck B
Freebody, Samuel sen, ck A
Freeman, Guinnit, hab B
Freeman, John, car B
Freeman, John, pai A
Freeman, Robert, mer B
Freeman, Robert, uph B
Freeman, Rowland, bar B
Freeman, Thomas, cp B
Freeman, Thomas, cut B
Freeman, Thomas, pai A
Freeman, William, sta B
Freind, George, uph B
French, George, dra B
French, James, far A
French, John, cur B
French, John, pou A
French, Joseph, gir A2B567
French, Thomas, bla A

86

Freshwater, William, but B
Friend, John, dra A23B8
Frind, Thomas, pla B
Frith, John, far B
Frohock, George, fou A
Frost, John, arm A
Frost, Joseph, fis A
Frost, Lawrence, glz B
Frost, Richard, vin A
Frowd, Lambert, car A
Fry, Edward, bri B
Fry, George, clo A
Fryar, Isaac, glz B
Fryer, George, lea A
Fryer, John, pew A
Fryer, Thomas, clo B
Fucknall, Hugh, pou A4B567
Fuller, Ezekiel, bro B
Fuller, John, joi B
Fuller, John, joi B
Fuller, John, joi B
Fuller, Robert, tai A
Fuller, Thomas, glz A
Fuller, William, but A
Fullwood, Richard, tal B58
Furse, John, bar B

Gage, Richard, tur A12B67
Gahtman, John, gir A
Gallately, John, dra A
Gamadge, Robert, joi A
Gamble, William, gol B
Gamlyn, Thomas, uph A34B58
Gamull, Thomas, hab B
Ganols, Thomas, dra B
Ganssan, Peter, glz A
Garbrand, Robert, fis A
Garbut, Richard, mas B
Gardener, John, mer A
Gardener, William, apo A
Gardiner, Charles, mas B
Gardiner, John, bro B
Gardiner, William, apo A124B6
Gardiner, William, dis A13B67
Gardner, Abraham, fis A
Gardner, Arthur, fou B
Gardner, Benjamin, dra A
Gardner, Robert, fis B
Gardner, Thomas, bla A
Gardner, William, bri B
Gardner, William, fou A
Gardner, William, gol B
Gardner, William, gol B
Gardner, William, joi A
Gare, Edward, sad B
Garler, Robert, bar B
Garlick, William, fis B
Garlike, John, tai A
Garmson, James, gol A124B6
Garnet, August, tai B

Garnet, Edward, but B
Garnett, Peter, apo A
Garnier, Paul, gro B
Garrard, Henry, sal A
Garrard, Samuel kt, gro B
Garrat, John, tai B
Garrett, Hugh, tai A
Garrett, John, tai A
Garrett, Jonathan, tai A
Garrett, Matthew, bla A
Garrett, Thomas, gir A
Garriot, Daniel, gir A124B6
Garthorn, Francis, gir B
Garthorn, George, gol B
Garthron, Ralph, inn B
Gartridge, John, but B
Gary, Thomas, sad B
Gascogne, Richard, joi B
Gascoyne, Robert, bla A
Gaskin, Ebenezer, bar A
Gason, William, bla B
Gathorne, Roger, fis A
Gatts, Thomas, joi A23B67
Gauden, Benjamin, clo B
Gaudy, Robert, wea B
Gawthorne, John, mer A
Gay, Robert, bar B
Gaynes, Oliver, apo A
Gayon, Samuel, joi B
Geare, Thomas, bla B
Gearing, Henry, wea B
Gearing, Thomas, dra A
Geary, Charles, apo B
Geary, John, mus B
Geary, Samuel, ck B
Gedney, John, lor B
Gee, Henry, cp B
Gee, John, wax A
Gee, Joshua, gro A
Gee, Orlando, ski B
Gee, Zachariah, ski A
Geekie, Alexander, bar A
Gelder, Valentine, lea B
Gembart, Godfrey, dra B
George, Edward, bar A123B6
George, William, dye A
German, William, dis B
Gerrard, Benjamin, fis A
Gerrard, John, iro A
Gerrard, John, tai A
Gerrat, George, joi A
Ghiselin, Nicholas, lor A
Gibbon, John, gol B
Gibbons, John, dye A
Gibbons, Joseph, tal B
Gibbons, Thomas, bla A
Gibbons, Thomas, sad A12B58
Gibbs, Ezekiel, fou B
Gibbs, Joseph, but A
Gibbs, Philip, clo A

Gibbs, Richard, pai B
Gibson, John, bak A
Gibson, John, bro B
Gibson, John, lea B
Gibson, Samuel, gro A
Gibson, Seth, mer B
Gibson, Thomas, dra A
Gibson, William, cp A3B678
Gibson, William, cp A
Gibson, William, gol B
Gibson, Zachariah, bar A
Giddings, Josiah, cp A
Gideon, Sampson, lor A
Gifford, Stephen, apo A3B567
Gifford, William, lea B
Gilbert, George, bla A
Gilbert, Henry, hab B
Gilbert, John, bar A
Gilbert, Josiah, sta B
Gilbert, Philip, fle B
Gilbert, Thomas, dye B
Gilbert, Thomas, mer A
Gilbert, Walden, clo A12B67
Gildersland, John, dye A
Gilding, Benjamin, ski A
Giles, Anthony, fou B
Giles, Samuel, but A
Giles, William, but B
Gill, Edward, pla B
Gill, John, bak A124B5
Gill, Robert, clo A
Gillam, John, joi B
Gillis, Thomas, ck B
Gilly, Stephen, cur B
Gilman, Thomas, fou A
Gilpin, John, gol A
Gilstrop, Peter, apo A
Gines, Richard, tai A
Gipps, Henry, pai B
Gipps, Richard, hab A
Girle, John, bar A
Gisborn, Zachariah, gir A
Gladwin, John, gol A
Glann, John, cp A
Glasbrook, Joseph, fis B
Glassop, Clifford, tai A
Glinn, Robert, sal B
Glover, Gabriel, iro A
Glover, Henry, coa A234B8
Glover, Henry, wea B
Glover, Joseph, tur B
Glover, William, dye B
Goad, Thomas, gol B
Goadby, Samuel, fou A
Goade, Thomas, cp A
Goare, Edward, joi B
Goare, Edward, joi B
Goatley, Thomas, vin B
Goddard, John, lor A
Goddard, Joseph, ski A

Goddard, William, bak A
Goddard, William, glz A
Godding, John, dra B67
Godfrey, Henry, lea B
Godfrey, Peter esq., mer A
Godfrey, Sherman, dis A23B68
Godfrey, Thomas, hab B
Godman, Richard, bak A
Godscul, John, iro B
Godwin, Edmund, lea B
Godwin, Edmund, lea A
Godwin, Richard, bak A
Goffe, Jeremiah, gro B
Goffe, Richard esq., dye A
Gold, Christopher, glo A
Gold, Henry, ck A
Gold, James, sal B
Gold, James, sal A124
Gold, John, dra A
Gold, William, tai A
Golden, William, ck A
Golden, William, far B
Golding, Edward, dye B
Golding, Stephen, joi B
Goldney, Henry, glo A23B57
Gom, James, hab B
Gomely, John, hab A
Gonier, James, dra A34B58
Good, William, bar B
Good, William, far B
Goodall, Joseph, pai B
Goodchild, Richard, bri B
Goodchilde, James, glz A13B58
Goodfellow, Edward, ski B
Goodhew, Thomas, fis B
Goodinch, John, lea A
Goodlad, John, tai A
Goodman, John, but A
Goodman, John, cut A
Goodman, John, pou B
Goodred, Matthew, dye B
Goodson, William, bri A12B58
Goodwin, Anthony, dis B6
Goodwin, Henry, bak B
Goodwin, James, vin B
Goodwin, Nicholas, dra A
Goodwin, Richard, uph B
Goodwin, Timothy, sta A
Goodwyn, Abraham, plu B
Goodwyn, Bethel, fis A
Goodwyn, Samuel, joi B
Goodwyn, Thomas, lea A
Goodyeare, Robert, ski A
Goodyer, Moses, dye B
Gopp, John, bre A
Goram, John, cp B
Goram, Thomas, bri A
Gore, Francis, dis B
Gore, John, bar B
Goseling, John, clo B

88

Gosslin, Robert, sta B
Goudet, John, fou A
Gouge, Edward, dra A
Gouge, William, ck B
Gould, Nath, dra A
Gould, Samuel, ski A
Gould, Thomas, hab A
Gould, William, hab A
Gournay, Rich, bro A
Gower, Robert, apo A
Gower, Waston, bla B
Grace, John, joi A
Grafton, Edward, tur B
Grafton, George, sta A
Grainger, John, pai A2B678
Grainger, Thomas, bro B
Grammar, James, gol B
Grange, John, clo A
Grant, Charles, tai B
Grant, Henry, gol A
Grant, John, inn A
Grant, Silvester, wea A
Grave, Joseph, glo A
Grave, William, bre B
Gravener, Richard, cp A
Graves, Benjamin, wea A
Graves, Edmund, tai B
Graves, James, far B
Graves, James, tai A
Graves, James, wax A2B567
Graves, Thomas, cp A
Graves, Thomas, wax B
Graves, William, fle B
Gray, Joseph, sal A
Gray, Philips, dra B
Gray, William, inn A14B56
Greaves, Benjamin, glo A12B78
Green, Edward, bar B
Green, Francis, bro B
Green, Henry, gol B
Green, James, clo B
Green, John, car B
Green, John, dis B
Green, John, joi A
Green, Jos, glo A
Green, Joseph, bar B
Green, Joseph, gol A123B8
Green, Joseph, vin A34B58
Green, Matthew, bro A
Green, Nathaniel, joi A
Green, Nicholas, bow B
Green, Richard, dis B
Green, Richard, gol B
Green, Richard, lea B
Green, Robert, clo A
Green, Robert, pla B
Green, Samuel, bre A
Green, Samuel, glo A
Green, Thomas, glo A
Green, Thomas, inn B

Green, Thomas, joi B
Green, Thomas, tai A
Green, William, bla B
Greener, John, cur B
Greener, Richard, cur A
Greening, John, tal A
Greenough, Robert, fis A
Greenway, Henry, mer A
Greenwell, William, wea B
Greenwood, John, dis B
Greenwood, John, mer B
Gregg, Edward, mer A234B7
Gregoore, Michael, but B
Gregory, Francis, inn A
Gregory, Humphry, wea B
Gregory, John, pla B
Gregory, Matthew, joi B
Gregory, Nathan, glo A
Gregory, Philip, fou A
Gregory, Philip sen, fou A
Gregory, Thomas, mer A12B67
Gregory, William, dis A
Grew, Richard, cp B
Grewry, Garland, gro B
Grey, John, bak B
Grey, John, lor A
Griffin, Francis, gol A
Griffin, Joseph, cut B
Griffin, Thomas, clo A
Griffith, Edward, ski A
Griffith, Joshua, cor A
Griffith, Thomas, joi A134B7
Griffith, William, uph B
Griffitts, John, bow A
Grigsby, John, tai B6
Grigson, John, cur A
Grimbalston, Valter, pai B
Grimes, Peter, fra B
Grimes, Peter, fra A124
Grimes, Robert, coa B
Grimsted, Joseph, tur A
Grinsell, John, pla B
Grolleau, Lewis, ck A
Gronose, Joseph, vin B
Gronouse, James, uph A123B6
Groome, John, tai B
Gross, Edward, bak A12B78
Grosvener, Robert, lea A
Groswell, Rich, car A
Grove, George, tal B
Grove, James, pai B
Grove, John, car B
Grove, John, cp A
Grove, Samuel, pai A13B78
Groves, James, car B
Grubb, William, sal B8
Grundry, Richard, dye B
Grunford, Thomas, joi A
Grunsill, Charles, pou B
Grunwin, Francis, ski A

89

Grunwin, Gabriel, pew A
Guaraudet, Claudy, wax A
Guarst, Tristrum, wea A
Guepin, David, bro A
Guest, John, hab B
Guest, Richard, cut A
Guest, Timothy, gro A
Guibert, Phillip, uph A
Guidion, Rowland, pai A
Guilam, John, bak B
Guillim, William, bow A2
Guillum, John, bar B
Guilt, Howell, pew A
Gundy, Radford, hab B
Gunn, George, bak A
Gunnell, John, joi B
Gunter, John, fru A
Gunton, Samuel, sad B
Gurpwell, George, sal B
Gutridge, Edmund, inn A
Guy, George, dra A
Guy, Thomas, sta A
Guynell, Henry, vin B
Gwillam, James, bro B
Gwillyng, Nathaniel, dra A
Gwilt, Daniel, wea A
Gwin, Charles, inn A
Gynas, Joseph, iro B

Hackett, John, ck A
Hackley, Thomas, bar A
Hackney, Joseph, dye A12B67
Hacks *see* Hucks
Hackshaw, Humphrey, vin A
Hackshaw, Robert, ski A
Haddock, Robert, hab B
Haddock, William, gir A
Haddon, Thomas, car A
Haddon, William, bar B
Haddon, William jun, bak A124B7
Haddon, William sen, bak A
Hadibald, William, inn B
Hadly, Isaac, fou A
Hadock, William, fru B
Haines, Clement, cor A
Haines, Isaac, bak B
Haines, James, dra B
Hakes, John, ck A
Hale, Friend, mus B
Hale, George, pai B
Hale, Jasper, hab A
Hales, John, cur B
Halford, Isaac, but B
Halford, Stephen, fis A
Halftide, Thomas, joi B
Hall, Benjamin, tai A
Hall, Edward, cp A2B568
Hall, Ezekiel, clo A
Hall, John, bla B
Hall, John, ck A

Hall, John, clo B
Hall, John, dis A
Hall, John, dra A
Hall, John, nee A1B568
Hall, Joseph, lea B
Hall, Nathan, tal A
Hall, Nathaniel, tal A
Hall, Robert, but A
Hall, Robert, uph A
Hall, Samuel, dis B
Hall, Thomas, bar A34
Hall, Thomas, gro B
Hall, Thomas, tal B
Hall, William, but A
Hall, William, cor B
Hall, William, tai A
Hallam, Richard, clo A
Hallett, James kt, gol B
Hallywell, William, sad A
Hals, John, pai A3
Halsam, Richard, sal B
Halsey, George, ski B
Halsey, John, bre A
Halsey, John, cur B
Halsey, John, tal A
Halsey, Thomas, mer A23B58
Halside, John, fou B
Halton, Edward, tai A
Halton, George, bre A234B6
Halton, Thomas bt, tai A
Ham, John, tal A
Hambleton, John, bla B
Hamers, John, dra B
Hamley, William, hab A13B56
Hamlin, Anthony, dye A
Hamman, Thomas, joi B
Hammond, Charles, sad B
Hammond, Christopher, apo B
Hammond, Edward, vin B
Hammond, Francis, sal B
Hammond, Thomas, joi A134B6
Hammond, Trice, bla A
Hammond, William, dra A1B567
Hammond, William, gol A134B8
Hamond, Charles, coa B
Hamond, George, pew A
Hamond, William, apo B
Hampton, James, pou B
Hanbury, Nicholas, clo B
Hancks, Thomas, cur A
Hancock, Daniel, fou B
Hancock, John, sta A134B5
Hancock, Samuel, pew A
Hancock, Thomas, dye A124B8
Handbury, John, bri A
Hands, James, pla A
Handy, Thomas, bro B
Hanes, Tho, nee B
Hanes, Tho, nee B
Hanford, Thomas, fis A

90

Hanger, John, mer A
Hankey *see* Haulkley
Hanley, Jervas, iro A
Hannell, John, wea A
Hannott, Samuel, dye A12B78
Hanshaw, Egerton, ck B
Hanvill, Nathan, car B
Harbert, Salter, gol B
Harbroe, Abraham, pai A13B78
Harcourt, John, cp B
Harcourt, Richard, pai A
Harcourt, Thomas, bla B
Hardgrave, William, bri B
Hardin, Thomas, joi B
Hardin, Ustus, fru B
Harding, James, mer A
Harding, John, cor B
Harding, John, sta B
Harding, John, vin A
Harding, Peter, vin B
Harding, Richard, dra B
Harding, Thomas, fie A
Harding, Thomas, joi A
Harding, Thomas, sta B
Harding, Thomas, sta B
Harding, Thomas, wax B
Hardmett, Richard, bar A24B58
Hardret, John, bar B
Hardret, Peter, bar B
Hardwick, Richard, clo A
Hardy, James, mas B
Hardy, Thomas, hab B
Hardy, William, bar A24B78
Hare, John, dra B
Hare, William, fru A24B68
Harford, Henry, pew B
Hargrave, John, dis A
Hargrave, Richard, uph B
Hargrave, William, sal B7
Haridon, John, sal B
Harman, John, clo A
Harmer, Jasper, sta B
Harne *see* Haynes, William
Harneis, Samuel, bar B
Harper, Charles, sta B
Harper, John, bak B
Harper, Lopwood, joi B
Harper, Miles, lea A
Harper, Samuel, but B
Harpor, Thomas, wax A
Harrice, Edward, wea B
Harrington, Thomas, clo A
Harriots, John, far A
Harris, Abraham, joi B
Harris, Benjamin, scr A
Harris, Benjamin, sta A234B7
Harris, Francis, clo A
Harris, Gyles, tal B
Harris, Jabes, pew A
Harris, Job, gol B

Harris, John, bla B
Harris, John, bla B
Harris, John, dis A
Harris, John, gir A
Harris, John, gol B
Harris, John, tai A134B6
Harris, John, tai A
Harris, Jos, hab A
Harris, Joseph, wea A
Harris, Philip, plu B
Harris, Richard, but A
Harris, Richard, dye B
Harris, Richard, sta A
Harris, Samuel, hab A
Harris, Thomas, sad B
Harris, Thomas, tai B
Harris, Thomas, vin A
Harris, William, glz A
Harris, William, gro A
Harris, William, vin B
Harris, William, vin B
Harris, William, vin A
Harrison, Benjamin, wea B
Harrison, Charles, glo B
Harrison, Edward, gol A
Harrison, Israel, sta A13B67
Harrison, John, bar A
Harrison, John, cut A
Harrison, John, hab B
Harrison, John, wea A
Harrison, Peter, cut B
Harrison, Robert, gir B
Harrison, William, gol B
Harrop, Ralph, vin B
Hart, Bartholomew, wea A
Hart, John, mer B
Hart, Jonas, bak A123B7
Hart, William, fra B
Hart, William, inn B
Hartley, Charles, bar B
Hartley, Ralph, iro A
Hartley, William, hab B
Hartly, John, gro B
Hartly, Thomas, gro B
Harvest, Maximilian, fou B
Harvey, Benjamin, hab A2B567
Harvey, George, clo A
Harvey, Richard, bar A
Harvey, St John, dye A
Harvey, Thomas, cur B
Harward, Edward, bro B
Harwood, John, clo A
Harwood, Jos, bla A
Harwood, Will, but A
Hasell, Eliazar, mer A
Hasey, William, but A4B678
Hassel, John, tai A
Hassell, John, bre B
Hassell, Ralph, sal B
Hassleborne, Jacob, pew A

Hastell, Matthew, cor B
Haswell, Matthew, cor A2
Hatch, Henry, lea B
Hatchett, Thomas, tai A
Hatfeild, Samuel, cor A
Hatfield, Thomas, ski A
Hathon, Joshua, cp A
Hatle, George, sal B
Hatley, Benjamin, gro A
Hatley, George, sal A124
Hatley, Henry, hab A
Hatley, Jonathan, uph B
Hatley, Ralph, bar A
Hatly, Gerrard, gro B
Hatly, Ralph, gro B
Hatly, Thomas, uph B
Hatsell, Lawrence, sta A
Hatt, Joseph (Joshua), pou A234B5
Hatt, Joseph, vin B
Hatton, George, plu A
Hatton, Henry, tai A
Hatton, Richard, hab B
Hatton, Richard, hab B
Hatton, Samuel, plu A
Hatton, Thomas, hab A
Hatton, William, dra A
Haulkley (Hankey), Henry, hab A123B7
Hawford, Francis, tur B
Hawgood, Thomas, bro B
Hawgood, Thomas, fou B
Hawkes, John, bre B
Hawkes, Robert, fis A
Hawkins, George, gro B
Hawkins, George, tur B
Hawkins, James, bow B
Hawkins, James, tai A
Hawkins, John, bla A
Hawkins, John, bre B
Hawkins, John, dis A
Hawkins, John, dis A
Hawkins, John, wea A
Hawkins, Michel, bla B
Hawkins, Richard, arm B
Hawkins, Thomas, bow A123B8
Hawkins, Thomas, but B
Hawkins, Thomas, inn B
Hawoop, George, wax B
Haws, Edward, fou B
Haws, Robert, lea B
Hay, Henry, gol B
Hay, Martin, bro B
Haydad, William, bla B
Hayden, James, tai A
Haydon, Robert, arm A
Hayes, Claude, dye A
Hayes, James, bro B
Hayes, John, bar A
Hayes, Robert, bar A
Hayes, William, pla A
Hayford, William, dis B

Haynes, Charles, fra B
Haynes, Edward, hab B
Haynes, John, joi B
Haynes (Harne), William, hab A12B67
Haynes, William, wax A
Haynes, William, wea B
Hays, Richard, pai A
Hays, Robert, sta A
Haysome, Thomas, fis B
Hayson, William, gro B
Hayter, Whitfield, gol A
Hayward, Giles, arm A
Hayward, John, bla B
Hayward, Philip, arm A
Hayward, Rich, bro A
Hayward, Richard, bla A
Hayward, William, fou A
Haywards, John, bri A
Haywood, David, tal A
Haywood, Elijah, joi A
Haywood, Samuel, gol A
Haywood, William, tai A
Hayword, Joseph, hab B
Hazard, James, fis A
Hazard, Joseph, sta B
Hazard, Roger, fis A
Hazzard, Richard, car B
Hazzard, Thomas, fis A
Hazzard, William, car B
Headland, John, car B
Heanes, Thomas, tal A
Hearn, Richard, cp A
Heart, Henry, mus A
Heasmen, Henry, uph B
Heaster, John, clo A
Heath, Francis, but B
Heath, John, bak B
Heath, John, dis B
Heath, Joshua, fis B
Heath, Richard, lea B
Heath, Richard, pew A
Heath, Thomas, tai B
Heath, Thomas, tai A3
Heath, William, sad A
Heathcoat, Thomas, fru B
Heathcote, Gilbert kt, vin A
Heather, Edward, bak B
Heather, Thomas, gro A
Heatly, John, bla B
Heaton, Abraham, pai A
Hebbert, Matthew, ski A
Hedgabout, James, tai B
Hedges, Robert, car A
Hedges, Thomas, tal A
Heele, Nicholas, gro A2B568
Hefford, William, but B
Hefford, William, but A12
Hegg, William, tai A
Heightfield, Watsinham, dis B
Helby, Joseph, bre A

92

Helthorne, John, bar A3B568
Heming, Edward, bri B
Henchman, Leonard, bar A1B678
Henchman, Robert, fou B
Hendley, John, tai A
Hendlyn, Thomas, but B
Henly, Francis, pla B
Henly, John, inn A
Henshaw, Benjamin, bro A
Henshaw, William, gro A2B568
Henvell, William, cor B
Heptinstall, John, sta B
Herbert, Denis, cor A
Herbert, Isaac, bla B
Herbert, Richard, cor B
Herbert, Robert, cp A
Herbert, Thomas, dye A
Herenden, Anthony, bar A4B678
Hermot, Jaspee jun, iro B
Hern, John, bri A
Herne, James, fra B
Heron, John, hab A
Herrad, Edward, joi A
Herriot, Roger, bak A134B7
Hesketh, John, bar A
Hester, Henry, bri A
Hetley, Thomas, uph A
Heughs, Richard, tal B
Heushman, Thomas, far B
Hewes, Caleb, pou A
Hewes, William, cut A
Hewet, Richard, but B78
Hewet, Samuel, gro A
Hewett, Alexander, cur B
Hewett, John, cur A
Hews, Francis, bar A
Hews, Thomas, wax B
Hewson, John, dra A
Heyham, Beningfeild, dye A
Heylin, John, sad A
Heys, William, uph A
Heysham, Robert esq., dra A134B8
Hibbert, John, ski A
Hibbin, Alexander, pou A
Hickes, Jonathan, tal A
Hickes, Michael, vin B
Hickman, Daniel, dis A
Hickman, Joseph, lea A
Hickman, William, joi B
Hicks, Henry, cor A
Hicks, James, bar B
Hicks, John, joi A
Hicks, Richard, lea A
Hicks, Thomas, iro B
Hide, John, sal A123B8
Hide, John, sal A
Hide, Thomas, but B
Hide, Thomas, mer B
Hide, William, sal B
Hidgcock, Richard, bow B

Higate, Humphry, mas B
Higby, David, fou B568
Higg, Samuel, bak B
Higgets, William, cur A
Higgins, Francis, joi A
Higgins, Thomas, lea A
Higgins, Thomas, pla B
Higgison, John, bla A1B578
Higgs, Castor, lea A
Higgs, Richard, ski B
Higgs, Thomas, apo B
Higgs, Thomas, inn B
Higgs, Thomas, pew A
Highmore, William, bar A
Hill, Benjamin, tai A
Hill, Edward, glo A
Hill, Humphrey, wea A
Hill, Humphry, bre A
Hill, James, tai A
Hill, John, apo B
Hill, John, bak A
Hill, John, cp A
Hill, John, vin B
Hill, Richard, gol A
Hill, Roger, bla A
Hill, Thomas, inn B
Hill, Thomas, inn A2
Hill, Thomas, inn A
Hill, Thomas, lea B
Hill, Thomas, mas B
Hill, Thomas, mas B
Hill, Thomas, wea A
Hill, William, cp A
Hill, William, sta B
Hilliard, Edward, tur A
Hilliard, Henry, tal A
Hilliard, Nicholas, mer A
Hilliard, Richard, inn B
Hilliard, Samuel, ski A
Hillier, John, bri A
Hills, Edward, tur A
Hills, Guillam, sta B
Hillyard, Benj, lea B
Hillyard, Richard, inn B
Hinckliff, Thomas, sal B
Hind, William, tur B
Hinder, William, cor B
Hindman, Michael, sad A13B67
Hinds, Henry, fou B
Hinks, Edward, joi B
Hinton, Benjamin, mer A
Hinton, Edward, ski B
Hinxman, Thomas, bri B
Hiorney, Robert, joi B
Hiscock, Robert, hab A
Hitchcock, Edward, tal B
Hitchins, Charles, joi B
Hitchins, Daniel, pla B
Hoar, Richard kt, gol B
Hoare, Francis, but A

93

Hoare, George, but A
Hoare, Henry, gol B
Hoare, John, dra A134
Hoare, John, wea B
Hoare, Samuel, bre B
Hoare, William, tur B
Hobbs, Joseph, cut B
Hobday, William, bar A
Hobday, William, glo A
Hobson, John, joi B
Hobson, Percival, dis A
Hodgekins, John, joi B
Hodges, Benjamin, dye A
Hodges, John, cor A
Hodges, Thomas, joi B
Hodgeskins, John, glo A
Hodgkins, Benjamin, ski A
Hodgkins, Joseph, dis B
Hodgkins, Thomas, ski A
Hodgkins, Thomas, sta B
Hodgson, Nicholas, gol B
Hodgson, William, tal A
Hodsdan, Edward, vin A
Hoe, Robert, bla A2B578
Hogg, John, dra A
Hogg, Thomas, glo A
Holbeck, Anthony, dis B
Holbetch, Samuel, dis B
Holbidge, Samuel, dis B58
Holbrook, Walter, cp A
Holden, Alexander, gro B
Holden, Daniel, mus A34B78
Holder, Richard, tai B
Holder, Richard, tai B
Hole, Francis, gro B
Holford, Joshua, tai B
Holgate, George, glo A
Holland, Char, but A
Holland, James, sta B
Holland, John, bro B
Holland, John, ck B
Holland, John, lea B
Holland, Richard, fru A
Holland, Thomas, gol B
Holland, William, mas A
Holland, William, sta B
Hollaway, John, wea B
Hollester, John jun, tai A
Hollett, Nathaniel, joi A4
Hollford, Frances, inn B
Hollier, William, clo A
Hollinghead, Francis, wea A
Hollis, John, dra A
Hollis, John, tai A
Hollis, Thomas, dra A
Hollis, Thomas jun, dra A
Hollis, Thomas yr, dra A
Hollister, John sen, tai A
Holloway, John, uph B
Holly, John, pew A2B678

Holly, Oakes, gro B
Holmden, Gabriel, arm A
Holme, John, sad A
Holmes, Abraham, hab B578
Holmes, James, pou B
Holmes, John, inn B
Holmes, John, vin B
Holmes, Samuel, sad B
Holmes, Thomas, fis B
Holmes, Thomas, hab A
Holsey, Edward, sad B
Holt, Andrew, bow A
Holt, John, cur A
Holt, Walter, mus A
Holton, John, mer A
Holton, Nathaniel, mer A
Holyoak, Thomas, gro B
Honard, Paul, bro A
Hone, John, joi A
Hone, William, pew A
Honer, James, sad B
Honeyman, John, dye B
Honner, Isaac, cp B
Honnor, Henry, sad A
Honour, Isaac, cp B
Hood, Joshua, fou A
Hook, James, vin B
Hooke, Caleb, mer A
Hooker, Samuel, wea B
Hooker, William esq., gro A2B678
Hool, John, dra A
Hoole, Samuel, hab B67
Hooper, Benjamin, sal A
Hooper, Charles, tai A
Hooper, Giles, vin B
Hooper, John, gro B
Hopegood, Francis, mer A3B567
Hopes, John, vin A
Hopkins, Henry, iro A
Hopkins, John, dye A
Hopkins, John, fou A
Hopkins, Lawrence, bla A12B78
Hopkins, Thomas, tal A24B67
Hopkins, William, arm B
Hopkins, William, lor A
Hore, Robert, bla B
Horlock, Robert, bla A
Horn, Henry, fou B
Horn, John, uph B
Horn, Robert, bak B
Horn, Thomas, cut B56
Hornblower, William, wea B
Hornby, Thomas, bow A
Horne, John, bri B
Horne, Thomas, mer A
Horne, Thomas, sta B
Horneblow, Richard, bla B678
Horrocks, Alexander, uph A
Horseman, Henry, gol A
Horseman, Henry, gro A

94

Horsenail, Hashaliah, far B
Horslety, John, tai B
Horton, James, dye A
Horton, James, gro B
Horton, James, tal A
Horton, John, mer B
Horton, Robert, car B
Horton, Robert, pai A123B5
Horton, Thomas, joi B
Horton, William, cp B
Hose, John, uph B
Hose, Thomas, joi B
Hosier, Charles, gol B
Hosier, Elias, cut B
Hoskins, Oswald, fis A
Hoskins, Thomas, tai A
Hoskins, Williams, sad B
Hougan, Francis, pai B
Hougham, Charles, cur B
Houghton, John, glo A
Houlditch, Richard, ski A
Househan, John, uph A
Houseman, Richard, glo A
Houseman, Thomas, cut B
Houserous, Thomas, glo A
How, Ephraim, cut A
How, Humph, bar B
How, John, cut A
How, Richard, wea B
How, Thomas, clo B
Howard, Francis, mus B
Howard, George, wea A
Howard, John, uph A
Howard, John jun, uph A
Howard, Matthew, hab A
Howard, Matthew, mer A
Howard, William, bak A134B7
Howard, William, gro B
Howard, William, mas A123B6
Howater, Richard jun, mer B
Howell, Daniel, vin B
Howell, Henry, pai B
Howell, John, sal B
Howell, Samuel, bre A124B6
Howell, Thomas, mer A
Hows, John, gol B
Hoyle, Charles, lea B
Hoyle, John, ck B
Hoyle, Samuel, sta B
Hubbard, Edward, joi B
Hubbard, James, but A
Hubbard, James, fou A
Hubbard, Robert, pew B
Hubbard, Tho, but A
Hubberd, William, joi B
Huboard, John, dis B8
Huck, Thomas, joi B
Huckle, Thomas, lea A
Huckle, Thomas jun, lea A
Hucks (Hacks), Thomas, bla A234B7

Huckwele, Richard, coa B
Hudd, Samuel, gol B
Huddle, Joseph, pou B
Huddleston, John, bar B
Hudlestone, John, bar A
Hudson, Charles, but B
Hudson, Daniel, fou A
Hudson, Henry, bak B
Hudson, John, bri A
Hudson, Joseph, uph B
Hudson, Richard, pai A
Hudson, Roger, gol B
Hudson, Thomas, cp B
Hudson, Thomas, dra A
Hudson, William, bri A
Hudson, William, hab B
Huet, Charles, bar B
Huggins, Daniel, joi B
Hughbank, Thomas, vin B
Hughes, Ellis, fou B
Hughes, Evan, bla A
Hughes, John, hab A
Hughes, Rees, pai A134B8
Hughes, Thomas, fou A123B8
Hughes, William, fou B
Hughs, John, hab B
Hughs, John, wea A
Hughs, William, cp B
Hughs, William, tai B
Hulbert, James, fis A
Huleap, John, tal B
Hulley, George, tai B
Hulls, John, pew A2B578
Hulls, William, tai A
Hulme, John, tal A
Humble, Joseph, wea A
Humerston, William, cor B
Humfreys, Charles, tai B
Humfreys, William, uph A12B67
Hummetsham, Francis, far B
Humphrey, Richard, vin B
Humphreys, John, sta A
Humphreys, Samuel, joi A
Humphreys, Thomas, mas B
Humphreys, William kt, iro A
Humphries, John, pou B
Humphry, John, bla B
Humphrys, John, tai A
Humphrys, Philip, wea A
Humphrys, Thomas, lea A
Huniborne, Thomas, tai A
Hunsden, Thomas, clo B
Hunt, Edmond, tal B
Hunt, Henry, cur A
Hunt, Henry, dye A
Hunt, James, bla A24B57
Hunt, John, cp B
Hunt, John, tal B
Hunt, Joseph, bak B
Hunt, Richard, gro A

95

Hunt, Thomas, tai B7
Hunt, William, apo B
Hunt, William, lea B
Hunter, Charles, hab A34B58
Hunter, John, dye A123B6
Hunter, Nathaniel, gro B
Hunter, Thomas, cor A
Hunter, Thomas, gro B
Huntingdon, Robert, apo B
Huntman, Joseph, tal A2B578
Hunton, Nathaniel, pla A
Hunton, Stephen, joi B
Hurst, George, cp A
Hurst, John, hab A
Hurst, Richard, fis B
Hussey, Paul, wea A
Hussey, Thomas, hab B
Husson, Robert, fis A
Hust, Richard, fis B
Hutchenson, Ralph, tai B
Hutchins, Thomas, fis B
Hutchins, Walter, far B
Hutchinson, Benjamin, pou A
Hutchinson, Edward, pou A
Hutchinson, Francis, dra A
Hutchinson, George, tur A
Hutchinson, John, sad A
Hutchinson, Walter, pou A234B5
Huthname, Nathaniel, sal A
Hutt, William, clo B
Hutton, Samuel, glo B
Hyde, Francis, cut A2B578
Hyde, Michael, fis A
Hyde, Ralph, vin B
Hyde, Thomas, dis B
Hyett, John, dis A
Hygden, John, lor B
Hymore, Thomas, pai B
Hymore, William, tur B
Hynde, Jacob jun, pai B
Hynde, Morgan, cp A

Iles, John, pew A
Ilive, Thomas, sta B
Immings, Jeremiah, sal A
Immins, Thomas, dis A
Imple, Authur, bla B
Ingle, Samuel, tai A
Ingleton, William, dis A123B7
Ingram, Antony, tai B
Ingram, Henry, dra B
Ingram, Joseph, glo A
Ingram, Robert, gir A
Ingram, William, fis A
Inns, William, pla A2B568
Innys, William, sta B
Insley, Josiah, bla B
Ireland, Daniel, bri B
Ironside, Edward, gol A134B6
Isham, Alexander, but B

Ives, Humphry, gls A
Ives, Joseph, joi B

Jack, Thomas, bro B
Jackman, Nicholas, pew A
Jackman, Richard, gro B
Jacks, William, wea B
Jackson, Charles, fra B
Jackson, Francis, clo A
Jackson, George, glo B
Jackson, Isaac, tal A
Jackson, James, bre B
Jackson, James, dra B
Jackson, John, bar B
Jackson, John, gol B
Jackson, John, hab B
Jackson, John, iro A
Jackson, John, pew B
Jackson, John, wea B
Jackson, Joseph, tai A
Jackson, Nathaniel, mer A
Jackson, Philip, hab A
Jackson, Richard, bak A123B7
Jackson, Richard, tai B
Jackson, Samuel, pew A
Jackson, Thomas, bar A1B567
Jackson, Thomas, cut B
Jackson, Thomas, tai B
Jackson, Thomas, vin B
Jackson, William, bar A
Jackson, William, dye A
Jackson, William, wea B
Jacob, Emanuel, fou A34B78
Jacob, Joseph, coa A
Jacques, John, fou A
Jaggard, John, tai A
James, Anthony, pew B
James, Benjamin, fou A
James, George, mus B
James, George, sta B
James, Jery, arm B
James, John, car B
James, Jonathan, gir A
James, Matthew, but A
James, Richard, but A
James, Thomas, fis B
James, William, but A
James, William jun, but A
Janson, Hugh, bro A
Jarman, William, dis A1B567
Jarmin, Matthew, glz B
Jarvis, George, gro A
Jarvis, George, tai A1B578
Jarvis, Nathaniel, dis A
Jarvis, Thomas, bla B
Jatt, John, coa B
Jaye, John, apo A
Jeams, William, tal B
Jefferys, Edward, but A
Jeffres, George, car B

Jeffreys, William, wax A
Jeffries, William, tai B
Jeffs, Robert, car B
Jeffs, Robert, cp A
Jeffs, William, bre B
Jeffson, Robert, bri B
Jellico, Samuel, inn B
Jellicoe, Adam, lea A
Jelly, John, cur A
Jenells, John, cut B
Jenkins, George, dra A
Jenkins, John, hab B
Jenkins, John, ski A
Jenkins, John, tai A
Jenkins, John, tal A
Jenkins, William, clo A
Jenkinson, Thomas, lea A
Jennings, Alexander, bar A
Jennings, George, clo B
Jennings, John, clo B
Jennings, John, pai A23B68
Jennings, Joseph, dye A
Jennings, Richard, car B
Jepson, Humphry, plu B
Jepson, John, sad A
Jermain, Edward, dye B
Jerrard, Ralph, wax A
Jerrimy, James, arm B
Jesse, John, ski A
Jesson, Cormet, iro B
Jesson, Cornelius, iro A23
Jetsome, Josiah, tai A
Jett, John, coa B
Jewson, William, tur B
Jinkins, Thomas, dra B
Job, Anthony, joi A
Joffs, Robert, bre B
Johnson, Abraham, dis A
Johnson, Benjamin, tai A
Johnson, Benjamin, tai A
Johnson, Charles, pou B
Johnson, Edward, mer B
Johnson, Edward, pou B
Johnson, Gerrard, joi B
Johnson, Henry, bre B
Johnson, Henry, dra A
Johnson, Jeremiah, gol A
Johnson, John, arm A23B68
Johnson, John, bro A
Johnson, John, glo A
Johnson, John, joi A
Johnson, John, tai B
Johnson, John, wea A
Johnson, John, wea A
Johnson, Mathias, dra A34
Johnson, Nathaniel, hab B
Johnson, Richard, gro B
Johnson, Robert, pou B
Johnson, Thomas, hab A
Johnson, Thomas, vin A

Johnson, William, arm A
Johnson, William, bla B
Johnson, William, bla A
Johnson, William, bro B
Johnson, William, lea A12B68
Johnston, John, bar B
Jole, Robert, sta A
Jolland, Thomas, ski B
Jolliff, William, mer A
Jolly, Thomas, wax A
Jolly, William, bow B
Jones, Charles, fou A
Jones, Charles, uph A
Jones, Ebenezer, scr B
Jones, Francis, pai B
Jones, George, bro A1B678
Jones, Hugh, inn B
Jones, Humphrey, lea B
Jones, James, joi B
Jones, James, joi B
Jones, Jeremiah, vin B
Jones, John, bar A
Jones, John, bla B
Jones, John, cut A
Jones, John, dye A
Jones, John, hab B
Jones, John, inn A
Jones, John, joi B
Jones, John, mer B
Jones, John, sad A
Jones, John, uph A
Jones, John, wax A
Jones, Lawrence, gol A
Jones, Peter, lea A3B568
Jones, Philip, bla A1B567
Jones, Richard, bla B
Jones, Richard, cur A1B678
Jones, Robert, joi B
Jones, Samuel, coa A
Jones, Thomas, inn B
Jones, Thomas, tai A
Jones, William, pai A
Jonson, Thomas, dra B
Jordan, Benjamin, ski A2B678
Jordan, John, wea A
Joseph, Benjamin, fis A
Joseph, Benjamin jun, fis A
Jourdan, Thomas, tur A
Joyce, Arthur, inn A2B567
Joyner, Edmond, joi B
Jube, Robert, pew B
Judge, William, cor A
Junt, John, sta A
Juskip, Edward, ck B

Kalloway, John, cor A13B56
Kanady, Silvester, sta B
Kate, Robert, cut A
Keach, Jos, iro A123
Keach, Ralph, clo A

97

Keate, William, gol A
Keckwich, Peter, clo A
Keeble, Samuel, sta B
Keeling, John, tur A
Keen, John, tai A
Keene, John, cur A
Keene, Jonas, but A
Keene, Samuel, bak A
Keep, Edward, pai A
Keep, Edward, ski A
Keetley, John, sad A
Kelam, James, fru B
Kelk, Thomas, ski B
Kelsey, Henry, fis A
Kemmis, John, but B
Kemmis, Will, but A
Kemmish, Richard, but B
Kemp, Robert, cur B
Kempster, Samuel, uph A
Kempster, William, mas B
Kendrick, John, gro A
Kenerstone, Edward, joi A
Kennet, William, bak A
Kenniston (Kinaston), Thomas, dye
A124B6
Kent, Griffith, bre A
Kent, Henry, bri A2B568
Kent, John, fis A
Kent, John, tur B
Kent, Thomas, vin B5
Kent, Walter, tai B
Kent, William, arm B
Kent, William, bar B
Kent, William, tai A
Kenton, John, cut A
Kenton, John, pew B
Kenyon, John, bar B
Kerby, Edward, tai B
Kerby, Thomas, vin B
Kerby, William, joi B
Kerfoot, Nathaniel, dye A
Kerison, Samuel, fou A
Kerradge, William, plu B
Kerver, Richard, fis A134B6
Ketchmead, Francis, ski A
Kettel, Philip, ski B
Ketteridge, Thomas, ski B
Kettle, Jeremiah, joi A
Kettle, Josiah, tai B
Kettlebutter, John, cut A
Key, James, gro B
Key, John, glo A
Key, Robert, fou A
Keys, Richard, cut B
Keyzer, Charles, hab A
Kidd, John, tai A
Kidgell, John, cp A
Kift, Henry, sta A
Kighly, Samuel, pai A
Kilby, Joseph, joi B

Killingworth, Thomas, bla B
Kilmister, Henry, bla A
Kimpton, William, wax B
Kinaston *see* Kenniston
Kinbey, John, pai B
Kinch, John, dis A
King, Bartholomew, bar B
King Charles, joi A
King, David, cp B
King, Henry, ski A
King, Her, tai B
King, Isaac, sal A
King, James, mer A
King, James, sal A
King, John, bak A
King, John, bar B
King, John, clo A
King, John, coa A
King, Jos, pew A
King, Joseph, hab A123B6
King, Lawrence, but A13B78
King, Maynard, hab A
King, Michael, ski B
King, Morris, mer A
King, Peter, tai A
King, Richard, clo A
King, Richard, joi B
King, Richard, pou B
King, Richard, pou A
King, Robert, pew A
King, Samuel, clo B
King, Stephen, dis B
King, Thomas, glz B
King, Thomas, mer A
King, Thomas, pew B
King, William, bro B
King, William, coa B
King, William, cor A
King, William, cut A
King, William, gol A34
King, William, pai B
King, William, vin B
Kingsley, Anthony, gro A
Kingston, Robert, tur A
Kingston, Samuel, tur B
Kingston, William, dra B
Kingstone, Dan, bro A
Kinning, William, plu A
Kinsey, William, bar B
Kinsman, Thomas, vin B
Kinton, Benjamin, lea B
Kipling, William, bla A23B58
Kirby, James, lea A
Kirby, Thomas, joi B
Kirby, William, glz A14B68
Kirhill, Elijah, bro B
Kirk, John, gol B
Kirk, Jonathan, gol B
Kirk, Joshua, dra B
Kirkham, John, bar A

Kirton, William, arm B
Kirwood, Matthew, gol B
Kistell, Philip, gir A
Kittle, John, gir B
Knap, George, wax B
Knap, John, wax B
Knaplock, Richard, pai B
Knaplock, Robert, sta B
Knapp, Clement, bak A
Knapp, John, vin B
Knapton, James, sta A
Knapton, Samuel, gls A
Kneetha, Samuel, ski B
Knight, Anthony, fou A
Knight, James, pai B
Knight, John, dye B
Knight, John, nee A
Knight, John, ski B
Knight, Peter, fou A
Knight, Richard, vin A14B78
Knight, Robert, fis B6
Knight, Robert, gro A
Knight, Thomas, dis A2B678
Knight, Thomas, gro A
Knight, William, plu B
Knight, William, tal B
Knight, William, vin B
Knightley, Giles, mer A
Knighton, John, cur B
Knipe, Benjamin, ski B
Knipe, John, scr B
Knipe, Randolph kt, clo A
Kniveton, John, tal B
Knott, Thomas, gol A
Knowles, John, car A
Knowles, John, hab A
Knowles, Samuel, hab A
Knowles, Stephen, tai A
Knowls, John, dra A
Kroger, John, bre A

Lacey, Roger, hab A
Lacoe, Francis, gro B
Lacy, Gilbert, tai B
Lade, John esq., lea A14B78
Ladyman, John, gol A
La Force, Stephen, ck A
Lamas, Jeremy, gol B
Lamb, Arthur, dra B
Lamb, Bazill, gir B
Lamb, James, hab A
Lamb, John, tai B
Lamb, John, uph B
Lamb, John, uph B
Lamb, Robert, lea B
Lamb, Will, cut B
Lambert, Thomas, wax A
Lammas, Edward, gol B
Lamme, Nathaniel, wea B7
Lancashire, James, apo A

Lane, Benjamin, gol B
Lane, Bray, cp A
Lane, Charles, hab A
Lane, George, fru A
Lane, John, wax A
Lane, John, wea B
Lane, Jonathan, gol A
Lane, Nathaniel, coa A2B578
Lane, Richard, bak A134B7
Lane, Richard, ck B
Lane, Thomas, ck A
Lane, Thomas, gro B
Lane, William, sal A
Langbridge, Thomas, bar B
Langerwood, John, wea A
Langford, Matthew, glo A
Langham, William kt, dra A
Langley, Henry, gol A
Langley, James, pou B
Langley, John, glo B
Langley, John, wea A
Langley, Robert, bro A
Langley, Samuel, gir B
Langley, William, pai B
Langly, Timothy, gro A
Langton, John, cp A1B678
Lansdell, John, gol A
Lapp, Gabriel, mer B
Lardler, Thomas, far A23B68
Lark, Richard, bre B
Larke, James, dra A
Lason, Abraham, gol A123B6
Lassells, Edmund, dye A
Lateward, John, pai A
Latham, Francis, lor A
Latham, Thomas, cut A
Lathwell, Joseph, cur A
Lathwell, Robert, sad A
Lattimer, John, cut B
Launee, David, cor B
Lavarick, Samuel, joi A
Lavender, William, bla B
Lavington, Richard, wea A
Law, Ed, bla B
Lawd, Mark, fis A4B568
Lawford, John, sal A
Lawford, Tho, bro A
Lawrance, John, pew B
Lawrance, Jos esq., vin B
Lawrence, Daniel, fou A
Lawrence, Edward, cp B
Lawrence, George, iro A
Lawrence, James, lea A
Lawrence, John, tai B
Lawrence, John jun, sta A
Lawrence, John sen, sta A
Lawrence, Richard, apo B
Lawrence, William, bla A
Lawrence, William, hab B
Lawrence, William, joi A

99

Laws, John, inn B
Lawson, James, gro B
Lawson, Richard, dis B
Lawton, Edmond, dye B
Lawton, William, cut B
Laxton, Martin, inn B
Lay, Timothy, fou B
Layne, Joseph, mer A
Lea, John, cp B
Leach, Dryden, sta A124B7
Leach, William, clo A
Leadbeater, James, fou A
Leadbeater, John, joi B
Leak, William, inn A
Leake, John, sta B
Leake, Samuel, bak B56
Leapidge, George, ski A
Leaver, James, cor A
Leay, Charles, vin B
Lee, Edward, bro A
Lee, George, fis A
Lee, John, lea B
Lee, Jonathan, apo A
Lee, Lancelot, mer A
Lee, Peter, tal B
Lee, Richard, bar B
Lee, Richard, tur A
Lee, Stephen, bak A123B7
Lee, Thomas, but B
Lee, Thomas, far A123B8
Lee, Thomas, pla B
Lee, Thomas, pla B
Lee, Thomas, vin B
Lee, William, cor A
Lee, William, dye B
Lee, William, fis B
Leeds, Edward, mer A
Leeke, William, glz A34B58
Leere, George, fru B
Leeson, George, bla A
Leever, Clement, joi B
Leffingham, Samuel, tai A
Legatt, George, fis A
Legg, Daniel, tai A
Legg, Thomas, cor A
Leggat, Abram, dis B
Legot, Henry, bro A
Leigh, Onisephorus, ski A
Leigh, William, ski B
Leigh, William *see also* Linch, William
Leithieullier, Christopher, dye A
Lekeux, Peter, wea A12B78
Leman, Ralph, wea B5
Lemon, Philip, pou B
Leneave, Edward, tai B
Lenoy, Timothy, bre B
Lenthall, John, sta B
Lepidge, Edward, pew A
Lepington, Lemuel, sal A
Le Plastrier, John, tai A134B6

Lester, John, fou B
Lester, Thomas, fou B
Letchmore, Richard, sal A
Lever, Francis, cur B
Lever, Nicholas, but A34
Leveridge, John, cur B
Leveridge, John jun, cur B
Levet, Francis, mer B
Levet, James, wax B
Levet, Richard, mer B
Levett, William, dra A
Levine, Peter, gro A1B578
Levingworth, Peter, wea A
Lewen, Edw, tai B
Lewen, William kt, hab B
Lewins, Anthony, but B58
Lewis, Charles, joi B
Lewis, George, gol B
Lewis, Henry, uph A
Lewis, John, gro A
Lewis, John, pla B
Lewis, John, pla B
Lewis, John, vin B
Lewis, Joseph, sad B
Lewis, Percival, dra A
Lewis, Thomas, iro B
Lewis, Thomas, sta A
Lewis, William, cor B
Lewken, Henry, apo A123B6
Lewkin, John, clo A
Libourn, William, sta B
Liddard, Richard, bla B
Liddards, Lemual, bla A
Liester, John, bar B
Ligar, Isaac, bro A
Light, Samuel, glo A
Light, Thomas, cur B
Lilly, William, apo A
Lime, Benjamin, dis B
Linch, Roger, cp B
Linch (Leigh), William, ski A34B78
Lind, Jos, bla B
Lindsey, Giles, cut B
Lindsey, Jos, bre A
Lingard, Thomas, plu B
Lingard, Thomas, sta A
Linley, Francis, but B
Lintott, Bernard, sta A
Linwood, John, vin B78
Lipcomb, Joseph, pou B
Lisseman, Richard, mas A
Lister, Charles, tai B
Litten, John, pou A
Little, John, ck B
Little John, pai A
Little, John, sal A
Little, Richard, coa A
Little, Robert, tal B
Littlebitty, John, sad B
Littlebury, George, sta A

100

Littlefeild, Edward, car A
Littlefeild, Walter, bri B
Littlefield, Edward, car B
Littler, William, dra B
Lloyd, Charles, ski A4B578
Lloyd, Cornelius, gro A123B7
Lloyd, John, pai A
Lloyd, John jun, scr A
Lloyd, John sen, scr A
Lloyd, Jos, sal A
Lloyd, William, cp A
Loader, William, cut A
Lock, Daniel, cor A
Lock, Matthias, mer A
Lock, Nathaniel, gol A
Lock, Richard, clo A123B5
Lock, Samuel, vin A
Lock, William, cor A
Locker, Joseph, tai A
Locker, Stephen, lea A
Lockier, John, lea A
Lockington, Thomas, fis A2B567
Lockwood, Thomas, car A
Locton, Eleazar, mer A
Lodes, Thomas, pou B
Lodge, Thomas, cut B
Lodwick, Charles, fis A
Lofthouse, Seth, tai B
Lombe, Thomas, mer A
London, John esq., iro A
Long, George, bla B
Long, James, dis B
Long, James, lea B
Long, Nath, vin A
Long, Solomon, glz B
Long, Thomas, tai B
Long, William, gro A
Long, William, pew B
Longbottom, James, mer A
Looker, John, bar A
Looker, Robert, far A
Lord, Job, bro A
Lord, Obediah, gol A
Lord, Robert, cp B
Lorimer, Nevill, bow A
Lorringe, Charles, fis B
Lorton, Thomas, joi A
Love, John, dra A
Love, Thomas, lea B
Love, William, fis B
Loveday, Thomas, tur B
Lovel, Robert, fou B
Lovell, Henry, fis A
Lovell, Michael, uph A
Lovell, William, hab A3B568
Lovett, William, cur B
Loving, Henry, bla B
Low, Anthony, fou B
Low, John, tal B
Low, Roger, bri A

Low, William, dye A
Lowdan, John, bro A
Lowen, John, gir B
Lowfeild, How, dra A
Lowfeild, Richard, dra A
Lownes, John, ski B
Lowth, Henry, uph B
Lowth, Robert, dra A
Loyd, Griffith, gol B
Loyd, John, bar B
Loyd, John, scr B
Loyd, Nathaniel, bar B
Loyd, Owen, sta B
Loyd, Walter, bak A14B78
Lucas, Edward, gol B
Lucas, James, glz B
Lucas, James, inn B
Lucas, Robert, bre A
Lucas, Stephen, tur B
Lucas, Thomas, tai A
Luck, George, wea B
Luckin, William, gol B
Ludlam, Francis, sal B
Ludlaye, George, wax B
Ludlow, John, cp A
Ludlow, Joseph, sal B
Luice, John, coa B
Lukus, Timothy, lea B
Lumby, Zephaniah, fru A
Lund, James, gls B
Lund, John, gol B
Lundsey, Thomas, tai B
Lunn, Thomas, coa B
Luport, Peter, fis B
Luquesne, John, gro A
Lutman, Josiah, glz A
Lutman, Thomas, hab A
Lutman, William, iro B
Lyd, Nehemiah, gol A
Lyddell, Robert, dra A134B6
Lydiard, Thomas, clo A
Lyell, Henry, tal A
Lyford, William, gro B
Lylliott, James, dis A
Lyme, Richard, dis B
Lympany, Robert, sta B
Lynch, Simon, bar B
Lyneal, John, joi B
Lyon, Joseph, dis A
Lyons, John, gro A

Mabson, John, bri B
Macascree, Nathaniel, arm B
Mace, Gilbert, wea A
Macham, John, coa A
Machin, Peter, bar A
Mackall, James, sal A
Mackett, William, tai A
Mackett, Zeph, tai A
Mackmorran, Robert, hab A

101

Madden, John, hab A
Maddocks, James, bre A
Maddy, John, bla B
Madewell, James, sal B
Madox, George, pai A
Maggs, Percival, pai A13B68
Maho, John, but B
Maidstone, Nathaniel, fis A
Main, Dorrington, mer A
Main, Jonathan, joi B678
Maine, Samuel, mer A
Makerness, Joseph, mus B
Maling, Jos, cut A
Maling, Thomas, bre A
Mallard, Joseph, but B
Malleroy, John, gro B
Mallery, John, lea B
Mallory, Eleazer, joi A
Malton, John, gol A
Malton, Samuel, wea A
Man, John, dra A
Man, Thomas jun, dra A
Man, Thomas sen, dra A
Man, Walter, cp A
Mandevile, Daniel, wea B
Mandevill, Jegon, tal A
Mandrell, Richard, sal B
Mane, Jonathan, joi A
Maneton, Robert, vin B
Manlove, Richard, scr B
Mann, Edward, vin A
Manning, Edward, cp B
Manning, Robert, cp A
Manning, Roger, joi A124B5
Mansfield, Lodwick, dis B
Manship, James, vin A
Manship, Samuel, sta B
March, John, bak A134B7
Marcross, Jonathan, dye B
Marcroyft, William, clo B
Mardin, Edward, joi B
Margary, Joseph, lor A
Margas, Jacob, but A
Markes, Joseph, lea B
Markham, Edward, but B
Markham, John, joi B
Markham, Richard, cur B
Markham, Robert, bla B
Markham, Robert, cur A
Markham, Robert, inn A
Marks, William, glo A2B678
Markum, John, apo B
Marler, Thomas, sta B
Marloe, Jeremiah, gol A
Marlow, John, bro A
Marlow, Joseph jun, gol A
Marlow, Michael, tai A
Marlow, Thomas, wea B
Marlowe, Joseph, gol A
Marriot, Augustine, gro B

Marriot, John, gro A
Marriott, Jacob, glo A
Marriott, James, tai B
Marriott, John, gir A
Marriott, Samuel, iro A
Marriott, William, apo B
Marscham, Mathew, lor B
Marsden, Thomas, dra B
Marsh, David, fru B
Marsh, Henry, ck B
Marsh, Isaac, wea A
Marsh, Samuel, hab A
Marshal, Joseph, ski A
Marshal, Simon, gro A
Marshall, Henry, dra B
Marshall, John, sta A
Marshall, John, tur B
Marshall, John, vin B
Marshall, Joseph, sta A
Marshall, Robert, gir B
Marshall, William, sta A
Marsland, William, tai A
Martin, Edward, hab A
Martin, George, ski B
Martin, James, far B
Martin, John, cut A
Martin, John, hab B
Martin, John, ski A
Martin, John, tur A
Martin, Joseph kt, hab B
Martin, Nathaniel, pai A134B6
Martin, Nathaniel, wea B
Martin, Simon, wea A
Martin, Thomas, bla B
Martin, Thomas, ck B
Martin, Thomas, gol A
Martins, Henry, tai A134B7
Mashham, Hugh, pew A
Mason, Adam, tai A134B6
Mason, Benjamin, pou A
Mason, Charles, joi B
Mason, Edmund, joi A1B678
Mason, George, gol B
Mason, Jeremiah, hab B
Mason, John, bre A
Mason, John, mus B
Mason, John, pew A
Mason, John, vin B
Mason, Joseph, dye B
Mason, Nathaniel, fle A
Mason, Robert, tal A
Mason, Thomas, lea B
Mason, Thomas, pla A
Mason, William, gro B
Mason, William, pai B
Mason, William jun, pai B
Master, John, tai B
Masters, Edward, cp A
Masters, Thomas, clo B
Masters, Thomas, clo B

102

Mathews, John, sta B
Mathews, Thomas, gol B
Maton, Samuel, but B
Matson, George, bro A
Matthew, Edward, pew B
Matthew, John, mer A123
Matthew, John, mer A
Matthew, Timothy, gro B
Matthews, Christopher, but B
Matthews, Edward, pew A14
Matthews, Emanuel, sta A
Matthews, John, inn B
Matthews, John, pai B
Matthews, Jonathan, ski A
Matthews, Richard, but A
Matthews, William, bow B
Matthews, William, clo B
Matthews, William, cur A
Mattocks, Charles, fis B
Mauby, William, pla B
Maud, Gamaliel, wea A
Maud, Gamaliel jun, wea A
Maud, John, wea A
Maulkin, Richard, uph B
Maund, Thomas, lor B
Mawer, George, but B
Mawhood, Samuel, fis B
Mawson, Thomas, gls A
Maxey, Charles, wea A
Maxey, William, wea B
Maxsee, Nath, dra A
May, Henry, dye B
May, Nathaniel, ski A134B5
May, Samuel, bre A
May, Tristram, bre A
May, William, ck B
May, William, tal A
Mayd, Thomas, lor B
Maydwell, Glison, gls A3B568
Mayer, John, lor A
Mayhew, Edward, dye A
Mayhew, William, dye B
Mayhoe, Will, but A
Mayhue, Steph, bro A
Maylin, Edward, joi A13B56
Maynard, Thomas, dis A3B678
Maynard, William, pla A
Mayne, John, but B
Mayne, Samuel, mer A
Mayo, Samuel, glo A
Mayor, Ralph, coa B
Mead, John, gro A
Mead, Richard, hab A2B568
Mead, William, dye A
Meader, John, joi A12B67
Meal, Nevill, bak B
Meard, John, tur A
Meares, Richard, fle A
Mears, William, mus B
Mears, William, sta A1B678

Meazey, Nath, apo A134
Mechan, Samuel, bla B568
Mechan, Samuel, bla A
Medcalfe, Lassells, tai A
Medders, Augustin, dye B
Meddows, George, cur A2B578
Medley, John, bla B
Medley, Robert, bla B
Mee, Benjamin, ski A
Mee, Hugh, ski A
Meekins, Edmond, vin B
Meekins, William jun, uph A134B6
Meekins, William sen, uph A134B6
Meeres, Stephen, cor A
Mekins, John, fou B
Melcher, Richard, apo B
Mellington, Thomas, dye B
Menzeys, William, lea A
Mercer, Thomas, sta A
Mercey, Isaac, cp A
Meredith, John, gro B
Meriall, Alexander, fis A
Meridith, Francis, bak B
Merredeth, Henry, hab B7
Merrett, Anthony, wea A3B567
Merrett, Stephen, lea B
Merrick, Francis, dis B
Merriden, John, cut B
Merridith, Henry, hab A234B7
Merrill, John, vin B
Merrill, Thomas, lea B
Merrit, Stephen, lea B
Merritt, Thomas, vin A234B7
Merriwether, Edmond, bla B
Merry, Kinghelme, wea A23B58
Merry, Thomas, gol B
Merrydale, Edmund, gro A
Merryfeild, Abraham, cp A
Merryman, Benjamin, tai A
Merryweather, Richard, hab A
Messinger, Edward, wea A
Metcalf, John, but B
Mettayre, Lewis, gol A2B578
Meux, Thomas, mer B
Meynell, Gerrard, inn A2B578
Meynell, John, gol A4B568
Michalson, George, car B
Michell, Edward, sal B
Micklethwait, Nathaniel, fis A
Micklewright, Samuel, hab B
Middleton, Arthur, lea B
Middleton, Henry, bar A
Middleton, John, joi B
Middleton, Ralph, hab B
Midford, John, glo A
Midwinter, Daniel, sta A
Mihell, Richard, bak B
Milbourn, John, lea B
Milbourn, John, pou B
Miles, Arnold, vin B

103

Miles, Henry, tal A
Miles, James, glo B
Miles, John, but B
Miles, Jonathan, dra A
Miles, Michael, gir A
Miles, Richard, but A23B68
Miles, William, nee A
Milla, Samuel, fle B
Millam, John, fis B
Mille, John, mer A
Miller, Benjamin, tai A
Miller, Bowler, ck B5
Miller, Isaac, bla A
Miller, James, tal A
Miller, John, fou B
Miller, John, mas B
Miller, John, tai A
Miller, Richard, fis A
Miller, William, vin A14B78
Millett, John, wea B
Millington, David, bow B
Millner, Nicholas, vin A1
Millner, Thomas, glo A
Mills, Bryan, sta A123B7
Mills, Edward, ski B
Mills, George, sal B
Mills, Henry, tai A
Mills, John, bla A
Mills, Richard, sta B
Mills, Stephen, clo A
Mills, William, pla B
Milner, James, sad A
Milner, James, uph B
Milner, Nicholas, vin B
Milton, Thomas, dis B
Milward, Thomas, joi B
Mingay, William, dra B
Minns, Richard, glz A
Minshall, Thomas, sta B
Minshell, Thomas, sta A2
Mitchell, Francis, mer A
Mitchell, John, wax A
Mitchell, Joseph, glo B
Mitchell, Robert, mer A
Mitchell, Theophilus, ck B
Mitton, Charles, bla A134B5
Mobbs, Robert, pla A
Molesworth, Thomas, but B
Molleson, Gilbert, dra A
Molt, George, hab A2
Moncaster, Peter, but B
Monger, Peter, gol B
Monk, George, dye B
Monk, Samuel, lor A
Monk, William, dra B
Moodey, Samuel, tai B
Moodey, Samuel, tai B
Moody, James, dis A
Moody, William, tai B
Moone, William, lea A3B678

Moor, Caleb, inn A
Moor, Jos, wea A
Moore, George, gro B
Moore, Isaac, fru B
Moore, John, car B68
Moore, Thomas, lea A
Moothin, William, mer B
Mordaunt, Charles, vin B
More, John, gol A
More, Joseph, cp A1B678
More, Thomas, sta B
Morehouse, Thomas, inn A
Morein, Thomas, bre A
Moreland, John, joi A
Moreton, John, bri B
Moreton, Thomas, fou A
Moreton, William, bri B
Morewood, Jos, gro A
Morey, Robert, gol B
Morford, William, joi B
Morgan, Edmond, bar A
Morgan, Edward, lea B
Morgan, Francis, bla B
Morgan, James, but B
Morgan, John, dra A
Morgan, Randall, tal B
Morgan, Thomas, fis A4B567
Moring, Anthony, ck A4B578
Morley, George, gro A
Morphew, John, sta B
Morrice, John, cut B
Morris, Edward, gro B
Morris, John, arm A
Morris, John, inn A
Morris, Joshua, iro A
Morris, Luke, bar B
Morris, Philip, hab A
Morris, Phillip, dye A
Morris, Robert, bla A
Morris, Thomas, mer A
Morrison, William, vin B
Morse, Nicholas, lor A
Morse, Richard, tur A
Morse, Robert, pew A
Morse, Robert, pou B
Morse, Robert, pou B
Morson, Richard, gol A
Morter, Rain, cor A
Mortimer, George, sta B
Mortlock, George, sta B
Mortlock, Henry, sta B
Morton, John, bro A
Moseley, Thomas, gol A
Mosely, John, ck B
Mosely, Richard, ck B
Mosely, Thomas, iro B
Mosely, William, mer A4B578
Moss, William, arm A
Mostyn, Richard, ski A
Motlow, Thomas, plu B

104

Mott, Roger, tai A
Mottershed, Richard, gro A
Mouldsworth, Thomas, but A
Moulins, Robert, pew A
Mounsey, Jonathan, bar B
Mount, Jerry, sal B
Mount, Richard, sta A
Mount, William, sta A
Mountague, Thomas, gro A
Mountford, Hezekiah, gol A123B6
Mowsley, Charles, hab B
Moye, Richard, lea B
Moyer, Lawrence, mer A
Moyer, Samuel bt, mer A
Moyer, William, mer A
Moyle, Charles, pai A
Muggleton, John, bak B
Mulcaster, Henry, wea B
Mullenay, Francis, tal B
Mumford, William, pou B
Munford, Edmund, gro A
Murdaine, John, sal A
Murden, John, joi A2B567
Murden, Robert, sal A
Murden, William, sal A
Murdin, Edward, joi A2
Murdin, Jeremy, tai A
Murdock, James, bak A
Murrey, George, pai A
Mussell, George, lea A
Mussell, Thomas, hab A
Musters, Francis, ski A
Myres, William, ski B

Nailer, Samuel, dra A
Narsh, Arthur, wea B
Nash, George, sal B
Nash, James, glo B
Nash, Richard, tai A
Nash, Robert, coa A24B68
Nash, William, gol A
Nayler, Williams, sad B
Neale, John, bla A
Neaton, Thomas, coa A
Nedwick, Joseph, fle B
Neele, John, lor A13B58
Negers, George, mer B
Neighbour, Robert, wea A
Nelham, Samuel, dra B
Nellis, William, but B
Nelmes, Anthony, gol B
Nelms, Robert, gro B
Nelson, Robert, fou A
Nelson, Thomas, apo B
Nelthorp, James, hab A
Nephine, Thomas, pou B
Nevell, John, nee B
Nevil, William, inn B
Nevill, Richard, fou B
Newberry, William, ski A

Newbery, John, ck B
Newbury, William, gol B
Newdick, Henry, pou A
Newdigate, Christopher, hab A
Newe, John, sal B
Newel, Thomas, but B
Newell, George, gol B
Newell, Ralph, tur A
Newell, William, joi A
Newham, John, fru A
Newland, George kt, joi B
Newman, Edward, joi B
Newman, Fossett, gls A
Newman, John, pou B678
Newman, Jonathan, joi A
Newman, Matthew, clo A
Newman, Richard, mer B
Newman, Richard, pai A
Newman, Robert, fou B
Newman, Robert, fou A
Newman, Thomas, clo A
Newman, Thomas, fou B
Newman, William, tal A134B6
Newnham, Lewis, gls A
Newnham, Nathaniel, mer A
Newstubb, Paul, bro A
Newth, Mark, bar A
Newton, George, fru A
Newton, James, hab A
Newton, John, gol B
Newton, John, sta A
Newton, John, tai A
Newton, Richard, bar A
Newton, Richard, gol B
Newton, Robert, gro B
Newton, Samuel, fou A
Newton, Samuel, lor A
Niblet, Andrew, arm B
Niccoll, Robert, lea B
Nicholas, Henry, tai A
Nicholas, John, bar B
Nicholas, Thomas, cp B
Nicholes, William, dye B
Nicholl, Roger, sal A
Nicholls, Anthony, gol A
Nicholls, Richard, fis A
Nicholls, Richard, gol A
Nicholls, Thomas, vin B
Nichols, Hen, wea B
Nichols, Soan, mus B
Nichols, Thomas, mus B
Nichols, Thomas, uph B
Nichols, William, bak A
Nicholson, James, apo B
Nicholson, James, sad A
Nicholson, John, clo A
Nicholson, John, sta A
Nicholson, Joseph, apo A123B7
Nicholson, Josiah, bre B
Nicholson, Robert, pew A

105

Nickholls, Samuel, pai A13B57
Nickless, Thomas, joi A
Nickolls, James, far A
Nicoll, Randolph, sta B
Nisbett, Thomas, dra A
Nitingale, Richard, fou A
Nixon, John, cor A
Noble, Francis, ski B
Noble, Matthew, inn B
Noble, Richard, bar B
Nockalls, William, bow B
Nockells, Christopher, bar B
Nodes, Benjamin, fis B
Nodes, John, mer A
Noel, Nath, sta B
Noell, John, tai A
Nooden, Hughs, tai B
Noon, John, plu B
Noone, John, bro A
Norbery, William, arm B
Norcliffe, Marmaduke, bar B
Normabell, Will, bro A
Norman, Edward, inn A
Norman, Henry, cur A
Norman, James, cp A
Norman, John, inn A
Norman, John, lea B
Norman, Joseph, bri A
Norman, Richard jun, car B
Norman, Richard sen, car B
Norman, Thomas, sta B
Norman, Thomas, sta A2
Norman, Tobias, cur A
Norris, Edmond, sal A
Norris, George, cp B
Norris, Hugh, iro A
Norris, John, gls B
Norris, Robert, apo B
Norris, Robert, wea A
Norris, Thomas, sta B
Norris, William, bla A
Norris, William, joi A
Norris, William, wea A
North, Daniel, cur B
North, George, pew B
North, Henry, ck B
North, Henry, ck A1
North, Robert, fou A
Northall, James, bar B
Northey, Thomas, hab B8
Northey, William, ski A
Northorne, Bryan, pou B
Norton, James, bar A
Norton, John, hab A
Norton, John, lea B
Norton, Thomas, bak B
Norton, William, hab B
Norton, William, hab B
Norton, William, ski B
Norwich, Erasmus, ski B

Norwood, John, cp B
Noss, Henry, pou A14B68
Nuce, Thomas, bak B
Nurser, John, iro B
Nut, William, gro A2B567
Nutcher, James, clo A
Nuthall, James, bar A
Nutt, John, mer A2B567
Nutt, John, sta B
Nutt, Joseph, bre A
Nutt, William, mer A3B567

Oade, Matthew, glo A
Oades, William, bar B
Oak, Joseph, sta A
Oakes, John, dra A
Oakes, Stephen, joi B
Oakly, Edmund, pou A
Oakly, Josiah, but B
Obee, John, glo A
Ogborn, William, car B
Ogle, Arthur, dra A
Oland, Thomas, nee A1B578
Old, Henry, tur A2
Old, William, tur B
Oldes *see* Ordes
Oldham, Thomas, clo B
Oldisworth, William, tai A12B8
Oldner, George, uph B
Oldsworth, Austin, tai B
Oldsworth, Austin jun, tai B
Oles, Edward, sad A
Oley, Daniel, gir B5
Oliver, Andrew, wea B
Oliver, Edward, car B
Oliver, John, but B
Oliver, Thomas, nee A
Oliver, William, pou B
Olley, Isaac, cor A
Olley, John, glo A14B56
Omans, Francis, cp A
Omant, James, dra A
Oncy, John, joi B
Ongley, Samuel, bro A12
Ongley, Samuel esq., bro B
Ongley, Samuel kt, tai B
Oram, Richard, inn A
Ordes (Oldes), James, sta A12B57
Orgwag, Henry, vin B
Orlton, John, vin B
Osborn, Samuel, arm B
Osborn, Thomas, gro B
Osborne, Anthony, gir B
Osborne, Arthur, uph B
Osborne, George, ski A
Osbourn, Richard, tai B
Osbourn, William, pla B67
Osgood, Benj, car A
Osgood, John, tal A134B7
Osland, Nehemiah, gro B

106

Osmond, George, bak B
Osmond, George, plu B
Osterland, Jacob, bro A
Oswin, John, bak A124B7
Ouring, Noah, bre A
Overall, Edmund, tai A
Overing, James, tur B
Overton, Henry, bro B
Overton, Humphry, tai B
Overton, Philip, sta B
Owen, Edward, ski A
Owen, Henry, cp A1
Owen, Richard, vin B
Owen, Robert, tur A
Oxwick, Robert, fis A

Pace, John, inn A
Pace, Joseph, sal A
Pace, Tho, tai B
Pack, Thomas, fou A134B8
Packer, Jacob, cor B
Packing, George, lea B
Packman, John, tai A
Page, Allen, wea B
Page, Charles, bar B
Page, Gilbert, bar A
Page, John, pew B
Page, John, tur A
Page, Stephen, but B
Page, Thomas, tal A
Page, William, but B
Page, William, hab B
Page, William, wea B
Page, Zephani, dis A
Pagett, James, mas A
Paggen, Peter, bre A
Paggett, William, wea A
Pain, Nathaniel, fis B
Paine, Jeremy, tur A
Paine, John, bak A
Paine, John, but A
Paine, John, hab A124B7
Paine, John, tur A
Paine, Richard, bro A
Paine, Richard, tur A
Paine, Robert, tai A14B56
Paine, Sampson, joi A
Paine, Thomas, fle B
Paine, William, arm A
Paine, William, mer A
Paine, William, tal A
Painter, Edmund, pai A12B68
Paitfeild, John, bro A
Pakeman, Timothy, gro A
Paling, Edmond, wax B
Pallady, John, joi B
Palledy, William, joi B
Pallington, Joseph, lor B
Palmer, Anthony, mer A
Palmer, George, cur A

Palmer, Henry, inn A
Palmer, Henry, iro A
Palmer, John, lea A
Palmer, John, tai A
Palmer, John, tur A1B578
Palmer, John, vin B
Palmer, Robert, bak A124B6
Palmer, Samuel, bar B
Palmer, Samuel, dis A
Palmer, Samuel, fis A
Palmer, Thomas, fru A
Palmer, Thomas, vin A
Palmer, William, cp A
Pampion, William, cp A
Pangbourn, Richard, cor A
Pankeman, John, bri A
Pansford, Tracy, lea A
Panting, Simon, gol A
Papillon, Samuel, fis A
Pappillion, Philip, mer A
Pargiter, William, fra A
Paris, Matthew, ski B
Parish, Isaac, fis A
Parish, William, mer A
Park, James, uph B
Park, Ruben, uph B
Parker, Andrew, sta B
Parker, Daniel, pew A
Parker, Edmond, sta A
Parker, Francis, pla B
Parker, Henry, sta B
Parker, James, fis A
Parker, John, but B
Parker, Lawrence, ski B
Parker, Nicholas, bar B
Parker, Richard, cp A
Parker, Thomas, bla B
Parker, Thomas, gls B
Parker, Thomas, pai B
Parker, William, bak A
Parker, William, bar B
Parker, William, tal B
Parker, William, wea B
Parkerson, Chester, plu B
Parkerson, Christoph, plu A14
Parkinson, Thomas, pou B
Parks, Samuel, dra B
Parme, William, joi B
Parnell, Robert, fis A
Parnidge, John, apo B
Parr, Henry, bla A
Parr, Thomas, gol A2B678
Parran, Benjamin, cp A
Parran *see also* Barron
Parrot, Abraham, hab B
Parrot, Edward, sad B
Parrot, Thomas, pai B
Parrott, Simon, fou A
Parrott, William, fis B
Parrson, John, dye B

107

Parry, Thomas, cp B
Parry, Thomas, wea B
Parsley, Thomas, glz B
Parson, John, coa A
Parsons, Henry, sta A124B7
Parsons, John kt, fis B
Parsons, Thomas, hab A
Parsons, William, fou A134B7
Partington, Thomas, dra A
Pasmore, Edward, bri A
Passenger, Thomas, sta A
Patcard, William, tal B
Patch, Robert, joi A
Pate, Robert, car A
Pate, William, tai A
Patrick, John, joi B
Patrick, Nicholas, uph B
Patrickson, John, bro A
Patridge, James, ski A
Patridge, John, gol A
Patridge, John, plu A
Patridge, Joseph, tai A123B7
Patridge, Richard, arm A
Patridge, Seth, gol A
Patridge, Thomas, pai A
Patsell, Joseph, bar A
Patten, Robert, gro A
Patten, William, lea B
Patterson, Robert, wax A
Pattison, Edward, cut B
Pattison, William, bla A
Pattrick, Henry, cp B
Paul, Josiah, bar A
Paulfreeman, John, clo A
Paulfreeman, Jonathan, hab B
Paulin, Edward, lea A
Pawlet, Robert, sta B
Pawley, Armstrong, joi B
Pawley, Francis, arm B
Pawley, Isaac, pla A
Payne, Benjamin, gol B
Payne, Hunphreys, gol B
Payne, Thomas, uph A134B8
Payne, William, mas A
Payton, John, glo B
Peachy, Edward, wea A
Peachy, John, ski A
Peacock, Barns, vin B
Peacock, Thomas, gro A
Pead, Len, ck A
Pead, Leonard, ck B
Peak, Richard, but B
Peake, John, hab A
Peake, Richard, pla B
Pear, Richard, bar B
Pearce, George, bak A
Pearce, James, gol A
Pearce, John, bar B
Pearce, John, sal A
Pearce, Matthew, gol A

Pearce, Richard, bar A4
Pearce, Thomas, dis A1B678
Pearce, Thomas, fou A24
Pearkes, James, fis A
Pearse, Thomas, ski B
Pearse, Thomas, wea A
Pearson, Thomas, fou B
Pearson, William, sta A23B56
Peaton, Jonathan, nee A
Peatson, Roger, bla B
Peatver, James, apo B
Pechin, George, sal B
Peck, Edward, dye A12B78
Peck, Simon, tur A
Peckings *see* Perkins, John
Pedmore, Peter, bri B
Peel, Thomas, fru B
Peele, John, fou A
Peele, Peter, bla B
Peer, Lewis, lea B
Peerman, James sen, joi B
Peerman, John, joi B
Peers, Charles kt, sal A
Peirce, James, tur A
Peirce, Jerem, tai B
Peirce, John, dye A
Peirce, Nathaniel, gol A123
Peirce, Richard, gro B
Peirse, John, dra B
Peirson, Edward, sal B
Peirson, Richard, gol B
Peirson, Robert, but B
Peirson, Thomas, but A123B7
Peirson, Thomas, glo B
Pelham, William, bak A
Pellet, William, fis A23
Pellett, William, fis B
Pember, Will, inn B578
Pemberton, Edward, fru A
Pemberton, George, mer A
Pemberton, John, fru A
Pemberton, John, sta A124B6
Pemberton, Roger, inn A1B678
Pemble, John, sad A
Pen, John jun, sta B
Pen, John sen, sta B
Pencill, Thomas, bla B
Pendleton, John, vin B
Pendred, Thomas, far B
Pengreve, Daniel, bar B
Penkethman, John, gol A
Penn, John, tai A
Penn, Thomas, arm A
Pennett, William, tal B
Pennington, William, coa B
Penny, John, gls A
Pepper, Christopher, gro A
Peppercorn, Edmund, inn B
Perce, Joshua, lea B
Percivall, Tho, but A

Perkins (Peckings), John, dye A12B58
Perkins, Solomon, glz A
Perkins, Thomas, joi A
Perkins, William, tal B
Perrey, Timothy, gir A
Perrier, John, ski A
Perrin, John, but B
Perrin, Jos, bla B
Perris, Henry, sta B
Perry, Benjamin, cur B
Perry, John, bre B
Perry, John, pla B
Perry, Matthew, nee B
Perry, Micajah, hab A123B7
Perry, Richard, hab A123B7
Perry, Samuel, apo A
Perry, Stephen, clo A
Pestell, Tho, tai B
Petche, John, gir B
Petche, William, cur B
Peter, Charles, fou A
Peter, Henry, sad B
Peter, Samuel, vin B
Peter, Simon, gol B
Peter, Simon, gol A124
Peters, James, scr A
Peters, Stephen, glo A134
Pett, John, gro A23
Petterson, James, scr A2B567
Pettey, Thomas, ck A
Pettifer, Abraham, joi A
Pettifer, William, pla B
Pettit, Edward, hab A
Pettit, Edward, wea A
Pettit, John, tai A
Pettitt, James, mer A
Petty, David, mer A134B6
Petty, John, joi B
Petty, Joseph, joi A
Petty, William, bar A2B568
Petworth, Henry, sad B
Pevishouse, Thomas, fis B
Pewsey, Christopher, glz B
Pewsey, Thomas, pou A
Peype, Samuel, bri B
Pheasant, John, nee A1B568
Phelps, Noble, lea B
Philip, William, ck B
Philips, Daniel, bla A
Philips, John, pla B
Philips, William, gro B
Phill, Thomas, uph B
Phillip, Thomas, ski B
Phillips, Andrew, tur A
Phillips, Charles, ski A1B568
Phillips, Daniel, bar A
Phillips, Henry, bri A
Phillips, John, pou A13B56
Phillips, John, ski B
Phillips, John, sta A

Phillips, Joshua, sta A
Phillips, Michael, cp B
Phillips, Nathaniel, dis B
Phillips, Randal, lor B
Phillips, Thomas, fou A
Phillips, Thomas, hab A
Phyll, Henry, sal A
Picant, George, bak B
Pickard, Edward, dye A
Pickard, John, bla A
Pickard, Thomas, dye A
Pickard, William, dye A
Pickerin, Edw, tai B
Pickering, Henry, lea B
Pickering, John, tai A
Pickering, Peter, tal B
Pickering, Peter jun, tal B
Pickering, Samuel, mer B
Pickering, William, pai A
Pickring, Richard, cp A
Picton, John, pou A
Piddell, Joseph, pew B
Pidgeon, Samuel, but B
Pierce, John, ck B
Pierson, Job, bla A
Piffing, William, uph B
Piggate, Richard, cut B
Piggott, John, coa B
Piggott, Thomas, hab A
Pigher, John, tur B
Pike, Richard, pou A
Pike, William, but B
Pike, William, fou B
Pike, William, uph A
Pincke, John, pai B
Pinckne, Philip, gol A
Pindar, Michael, fis A124
Pindar, Samuel, mer A
Pinder, Michael, fis B
Pinder, Thomas, sal B
Pinfold, Edward, gol B
Pink, John, pai B
Pinkney, Philip, ski A
Pippin, Matthew, dye B
Pitcher, Thomas, bro B
Pitkin, Roger, uph A
Pitkin, Thomas, bla B
Pitkin, Thomas, hab B
Pitman, William, bak A
Pitson, James, apo A
Pitson, William, ski A
Pitt, Andrew, glo A
Pitt, Thomas, mer A
Pitt, William, coa B
Pitt, William, gro B
Pittman, Joseph, tur A12B58
Pittman, Robert, pou A
Pitts, James, hab B
Pitts, Thomas, tai A
Pixley, Thomas, tai A

109

Place, Law, sta B
Plaistow, Henry, hab A
Plampin, Richard, far B
Planner, Jeremiah, vin B
Planner, John, tai A
Plant, John, wea A
Plasted, Richard, fou B
Plasted, Stonyeire, dis A
Plasted, Thomas, dis A
Plat, John, fou B
Platt, Nathaniel, clo A
Platt, Richard, bla A
Plattell, Peter, gol A
Player, Gabriel, gol A
Player, John, lea A1B578
Pledger, Elias, apo A
Plimley, Humphrey, dis A
Plowman, Richard, vin B
Plucross, Joseph, gls B
Plumbston, Matthew, dra A
Plummer, Richard, cur B
Plummer, William, cp A
Plumsted, Robert, dra A12B78
Podmore, Robert, sta B
Point, William, uph B
Polehampton, Edward, pai B
Polhill, Edward, gro A
Pollard, John, gir B
Pollet, William, gol B
Pomeroy, William, tai A
Ponton, Daniel, bri B
Pool, Benjamin, tai A
Pool, Rowland, bak B
Poole, Benjamin, gol B
Poole, Henry, bar B
Pooll, William, sad B
Pope, Henry, hab A
Pope, Ralph, pou B
Pope, Robert, tai B
Pope, Samuel, dra A
Pope, William, pla B
Popleton, Edward, nee A
Porteene, Francis, mer A
Porten, James, dra A
Porter, Benjamin, mer A
Porter, Francis, gro B
Porter, George, dis B
Porter, John, cp B
Porter, John, lea A
Porter, Kowland, bla B
Porter, Robert, apo A
Porter, William, bro B
Portress, Richard, mer A1B678
Portress, William, fra B
Portsmouth, William, gls B
Pothinton, Joshua, but B
Potter, Hamond, sal B
Potter, Ralph, tai B
Potter, Thomas, far B
Potts, Henry, inn B

Potts, Joseph, tai A234B5
Potts, Percivall, fle B
Poulter, John, cur A
Poultney, Thomas, joi B
Poulton, Richard, tai A
Powel, Benjamin, uph B
Powel, John, wea A
Powel, Samuel, gro A
Powel, William, far A
Powell, Edmund, sta B
Powell, Giles, vin B
Powell, Jeremiah, hab A
Powell, John, lor A2B678
Powell, Joseph, joi A
Powell, Robert, pla A
Powell, Thomas, but B
Powell, Thomas, cut A
Powell, Thomas, pla B
Powell, William, cut A
Powell, William, plu A
Powett, John, tur B
Powle, Daniel, dye A
Powle, Henry, gro A
Powle, Thomas, clo A
Prady, Edward, joi B
Prankard, George, wea A
Prat, Joseph, bri B578
Prat, Thomas, inn A
Pratchett, Richard, clo B
Pratt, John, tur A
Pratt, Joseph, pew A
Pratt, Samuel, mer B
Pratt, Thomas, bak B
Pratten, Charles, mus B
Prayton, John, car B
Predy, James, pai B
Prentice, John, inn B
Prescot, Roger, inn B
Prescott, Inglis, but A
Preston, Bartholomew, vin B
Preston, Nath, far A
Preston, Thomas, dye B
Preston, Thomas, vin B
Prestridge, Richard, gro B
Prett, Richard, bar B
Price, Charles, hab B
Price, Edward, bro B
Price, George, cor A
Price, James, coa B
Price, John, apo B
Price, Joshua, glz B
Price, Nathaniel, cur B
Price, Nathaniel, tai A
Price, Richard, wea A
Price, Tho, tai B
Price, Thomas, hab B
Price, Thomas, wea B
Price, William, fis B7
Prichard, John, sta B
Priddith, Christopher, dye B

110

Pridie, Thomas, cor B
Primate, Humphrey, gro A123B6
Prime, Matthew, tai A
Prince, William, tal A
Prince, William, wax A
Prine, John, fou A23B67
Prior, Thomas, bak B
Prittin, Thomas, car B
Proble, Matthew, dis A
Prockter, Marmiduke, gro B
Procter, Samuel, gro A
Procter, William, fis B
Procter, William, fis A124
Proctor, Henry, wax B
Proctor, Henry, wax A34
Proctor, William, hab A34B56
Proudfoot, Edmond, dis A
Proudman, William, tal B
Proudwood, Jos, tai B
Prowe, Richard, tur A
Pruden, John, clo A
Pryard, Edward, pou B
Puckard, William, bla B
Puckle, Thomas, iro A
Puckle, William, hab A
Pugh, Evan, clo A124B8
Pugh, Samuel, dye A
Pullen, James, sta B
Pullen, William, gro B
Puller, Samuel, pew A
Pullin, Samuel, far B
Pulling, John, nee A
Pumfrey, Ezekiel, joi A
Punter, Daniel, glz A
Purcass, Thomas, gro A
Purchase, James, tai A2B678
Pure, Thomas, bla A
Purnell, John, iro A
Purse, Robert, gro A
Pursloe, John, mer A
Pursloe, John, mer A
Purss, Nicholas, gro B
Puryour, William, glz A
Pycroft, John, bre B
Pyke, Benjamin, ski A
Pyke, James, wea B
Pyke, John, tal A
Pyke, Robert, joi A
Pyott, Alexander, glo A

Quaite, John, bak A
Quamell, Richard, but B
Quantock, Henry, tur B
Quantock, Joseph, tur B578
Quare, Jeremiah, glo A
Quarles, Anthony, cp A
Quartermain, Daniel, bla A
Quatremain, John, cut A
Quelch, William, dra B
Querendon, William, far B

Quick, Hugh, pew A
Quilter, John, but A
Quilter, William, but A2B568
Quineo, Andrew, apo B
Quinton, Nathaniel, cut A

Radams, John, hab B
Radman, Henry, tai A1
Ragdale, John, glz A
Ragg, William, dra A2B678
Rain, Thomas, vin B
Rainer, Richard, vin B
Rainsford, Richard, mer A14B58
Rainsford, Thomas, iro B
Rakestraw, Thomas, tal B
Rakins, Thomas, glo A
Ram, Stephen, gol A
Rammell, John, wea A
Randal, Edward, pew B
Randal, Robert, joi B
Randall, Bruce *see* Randolph
Randall, Henry, dye A
Randall, John, bar B
Randall, John, sta A
Randall, John, wea B
Randolph (Randall), Bruce, bak A123B7
Ranney, Henry, apo B
Ranshall, John, wea A
Raper, Henry, pai A
Raper, Moses, cor A
Raper, Thomas, lea A
Rapson, William, gls B
Rash, Samuel, tai B
Ratcliffe, Henry, cur A
Ratcliffe, Ralph, lor A
Ratcliffe, Thomas, tai A
Ratcliffe, William, fou A
Ratford, Daniel, wax A
Raven, Andrew, gol B
Raven, Joseph, sta A13B56
Ravencroft, Thomas, dra A2B568
Ravis, John, pla B
Raw, Adam, bar B
Rawbone, Joseph, lea A
Rawlins, James, sta B
Rawlins, John, but B
Rawlins, John, tai A
Rawlins, Nathaniel, hab A
Rawson, Charles, tai B
Rawson, Thomas, sta A
Ray, Walter, gro A1B678
Rayman, John, bre A
Rayman, William, uph B
Rayment, John, tur B
Rayment, Robert, gro B
Raymond, Jos, bre A
Raymond, Samuel, mer A
Raymond, Thomas, nee A
Rayne, Robert, wax B
Rayner, John, gls A

111

Raynsford, Edward, car A134B8
Rayson, Samuel, bar A
Rea, James, bla B
Rea, Roger, cor A
Read, George, cp A
Read, George, sta B
Read, James, cp A123B6
Read, James, sta A
Read, John, dra A
Read, John, gol B
Read, John, tur B
Read, Len, ck A134
Read, Richard, gro A123B6
Read, Richard, joi B
Read, Samuel, sal A
Read, Samuel, sal A
Reading, Nicholas, bak A
Reading, William, bri B
Readman, John, cp A
Redding, Edward, pai B
Reddish, Edward, apo B
Reding, William, bla A4B568
Redman, Henry, tai B
Redshaw, Joshua, gol B
Redwood, John, dra B
Reed, Alexander, tai A
Reed, Ely, bla B
Reed, Major, dye A
Reeve, George, fou B
Reeve, John, but A
Reeves, Hampden, ski B
Renaud, Lawrence, ck A
Renger, Thomas, cut B
Revell, Henry, clo B
Revell, John, dye A134
Reynell, Carew, fou A123B6
Reynold, John, tai A
Reynolds, Charles, cor A
Reynolds, Edmund, wea A
Reynolds, George, joi A
Reynolds, Hazariah, nee A
Reynolds, John, hab A
Reynolds, John, joi A
Reynolds, John, sal B
Reynolds, Richard, dye B
Reynolds, Robert, joi A
Reynolds, Samuel, ck B
Reynolds, Stephen, fou B
Reynolds, Stephen, gro A
Reynolds, Thomas, but A23B68
Reynolds, Thomas, wea A
Reynolds, William, gol B
Reynolds, William, pai A13B56
Reynoldson, Charles, cp B
Reynoldson, Joseph, hab A
Rheame, William, ck B
Rhodes, Henry, sta A
Rice, John, but A
Rice, William, but B
Rich, Elias, sad B

Rich, Thomas, dye B
Richards, James jun, iro A
Richards, James sen, iro A
Richards, Richard, glz B
Richards, Samuel, iro A
Richards, William, bla B
Richardson, Jeremiah, lea A
Richardson, John, fis A234
Richardson, John, fou A24B56
Richardson, John, lea A
Richardson, John, sal A
Richardson, John, wea A
Richardson, Joseph, uph A
Richardson, Nath, joi B578
Richardson, Richard, fis B
Richardson, Thomas, far B
Richardson, William, inn B
Richardson, William, joi B
Richardson, William, lea A
Richardson, William, pai B
Richbell, John, pai A12B57
Richier, Edward sen, wea A
Richins, William, cur B
Richmond, Andrew, vin B
Rickaby, William, fru A
Rickburd, John, bar B
Rickets, Francis, cp B
Rickles, Thomas, bak A124B7
Rickles, Thomas, bak A234B7
Rickword, Sam, car A
Riddle, Giles, tai A134
Ridge, George, clo A234B6
Ridge, Jeremiah, tal B
Ridgeway, William, pou A
Ridgway, Edward, bar A
Ridley, Giles, tai B
Ridley, John, gol B
Ridly, Anthony, but B
Ridly, Thomas, bla B
Ridly, Thomas, bla B
Ridock, Simon, cor A
Ridout, John, hab A
Ridout, Joseph, bar B
Ridout, Simon, bar A
Ridout, Thomas, cor A
Rigbey, Richard, tai A
Righton, John, uph A
Ring, Samuel, tai A
Ripert, Peter, wax A
Risheir, Edward jun, wea A
Rivett, John, tai A
Roades, Robert, tai A4B678
Roadeway, Richard, tur B
Robert, Joseph, plu B
Robert, Sisson, dis B
Roberts, Adam, tai A
Roberts, Edward, tai A
Roberts, George, clo A134B5
Roberts, Griffith, bla A
Roberts, Hugh, gol B

112

Roberts, James, sta A
Roberts, John, cur B
Roberts, John, dis B
Roberts, John, hab B
Roberts, John, inn B
Roberts, Joslin, mer A
Roberts, Nic, pla B
Roberts, Samuel, hab A
Roberts, Samuel, lea A
Roberts, Thomas, cut B
Roberts, Thomas, joi B
Robince, John, clo A
Robinett, Jonathan, joi A
Robins, John, far A
Robins, Thomas, bar B
Robinson, Benjamin, hab A
Robinson, Charles, joi B
Robinson, Charles, vin B
Robinson, Edward, vin B
Robinson, James, bak A23B78
Robinson, John, bla B
Robinson, John, bri B
Robinson, John, inn B
Robinson, Matthew, glo A
Robinson, Nath, dra A
Robinson, Peter, bri A
Robinson, Samuel, joi B
Robinson, Thomas, apo B
Robinson, Thomas, apo A
Robinson, Thomas, bla B
Robinson, Thomas, but B
Robinson, Thomas, dye A
Robinson, Thomas, gol A
Robinson, Wadder, joi A134B6
Robinson, William, mer A
Robotham, Walter, cut A
Rochdale, Joseph, cp A
Rochester, James, dra B
Rochester, Matt, dra B568
Rodway, John, mer B
Rodway, Robert, clo B
Roe, Peter, cur B
Roe, Richard, fou A
Roger, Humphry, ski B
Roger, William, tur B
Rogers, Benjamin, mer B
Rogers, Edward, tur A
Rogers, George, bro B
Rogers, Henry, gol B
Rogers, James, bak A
Rogers, John, hab A24
Rogers, John, mer B
Rogers, Richard, fra A
Rogers, Richard, pai B
Rogers, Robert, bri A
Rogers, Robert, tur A
Rogers, Thomas, but B
Rogers, Thomas, tai A
Rogers, Thomas, vin B
Rogers, William, far B

Rogers, William, tur B
Rogerson, Phillip, car B
Rogerson, Richard, car B
Rokeby, Nathan, apo A
Rolfe, George, bar B
Rolleston, James, gol A
Rolleston, John, lea A
Rollus, Phillip, gol B
Rondell *see* Rowdell
Rood, William, dra A
Rooe, Thomas, pai B
Rook, Thomas, cp A
Rooke, Benjamin, bla B
Rooke, John, fis B
Rooke, William, bar A
Rooker, Joseph, glz A1B578
Rooks, John, dye A23B78
Roome, Stephen, clo A123B6
Roome, William, ski A
Roper, Abel, sta B
Rose, Jerr, cur B
Rose, John, cor B
Rose, John, dye A
Rose, Joseph, tur A3B678
Rose, Matthew, sad B
Rose, Quince, sal B
Rose, Thomas, joi A
Ross, John, gol B
Rossell, Matthew, cor A
Rothbotton, Daniel, iro A
Rothmeal, John, vin B
Round, Edward, hab B
Round, James, sta A
Rouse, Nathaniel, gro A
Rouse, Robert, vin B
Row, James, uph B
Row, Thomas, coa B
Rowbery, John, glo A
Rowcliffe, Hugh, hab A
Rowdell (Rondell), John, bak A134B7
Rowe, John, gol A
Rowe, Martin, pla B
Rowe, Samuel, joi A
Rowe, Stephen, ck B
Rowell, John, far B
Rowfield, Thomas, dra A
Rowland, John, pai A13B6
Rowland, Richard, fru B
Rowland, Robert, arm A1B567
Rowland, Thomas, bar A
Rowleidge, William, but B
Rowles, Mich, tai A
Rowles, Thomas, apo B
Rowley, John, bro A
Rowly, Thomas, bar B
Rowse, Anthony, mus A
Rowse, William, apo A24B56
Rowton, John, cor A
Royal, Walter, clo B
Roycroft, Samuel, sta B

113

Roystone, Edwin, gro A1B568
Roystone, William, gro A1B567
Ruck, James, mer A
Ruck, Thomas, gir A
Rudduck, Thomas, ck A
Rudgby, Andrew, pew A
Rudrup, Benjamin, bla A
Rudsby, Philip, plu A
Rufford, Tamerlane, mer B
Rule, Ambrose, wea B
Rumsey, Robert, joi A
Rush, Samuel, hab A
Ruslen, John, gol A134B6
Russ, John, bro A
Russel, Anthony, cut B
Russel, Benjamin, wea B568
Russel, Charles, clo B
Russel, Cornelius, fis A
Russel, John, iro A
Russel, Joshua, bla A
Russel, Richard, gir B
Russel, Richard, pai B
Russel, Robert, uph B
Russel, Samuel, ck A
Russell, Abraham, tur B
Russell, John, car A
Russell, Michael, wea A
Russell, Thomas, bla B
Russell, William, bar B
Russell, William, tai A12B57
Rust, John, tai B
Rutbach, Benjamin, pai A13B78
Rutt, Richard, glo B
Rutter, Timothy, dra A4B5
Rutter, William, glo A
Rutty, John, hab A
Ryal, Francis, gir A
Ryder, Richard, ski A
Ryland, Thomas, lea B
Ryley, Ambrose, tai B
Ryley, Samuel, apo A
Ryley, Thomas, mer B
Ryly, Christopher, gol B
Rymer, Edward, but B
Rymil, John, joi B
Ryols, John, far A

Sadler, John, mer A
Sadler, Thomas, gol B
Safe, Peter, wea A124B7
Sage, Thomas, but A
St John, James, gol A
St Paul, James, mer A2B568
Sale, Samuel, ski B
Sale, William, ski B
Salisbury, Edward, sad B
Salisbury, Fulk, tai B
Salisbury, Norwich, sad A
Salisbury, Thomas, coa A
Salt, Samuel, vin B

Salter, John, bar B
Salter, John, tai A13B56
Salter, Robert, tai B
Salter, Samuel, ski B
Salter, Thomas, tai A13B56
Salway, Edward, hab A
Samm, Nathaniel, wea A123
Samwayes, John, tai A
Sandall, Thomas, tur B
Sanders, Nathan, cp A
Sanders, Samuel, joi A
Sanders, Thomas, lea B
Sanders, William, cp A
Sanderson, Andrew, bro A124B5
Sanderson, Edward, bri B
Sanderson, Edward, lor A
Sanderson, John, uph B
Sandford, Thomas, hab B
Sandon, John, cor A
Sandon, Thomas, gro A
Sands, William, wea A
Sands, Windsor, uph B
Sandwell, James, gir B
Sandwell, Joseph, gir B
Sanford, James, sal B
Sanford, Joseph, bar B
Sanguell, Richard, cur B
Sanny, Robert, but B
Sapsford, Luke, wax B
Sarasine, James, bro A
Sare, Richard, sta B
Sarfata, Matthias, fou B
Sargenson, James, fou B
Sarney, Thomas, glz A
Sarson, John, wea A
Satchivell, John, wea B
Saton, Joseph, but B578
Saunders, Henry, mer B
Saunders, John, joi A
Saunders, Joseph, cor B
Saunders, Joseph, hab A
Saunders, Richard, joi B
Saunders, Richard, wax B
Savage, Charles, tai A
Savage, Henry, plu B
Savage, Isaac, tai A
Savage, Michael, joi A2B578
Savage, Purbeck, uph A
Savage, Richard, pla B
Savage, Richard, pou B
Savage, William, gro B
Savage, William, sal B
Savary, Michael, lor A
Savidge, Richard, ck B
Savill, Richard, clo A
Sawbridge, Jos, cut A
Sawcer, John, fis B
Sawen, Abraham, joi B
Sawtell, Edmund, gro B
Sawyer, James, dis B

114

Sawyer, Thomas, car B
Saxton, Joseph, gir B
Sayer, Francis, hab B
Sayes, William, sta B
Saywell, John, lea B
Scamadine, Thomas, fis B
Scantlebury, Robert, joi A
Scarborough, Thomas, lor A
Scarborough, William, bla B
Scoffin, Joseph, tur A
Scot, Robert, ck B
Scot, Thomas, gro B
Scott, Daniel, tai A23B56
Scott, Daniel, tal A
Scott, John, arm A123B5
Scott, John, fou B
Scott, John, uph A
Scott, John, vin B
Scott, John kt, lea A
Scott, Richard, bro A
Scott, Richard, fis A
Scott, Richard, pai B
Scott, Robert, cp A
Scott, Samuel, but B
Scott, Samuel, lea A
Scott, Stephen, mer A
Scott, Thomas, inn A1B678
Scott, Thomas, pou B
Scott, William, fis A
Scotting, Joseph, glo A
Scrimshaw, Joshua, iro A
Scrimshire, Will, uph A34B67
Scruby, James, vin A
Seabrooke, Robert, uph A4B678
Seabrooke, William, hab A
Seagood, Francis, hab A
Seagrave, Samuel, wea A
Seamer, John, tai B
Seaquer, William, car B
Searle, John, bla A
Searle, Robert, inn A
Searlet, William, bro B
Searls, Thomas, sad B
Seawell, Thomas, vin B
Secher, Richard, lea B
Sedgewick, Tobias, bar B
Sedgley, Samuel, fru A
Sedwell, John, fou A
Sedwick, Samuel, pai A
Sedwick, William, bak A234B5
Seemer, James, dra A
Seer, John, bar B
Seewell, Thomas, lea B
Seigniorett, Stephen, tai A
Seivel, William, fru B
Sekip, Thomas, tai B
Selby, Robert, gol A134B6
Selby, Thomas, lea A34B58
Selby, Thomas, lea A
Selfe, Anthony, mer A14B68

Sells, John, pou B
Sellwin, John, tai A
Selwyn, William, ski A
Sendal, Joshua, lea B
Sender, John, bro A
Sereston, William, sal B
Serjant, Edward, vin B
Serjeant, John, but A
Serjeant, Sherard, tai B
Serman, John, coa A
Serman, Philip, hab A
Serocole, Thomas, mer A
Sewdley, Henry, pew A
Seyle, John, bla A
Shackleton, John, glz B
Shad, Thomas, but B
Shadell, Henry, inn B
Shadforth, George, bar B
Shadwell, Jeremiah, fis A
Shakepear, Benjamin, pai B
Shakespeer, Jonathan, bro B
Shakespere, George, lea B
Shakle, Thomas sen, pew A
Shales, Charles, gol B
Shaller, William, lea B
Shallpratt, John, bri A
Sham, Robert, pla B
Shannet, John, bla B
Shard, Isaac kt, glo A14B78
Shard, John, arm A
Sharp, Francis, tai A
Sharp, John, bre B
Sharp, Sutton, nee A
Sharpe, John, dis A
Sharpe, Lionel, joi A
Sharpe, Nathaniel, bak A
Sharpe, William, bri B
Sharples, Nicholas, inn A34B56
Shaw, John, cp A2B568
Shaw, Joseph, dra A
Shaw, Richard, cp A234B7
Shaw, Richard, cur A
Shaw, Robert, uph B
Shaylor, Thomas, apo A
Sheafe, Samuel, fis A
Sheaphead, Henry, dis B
Sheapheard, Richard, tai A
Sheapherd, Daniel, plu A
Sheapherd, John, plu A
Shearing, Thomas, glo A
Sheekle, Edward, ski A
Sheffield, Benjamin, fis A
Sheibell, Henry, apo A
Sheibell, John, apo A
Sheldon, Samuel, inn A
Sheldon, William, dra B
Shelley, John, tai B
Shelly, Charles, gol B
Shelly, Robert, ski A
Shelmerdine, Thomas, sta A

115

Shelston, John, wea B
Shelton, Henry, far A
Shelton, John, bar A
Shelton, John, but B
Shelton, John, sad B
Shelton, John jun, sad B
Shenton, Robert, dis B
Shephard, Edmund, pai B
Shepheard, John, bak A
Shepheard, Jos, mus B
Shepheard, Joseph, cut B
Shepheard, Richard, pai B
Shepheard, Vincent, hab A
Shepherd, William, uph B
Sheppard, Dormer, sal A
Sheppard, Gregory, dis B
Sheppard, John, bar B
Sheppard, John, vin B
Sheppard, John, wax B
Sheppard, Joseph, clo A23B67
Sheppard, Matthew, bar A
Sheppard, Phillip, dis B
Sheppard, Richard, dis B
Sheppard, Richard, joi B
Shepperd, William, gol A123B8
Sheppherd, Benjamin, mer A
Sherbon, William jun, joi A
Sherbourne, William, joi A
Sheriff, William, joi B
Sherley, Thomas, dis B
Sherley, Thomas, glz B
Sherlo, Thomas, clo B
Sherman, John, ski A4B578
Sherman, Paul, clo B
Sherman, Richard, arm B
Sherman, Thomas, sad A
Sherman, Thomas sen, sad A
Shermer, Thomas, clo B
Sherrard, Will, bro A
Sherriff, Thomas, cut B
Shervil, Richard, cur B
Sherwill, William, dra A
Sherwood, Francis, dye A
Sherwood, Henry, glz A124B5
Sherwood, Samuel, apo B
Sherwood, William, cor A
Sherwood, William, vin B
Shethell, Robert, apo B
Shewel, Thomas, fis B
Shewell, James, hab B
Shield, John, mas B
Shiers, William, pai B
Shilborn, Richard, vin B
Shilling, Daniel, scr A
Shipley, Jonathan, lea A
Shippy, Samuel, fis A
Shippy, William, glo B
Shipside, George, gro B
Shipton, John, bar A12B67
Shipton, John, joi A4B568

Shipton, Peter, glz A
Shipton, Samuel, tai A
Shipton, Thomas, sal A
Shoemaker, Abraham, bro B
Shorey, John jun, pew A
Shorey, John sen, pew A
Short, John, tai B
Short, Samuel, fis B
Short, Samuel, sal A
Shortridge, John, cur B
Shott, John, bar A
Shribb, Robert, gir A
Shrosbridge, John, bar B
Shrubsall, William, fru B
Shut, George, iro B
Shute, Benjamin, fis A
Sibbald, Babb, dra B678
Sibley, George, mer B
Sibley, Thomas, lea A
Sibthorpe, Christopher, joi B
Siddall, James, apo A
Silk, John, fis B
Silk, Tobias, iro B
Sill, Richard, hab B
Silles, Richard, hab A
Silver, John, pla B
Silver, Richard, hab B
Silvester, John, dra A
Simes, William, pai A
Simkins, Fran, tai A
Simmonds, William, cor B
Simmons, Henry, gro B
Simmons, Richard, dye B
Simmons, Richard, fou B
Simmons, Thomas, mas A
Simms, John, sta B
Simond, Robert, fle B
Simons, John, pla B
Simons, Richard, fis B
Simpson, John, lea B
Simpson, Lloyd, cor B
Simpson, Ralph, sta A
Simpson, Richard, sta A134B7
Simpson, Thomas, sta A
Sing, Richard, gol A
Singleton, Thomas, joi B
Sire, Samuel, vin A
Siritt, Simon, fou A
Sison, Henry, bow B
Sisson, Thomas, bow B
Sitwell, Francis, mer A
Skattergood, Thomas, pew A
Skeet, John, arm B
Skelton, Thomas, bar B
Skey, John, dra A
Skilton, Humphrey, uph B
Skimpton, George, cor B
Skinner, Abel, joi A
Skinner, Abel, joi A
Skinner, Edmund, hab B

116

Skinner, John, hab B
Skinner, John, sal B
Skinner, Lancet, clo B
Skinner, Obadiah, bak B
Skinner, Richard, apo A
Skinner, Samuel, scr B
Skinner, Stephen, fou A23B56
Skipp, Thomas, glz A
Skrine, Henry, vin A
Slack, Nathaniel, cut B
Slade, John, hab B
Slade, Richard, arm A
Slany, Abel, tai A3B567
Slany, John, tai A
Slapp, John, lea B
Slater, John, arm B
Slaughter, Chambers, sal A
Slaughter, Edmund, mer B
Slaughter, Matthew, but B
Sleighton, Robert, cor B
Sleith, Gabriel, gol B
Slemaker, Richard, tai A
Slemaker, Thomas, mas A
Slenny, Richard, mer A
Slocombe, John, lea A
Smallbones, Jos, cp B
Smalley, Thomas, lea A1B567
Smalwell, John, joi B
Smart, Adam, bro A
Smart, Francis, arm A
Smart, Richard, bre A24B58
Smedley, John, glz B
Smelt, Samuel, bla B
Smirke, Sampson, tai B
Smith, Anthony, pew A
Smith, Benjamin, bar B
Smith, Benjamin, cor B
Smith, Benjamin, fou A
Smith, Braban, clo B
Smith, Charles, gir B
Smith, Daniel, plu B
Smith, Edward, clo B
Smith, Edward, clo A4
Smith, Edward, gir A
Smith, Edward, hab A
Smith, Eleazer, mer B
Smith, Francis, gro B
Smith, Gabriel, gro A
Smith, George, apo A
Smith, George, clo A
Smith, George, dye A
Smith, George, hab B
Smith, Henry, apo A
Smith, Henry, ck B
Smith, Henry, gro A
Smith, Henry, tai B
Smith, James, fou A
Smith, James, pou B
Smith, James, sad A
Smith, James, vin B

Smith, John, arm A
Smith, John, bri A134B5
Smith, John, but A
Smith, John, dye A
Smith, John, fou B
Smith, John, hab A4B567
Smith, John, lea B
Smith, John, lor A
Smith, John, mer A134B6
Smith, John, pew A
Smith, John, pou A
Smith, John, tal B
Smith, John, tur B
Smith, John, tur B
Smith, Josiah, dra A
Smith, Launder, gol A
Smith, Lawrence, dra B
Smith, Lawrence, iro B
Smith, Mark, iro B
Smith, Matthew, joi A
Smith, Nathaniel, bar A2B58
Smith, Nicholas, gol B
Smith, Nicholas, hab B
Smith, Nicholas, lea B
Smith, Obed, sta B
Smith, Peter, bar B
Smith, Richard, bak B
Smith, Richard, bla A
Smith, Richard, pew A
Smith, Richard, pla A
Smith, Richard, plu A
Smith, Richard, tai B
Smith, Robert, apo B
Smith, Robert, cp B
Smith, Robert, pou B
Smith, Samuel, bar B
Smith, Samuel, bre A
Smith, Samuel, but B
Smith, Samuel, cp A
Smith, Samuel, cut A
Smith, Samuel, vin B
Smith, Samuel, wax B
Smith, Thomas, bla B
Smith, Thomas, cp B
Smith, Thomas, cut B
Smith, Thomas, hab B
Smith, Thomas, ski A
Smith, Thomas, tai B
Smith, Thomas, wea A
Smith, Thomas jun, gir A
Smith, Thomas sen, gir A
Smith, William, bar B
Smith, William, bar B
Smith, William, bar B
Smith, William, bla A
Smith, William, but B
Smith, William, car B
Smith, William, cp B
Smith, William, cp A
Smith, William, cut A1B678

117

Smith, William, cut A
Smith, William, fis A
Smith, William, joi B
Smith, William, mer A
Smith, William, tal B
Smith, William, tal B
Smith, William, wax B
Smith, William, wax A14
Smith, William, wea B
Smithen, Richard, bla A
Smithen, Samuel, gol B
Smithlyer, John, gol B
Smithson, Robert, gro A
Smythe, Benjamin, mer A
Snabling, Matthew, dra A4B567
Snagg, Richard, gol B
Snare, John, pou A1B578
Snart, John, bla B
Sneath, John, wea A
Snell, George, gol A
Snell, John, gol B
Snell, William, gol A
Snooke, Robert, lor A
Snow, Ralph, sta A
Snow, William, pai A
Snowden, Joshua, ski A123
Soame, Richard, gol A123B7
Soames, Henry, wea A
Soane, Thomas, gol A
Soanes, John, bla A
Sochon, Daniel, gol A
Solley, Joseph, tai A
Some, Bartholomew, gol A
Sopp, Robert, bri A2B678
Souch, Benjamin, tur A
South, Humphrey, fis A
South, Thomas, hab A
Southby, John, sta B
Southerland, Thomas, gro A
Southern, Henry, bar B
Southern, John, lor A
Southwerth, Robert, wea B
Southwood, Robert, tal A
Soutly, Thomas, hab A13B57
Souton, John, dye B58
Sowlter, Thomas, lea B
Spakeman, Thomas, gol B
Spakman, John, gol A
Sparham, John, bak A
Sparke, Robert, iro A1B678
Sparke, Thomas, pou A3B568
Sparkes, Jeremiah, dye A
Sparkman, William, bro B
Spearing, William, fis A
Spearman, James, joi B
Spearman, Josiah, cp A
Spence, Henry, dye B
Spence, Henry, dye A13
Spencer, Edward, fis A2
Spencer, George, pou A2B568

Spencer, Hugh, cur B
Spencer, Isaac, ck B
Spencer, John, ck B
Spencer, John, sal A
Spencer, Joseph, car B
Spencer, Thomas, bla A
Spensley, Miles, cp B
Sperink, Joseph, bak B
Speyngwell, John, bro B
Spicer, Christopher, fis A
Spicer, Robert, hab A
Spicer, Samuel, tai A
Spicer, Thomas, cut B
Spike, John, inn B
Spillett, John, mer A
Spillett, John jun, mer A
Spinkes, Elmes, gol B
Spinks, Seth, uph B
Spinler, Nathaniel, uph A
Spinnage, Anthony, fra B
Spitser, Peter, cut A
Spittle, Thomas, fou A
Spooner, Abraham, vin B
Spracley, Thomas, pou B
Spragg, Samuel, lea A
Sprakeling, Giles, joi A
Sprigg, Simon, ck B
Sprigg, Thomas, cp B
Spring, William, gol B
Springate, Richard, apo A
Springthorpe, Henry, bro A
Sprint, Benjamin, sta A
Sprint, John, sta A
Spurling, Edward, but B
Spurling, Nath, bla B
Spurrier, Henry, dis A
Squire, Nicholas, far B
Squire, William, clo A
Srent, Thomas, clo B
Stacie, Thomas, vin B
Stacy, Richard, cor B
Stacy, Richard, cor B
Stafford, William, cp A
Staley, John, bar B
Stallard, Abraham, gol A
Stamp, John, dra A
Stamper, Robert, scr B
Stancliff, James, hab A
Standard, William, bow A12B67
Standey, Henry, clo A
Standish, Charles, cut A
Standish, John, dra A123B7
Standish, John, hab A
Stane, George, wea B
Stanier, North, pai B
Stanlake, William, scr B
Stanley, Edward, arm B
Stanley, James, dra B
Stanley, Randal, pla B
Stanly, Christopher, but B

Stanton, Edward, mas B
Stanton, Fredrick, gls A14B67
Stanton, John, cor B
Stanton, Richard, mus A123
Stanton, Thomas, bar A134B6
Staples, John, gro B
Staples, John, uph A
Staples, Jos, lea A
Staples, Thomas, dra B
Staples, Thomas, uph B
Staploe, John, cp A12B67
Starling, Thomas, bla B
Starr, Joseph, cp A
Starth, Philip, gro B
State, John, joi A
Staverton, Deodatus, hab B
Stayner, Thomas, mas A123B8
Stead, George, mer A
Stead, Thomas, tai A
Steapman, Edward, uph A
Stebbin, Robert, cut B
Stebbing, John, pai B
Stedwell, Thomas, pai A
Steed, Matthew, cor B
Steel, Matthew, but B
Steel, Richard, hab A
Steevenson, John, gol B
Stephens, Henry, glo B
Stephens, John, glo A
Stephens, Nath, bla B
Stephens, Natth, ck B
Stephens, Robert, but B
Stephens, Samuel, dye A
Stephenson, Humphry, car A
Stephenson, Thomas, cur B
Stephenson, Thomas, fis B
Sterman, Shernall, hab A
Stert, Richard, lor B
Stevens, John, pai A2B568
Stevens, Nathaniel, dra B
Stevens, Robert, wea A134B5
Stevens, William, far B
Stevens, William, pew A
Stevenson, Christopher, tai B
Stevenson, Hen, but A
Stevenson, Peter, pla A3B578
Stevenson, Samuel, tur A
Stevenson, Thomas, bak A13B78
Stevenson, Thomas, cur B
Stevenson, William, mus B
Steventon, Anthony, gol B
Steward, Benjamin, gls A
Steward, Rowland, pew A
Steward, William, pai B
Stewart, Charles, bak B
Stewart, James, fis A
Stewart, John, dra B
Stewart, William, tai A
Stewart, William kt, bar B
Stiff, Isaac, joi B

Stiffe, Thomas, cp A
Stiles, Lazarus, joi A
Stiles, Thomas, hab A
Stillman, Anthony, cor A
Stockdale, Robert, fis A
Stocker, Henry, cur B
Stocker, Jasper, but B
Stoker, Richard, inn A3B678
Stokes, Jacob, pai B
Stokes, James, wea A
Stokes, John, gro A
Stokes, Joseph, gol A
Stonard, John, inn A
Stone, Guy, cut A1B678
Stone, Joseph, gro B
Stone, Thomas, joi A
Stonell, John, sad B
Stoner, Francis, dis B
Stonier, Samuel, ski A
Story, Richard, wea B
Stoughton, Richard, apo A
Stouton, William, bak A
Straham, George, sta B
Strainge, Samuel, cut A134B7
Strange, John, tai A
Strange, Samuel, bak B8
Strange, William, clo B
Stratford, Joseph, dis A
Stratton, Rich, coa A
Stratton, William, iro A
Streater, Samuel, gro A
Streatfeild, Thomas, gro A
Streek, John, plu A
Stretfield, George, tai A
Stretfield, William, hab B
Stretton, William, fis B
Strickland, Samuel, gol B
Stringer, George, pou A134B5
Stringer, Nathaniel, fou A13B58
Stringer, Thomas, joi A
Stringfellow, John, fou A
Strod, William, bri A
Strode, Thomas, bri B
Strong, David, lor A
Strong, Edward, mas B
Strong, Edward jun, mas B
Strong, William, mer A4B567
Strude, Samuel, bar B
Strudwick, George, fis A12B67
Strudwick, Henry, sal B
Strutton, Robert, but B
Strutton, William, mas B
Stubbin, John, hab A
Stuckwell, Francis, fis B
Sturt, John, gol B
Styles, John, lea B
Styles, John, pew A134B8
Styles, Thomas, gro A
Styles, Thomas, hab A
Suffil, John, but B

119

Summer, Thomas, joi B
Sumner, William, bla A
Sumpner, Regenald, bla A
Sunderland, John, fou B
Sunthorpe, John, sad B
Sureties, Samuel jun, joi A
Sureties, Samuel sen, joi A
Surman, William, tal B
Sussex, John, tal A14B68
Sussex, William, sta A
Sutton, David, lor A
Sutton, Jacob, lor A
Sutton, John, gol B
Sutton, Samuel, tai B
Swadlin, William, gol B
Swadling, John, dis B
Swain, Thomas, joi A
Swaine, Thomas, uph A
Swall, Abel, sta A
Swallow, Joshua, fou A
Swan, Thomas, plu B
Swann, Owen, vin A4B567
Swann, Ralph, clo A
Swann, Robert, tai B
Sweetapple, John, gol B
Sweetapple, Thomas, nee B
Sweeting, Nicholas, tur B
Swinhow, George, glo A
Swinstead, Rich, but A
Sylk, John, pew B
Symmons, Abraham, lea B
Symonds, Will, but A

Talford, James, glz B
Tallbott, Luke, wax A
Talmon, James, arm B
Tame, Henry, inn B
Tancy, Hen, bla B
Tandy, Richard, plu A
Tanner, John, glo A
Tanner, Joseph, bar A
Tanner, Martin, mer A
Tanner, Michael, gls B
Tanner, Michael, glz B
Tanner, Thomas, gir A
Tanner, William, cor A
Taping, John, mas B
Tapp, Richard, tai B
Tapp, William, lor A2B578
Tarbox, Joseph, glz B
Tarrant, Thomas, bla B
Tarrant, Thomas, bla B
Tarrant, Thomas, bro A2B567
Tarry, George, uph B
Tart, John, but B
Tarver, William, tai B67
Tarver, William, tai A
Tash, John, vin B
Tash, William, tai B
Tate, William, bre B

Tatem, Samuel, tai A
Tatham, Joseph, tai A3B568
Tatlock, Henry, mer B
Tatlock, Thomas, bla A
Tatlocke, Thomas, gro B
Tatnall, John, uph A
Taverner, Jeremiah, vin A1B567
Tavernor, John, scr B
Tay, Edward, dra A124B6
Taybeure, William, bre A123B6
Tayler, Anthony, arm A
Tayler, Joseph, cp A3B678
Tayler, Joshua, fra A
Tayler, Thomas, glo B
Tayler, Thomas, pew A
Taylor, Abraham, cur B
Taylor, Benjamin, wax A
Taylor, Cornelius, gir A
Taylor, Daniel, arm B
Taylor, Henry, arm A123B6
Taylor, James, arm A124B6
Taylor, James, glo A34B57
Taylor, John, bak A
Taylor, John, bla B
Taylor, John, dra A
Taylor, John, gir B
Taylor, John, glo A
Taylor, John, glz A
Taylor, John, hab A
Taylor, John, joi B
Taylor, John, mer B
Taylor, John, sta A
Taylor, John, tai B
Taylor, John, vin B
Taylor, John, wax A
Taylor, John, wea B
Taylor, Oliver, cur B
Taylor, Richard, dra A
Taylor, Richard, dra A
Taylor, Richard, fou A
Taylor, Robert, inn A
Taylor, Tho, bro A
Taylor, Thomas, coa B
Taylor, Thomas, fru A
Taylor, Thomas, gol A
Taylor, William, inn B
Taylor, William, sta A
Taylour, Charles, ski B
Teague, Daniel, fis A
Teaton, John, bak A
Teem, Matthew, bar B
Tempest, John, bar B
Temple, Richard, dye A
Temple, Richard, gir A
Terrad, Edward, joi A
Terret, William, wea A
Terrett, Isaac, lea B
Terrett, William, plu A
Terrie, Richard, tal A
Terry, John, mer A

Terry, Robert, fou A
Terry, Robert, wax B
Terry, William, sta B
Testard, James, bro A
Tew, Thomas, bak A
Thackary, William, sta A14B67
Thacker, Thomas, but B
Thacker, Thomas, tal B
Thacther, Charles, tal B
Thacther, William, tal B
Thatcher, Thomas, tal A23
Thayre, Humphrey, ski A
Thayre, Samuel, ski A12B56
Theed, John, sal A
Theed, William, hab A
Theedum, Edward, bre B
Theobald, John, sal A
Theobald, Peter, bar A
Thirsturn, Edward, vin B
Thomas, Charles, joi B
Thomas, John, fis B
Thomas, Jonathan, joi A
Thomas, William, joi B
Thomason, James, wax A
Thompson, Charles, cut A
Thompson, James, glz A
Thompson, John, hab B
Thompson, John, tal A
Thompson, Joseph, sal A
Thompson, Joshua, pai B
Thompson, Ralph, sal A
Thompson, Robert, iro A
Thompson, Samuel, bar A
Thompson, Samuel, hab A
Thompson, Stephen, cp A
Thompson, Thomas, bla A
Thompson, William, cp A
Thompson, William, fis B
Thompson, William, inn A12B68
Thomson, Peter, pai A
Thomson, Robert, wax B
Thomson, William, pla B
Thornborough, John, bro B
Thornborough, John, but B
Thornhil, James, pai B
Thornhill, Joseph, bla B
Thornton, John, wea A
Thornton, Samuel, dra A24B67
Thornton, Thomas, bla A
Thorowgood, Thomas, fou B
Thorp, Robert, lea A
Thorp, Thomas, gir A134B5
Thorp, Thomas, wea A
Thorpe, Francis, uph B
Thorpe, John, apo A
Thorpe, John, but B
Thursfield, Edward, wax A
Thurston, James, but B
Thwaites, John, cut B
Thwaites, Richard, vin B

Tibbee, Edmond, bak A
Tidford, Ralph, wea B
Tidmarsh, Richard, dye B
Tidmarsh, Thomas, pew A134B7
Tidmarsh, Wall, uph B
Tidswell, Richard, hab A
Tignell, Henry, dye B
Tilbury, Henry, bak B
Tilden, Richard, bro A
Till, John, gro B
Tillet, George, bro A
Tillier, John, pla A
Tilly, John, tal B
Tilly, William, ski A14B68
Timberliack, James, coa B
Timbrell, Robert, gol A
Timbrell, Thomas, clo A
Timm, William, bar A
Timm, William, ski B
Timms, John, cor B
Timms, John, wax A
Timms, William, cor B
Timwell, Charles, bla A
Tindall, Charles, apo B
Tindall, Edward, bla B
Tindell, John, vin B
Tingin, John, glo A
Tinson, Charles, inn A
Tipper, Morice, sal B
Tipping, John, cut A
Tipping, William, ski A
Tisdale, Benjamin, ski B
Tisdale, William, tai B
Tisdall, William, cor B
Titterton, Richard, bri B
Tobin, Morris, apo B
Tocketts, Roger, bar A
Toll, William, gro A
Tombs, Christopher, bar B
Tomkins, Benj, but A
Tomkins, Edward, cut A
Tomkins, Edward, joi A
Tomkins, Edward, joi A
Tomkins, John, sad A
Tomkins, Matthew, tai A
Tomkins, Nicholas, joi A
Tomkins, Richard, tur A
Tomlin, Samuel, lea A
Tomlin, Thomas, but A
Tomlin, Thomas, mer A
Tomlins, Hugh, bla B
Tomlins, Joseph, sad A
Tomlinson, Benjamin, tal B
Tomlinson, John, but A13B67
Tomlinson, Samuel, but B
Tomlinson, William, bar B
Tomms, Thomas, bar B
Toms, Philip, mer A
Tomson, John, but B
Tomson, Ralph, fra A

121

Tomson, William, clo A
Tong, Thomas, ski B
Tonicliff, Joshua, bla A
Tonson, Jacob, sta A
Tonson, John, vin A
Tonson, Thomas, cp B
Tonstall, George, bar A134B7
Tooke, Benjamin jun, sta B
Tooke, Benjamin sen, sta B
Tooke, Edmond, sal A
Tooke, Nicholas, lea A123B6
Tooley, William, pla A12B78
Tooly, John, pla A
Toone, Hamlett, bla B
Toone, William, clo A
Toone, William, wea A
Toosands, Edmund, but A
Toosley, James, cut B
Toosly, James, cut A123
Topham, Christopher, scr B
Toriano, Charles, tai A
Torver, John, joi B
Tothill, Thomas, bar B
Totton, Samuel, mer A
Tough, Charles, pew A
Tounton, Thomas, iro B
Tournay, Anthony, ski B
Tourney, John, joi A
Tourton, Thomas, iro B
Tourton, Thomas, iro B
Tovey, John, apo A4B568
Tovey, Joseph, tai A
Tovey, Joseph, tal A124B7
Towell, Nicholas, but B
Towers, Edward, gir A
Towers, John, fis A
Towers, John, joi A
Towers, Robert, joi A
Towers, Samuel, joi A
Towers, William, iro A
Towersey, Richard, joi A
Towes, Christopher, hab A
Town, Thomas, mer B
Towne, Leonard, hab A134B6
Townsend, George, gol B
Townsend, Horatio, dra A
Townsend, James, bow A
Townsend, John, lea A
Townsend, John, tal B
Townsend, Jonathan, bow A
Townsend, Jos, bre A
Townsend, Tho, but A
Townsend, Thomas, but B
Townsend, Thomas, tai A
Townsend, William, tai A
Townsend, William, tal A124B8
Tracey, Ebenezer, sta A
Tracey, John, glz B
Traherne, Edward, pew A
Tramwell, Thomas, hab A

Tranton, John, inn A
Trapp, John, hab A
Trapp, Michael, wea A
Travel, Samuel, tur B
Travell, John, bla A
Travell, John, bri B
Travell, John, fis A
Travers, Benjamin, vin A
Traynton, Thomas, inn B
Tredway, Walter, glo A
Tredwell, John, wea A
Tree, Lambert, cor A
Treesar, John, bla B
Treidneck, James, cor B
Trench, Edmond, sal A
Trench, Samuel, sal A
Trench, William, dra B
Trent, Henry, iro A
Trevers, John, scr A
Trevers, Samuel, scr A
Trevett, Robert, pai B
Treyhern, Thomas, cor A
Trigg, John, gro B
Trigg, Joseph, iro A
Trigg, Math, mer A
Trimer, William, gro A
Trimmer, John, dye A
Trimmer, William, mas A
Trinquand, Charles, ski A
Triston, Thomas, dis B
Trossell, William, vin B
Troughton, Miles, wea B
Troughton, Nath, bla A
Trow, Charles, vin B
Trowe, Richard, sta A
Trowel, Samuel, bro B
Trowell, John, bro B
Trowell, Samuel, but B
Truby, Richard, vin B
Truelock, Thomas, bla A
Truelove, James, fis B
Trueman, Jos, lor A
Trumble, James, coa B
Truss, Christopher, wax A
Tryon, Rowland, tai B
Tuck, Arthur, ck A
Tuck, Samuel, dye B
Tucker, Humphrey, but A
Tucker, James, lea A
Tucker, James, pla A
Tuckey, Alexander, ck B
Tuffnell, John, wax B
Tufnell, William, wax B
Tull, Samuel, tai B
Tunson, Edward, but B
Turbevill, John, pai B
Turlis, Thomas, fou B
Turner, Daniel, sal A
Turner, Henry, pai B
Turner, James, ski B

Turner, James, wax B
Turner, John, fou A2B678
Turner, John, ski B
Turner, Joseph, pla B
Turner, Nathanael, ski B
Turner, Richard, gol A
Turner, Richard, hab B
Turner, Richard, tai B
Turner, Robert, fou B
Turner, Samuel, tai A
Turner, Thomas, glz A
Turner, Thomas, tai B
Turvey, George, bla A124B8
Turvie, George, fis B
Tuther, Hugh, bri B
Tutt, James, tai A123B5
Tuttle, Henry, tai A134B6
Twichell, James, bak B
Twiford, Owen, but B
Twine, Anthony, lea A
Twine, John, fis B
Twinn, Samuel, hab B
Twisden, John, mer B678
Tye, Joseph, cor A
Tyler, Thomas, bak B
Tyrrel, Charles, ski B
Tyrrell, Francis, mer B

Underwood, Edward, apo B
Underwood, Francis, uph A
Underwood, John, fra A
Underwood, Richard, coa B
Unit, William, hab B
Upfolde, Thomas, tai A
Upington, Robert, tal A3B567
Upp, Robert, gls A
Upton, Jonathan, inn B
Usborn, John, sta A
Usburn, William, hab A
Usher, John, hab A
Uvebale, Thomas, dra A
Uxley, Benjamin, cut B
Uzzell, John, dye A

Vale, George, dis B
Vandatseller, John, bro A
Vanderspreat, John, pai A
Vandewald, John, dra A
Vandike, George, glo A
Vannam, John, fis A4B578
Vare, William, bow A
Vaston, Benj, bro A
Vaston, William, bro A
Vaughan, John, glo A
Vaughen, Richard, tur B68
Vaune, Philip, cor B
Veal, Henry, iro B
Veinon, Edward, tai B
Vellett *see* Voilet
Venables, Stephen, gol A124B6

Venimore, Roger, but B
Vere, Job, vin B
Vere, Samuel, gol A
Vere, William, tai B
Vere, William, tai A
Vernam, Thomas, sta A
Verneon, Thomas esq., hab B
Vialls, Edmond, coa B
Vibert, Lawrence, tal A
Vicars, Richard, tai A
Vicars, Thomas, tai A
Vice, Nathaniel, cur A
Vickery, William, hab A134B5
Vickridge, Thomas, cut B
Villers, Joseph, gir B
Vince, John, fis B
Vincent, Emanuel, but A14B8
Vincent, Robert, sta B
Violett, Francis, cor A
Virgoe, George, fis B
Voilet (Vellett), David, glz A124B6
Vokins, Avery, tal B
Vorley, Edward, bak A134
Vowkins, Thomas, plu B
Voyce, John, gir A
Voyce, William, bro A

Waddell, William, plu B
Waddis, William, cor A
Wade, Edward, cp A
Wade, Ferdinando, bar A24B78
Wade, John, but A
Wade, John, fou B
Wade, John, mus A134B5
Wade, Joseph, joi B
Wade, Joseph, joi A
Wade, Nicholas, lea A
Wade, William, bak B
Wadnell, John, far A2B568
Wafer, Lionell, bar B
Waggitt, Christopher, dye B
Waggot, John, far A
Wagstall, John, mer B
Waine, Daniel, tal A
Wainhouse, John, pai A
Waite, Daniel, lea A
Waite, James, tai A24B57
Wakefield, James, fle A1B678
Waker, Thomas, vin B
Waklin, Thomas, apo A
Walden *see* Walkden, Samuel
Waldoe, Isaac, gro B
Waldron, Boys, glz B
Waldron, William, vin B
Wale, George, gro B
Wale, Thomas, gol B
Walkden, Charles, sta B
Walkden (Walden), Samuel, joi A134B5
Walker, Edw, bro A
Walker, Edward, inn B

Walker, Francis, but B
Walker, Heikin, plu B
Walker, Hezekiah, plu A4
Walker, James, bla B
Walker, John, inn B
Walker, John, mas A
Walker, John, sal B
Walker, Jos, car A
Walker, Jos, mer A
Walker, Joseph, glz B
Walker, Richard, arm B
Walker, Richard, tal A
Walker, Robert, inn B
Walker, Thomas, ck A
Walker, Thomas, coa A
Walker, Thomas, cp A
Walker, Thomas, lor B
Walker, Thomas, pla A
Walker, Thomas, wea B678
Walker, Thurston, inn B
Walker, William, cur B678
Walkwood, Richard, hab A
Wall, John, gol B
Wall, Samuel, clo A
Wall, Thomas, bla B
Wallden, Richard, pou B
Wallen, John, pla B
Waller, David, bro A
Waller, Henry, clo A
Waller, John, glz B
Walley, John, bre A
Wallis, Jacob, sad A
Wallis, John, clo A
Wallis, John, cp A
Wallis, John, mer B568
Wallis, John, mer A124B8
Wallis, Richard, dye B
Wallis, Richard, pai B
Wallis, Thomas, bla B
Wallis, Thomas, fis A134
Wallis, William, bak B
Wallis, William, gol A
Wallis, William, mer A
Wallmsley, William, fou B
Walsh, Thomas, hab B
Walsham, Robert, fra B
Walter, John, iro A
Walter, Richard, fis A
Walter, Richard, gol B
Walter, Samuel, fis A
Walter, William, sta B
Walters, Robert, mas B
Walthall, Hambury, hab B
Waltho, John, sta B
Walton, John, gol A134B6
Wandell, Henry, gro B
Wandell, Jos, tai B
Wandell, Thomas, lea A1B578
Wanley, George, gol B6
Wansel, Daniel, joi B

Ward, Downes, fle B
Ward, James, cp A
Ward, James, gol A
Ward, John, cor A
Ward, John, tai A1B568
Ward, John, tur B
Ward, Joseph, bak A
Ward, Joseph, gol B
Ward, Joseph, gol A
Ward, Nathaniel, car A
Ward, Richard, wea A
Ward, Thomas, dis B
Ward, Thomas, mer A
Ward, Thomas, uph A
Ward, William, bro B
Ward, William, wea A
Ward, Zachariah, gol A
Ware, Nicholas, tai A24B67
Wareham, William, bar A
Wareing, Michael, vin B
Wargan, Zouch, tai A
Warham, Thomas, ck B
Warham, William, gol B
Warkman, Mark, cp A
Warkman, Richard, pew A
Warkup, Henry, bak A4B578
Warlepoole, Richard, joi A
Warman, Edward, tai A
Warman, John, tal B
Warman, Richard, lea B
Warne, Thomas, ski B
Warner, Edward, dis A
Warner, John, cp A
Warner, John, gol A
Warner, Samuel, bla A
Warner, Thomas, ck A
Warner, William, cur B
Warren, Edward, uph A
Warren, John, bar B
Warren, John, car A
Warren, Joseph, gol A123B6
Warren, Martin, bar B
Warren, Peter, car B
Warren, Thomas, pai A3
Warren, William, car B
Warren, William, dra A
Warren, William, fou B
Warren, William, glo A
Warren, William, joi B
Warrin, James, joi B
Washbourne, Richard, bow B
Wastfield, Arundel, clo A
Waterman, Christo, pla B
Waterman, William, tur B
Waters, Jasper, mer A
Waters, Samuel, joi A
Waters, Samuel, ski A
Waters, William, car B
Waterson, Edmond, iro A
Waterworth, John, hab A

124

Watkins, Richard, wea A
Watkins, Thomas, fis A
Watkins, William, bar A
Watkinson, Edmond, tai A
Watkinson, Godfrey, cp A
Watmore, John, tai A
Wats, Stephen, fou B6
Watson, David, clo B
Watson, Edward, fis A
Watson, John, dra A
Watson, Joseph, hab A
Watson, Josiah, dis B
Watson, Marten, bro B
Watson, Robert, glz A123B6
Watson, William, dra B
Watson, William, fis A2B568
Watterson, William, cor B
Watts, Benjamin, gol B
Watts, Edmund, hab A
Watts, Henry, inn A2B578
Watts, James, mas A
Watts, John, bar B
Watts, John, gol B
Watts, John, lor B
Watts, John, tal B
Watts, Jonas, tal A
Watts, Joshua, sta A
Watts, Reder, bro A
Watts, Richard, hab A
Watts, Robert, wea A234B7
Watts, Thomas, bak B
Watts, Thomas, bla B
Watts, Thomas, mas B
Watts, Thomas, mas B
Watts, Thomas, tal A124B8
Waylet, George, hab B
Wayman, Robert, bri B
Wayt, Robert, pou A
Waytt, John, cor A
Weakes, James, ski A
Weakly, Thomas, mer B
Weale, John, ski A
Wearg, Charles, tur B
Weathen, Charles, dra A
Weatherly, William, fis A34
Weaver, Grave, bak A134
Weaver, Simon, cut A
Web, Thomas, bro B
Webb, Ebenezer, tai A
Webb, George, bow B
Webb, George, bre B
Webb, John, bar A
Webb, John, fra A234B8
Webb, John, tai A
Webb, Joseph, gro B
Webb, Joseph, lea A123B8
Webb, Joseph, pew A
Webb, Leader, scr B
Webb, Richard, iro B
Webb, Samuel, dra A12B68

Webb, Thomas, fou A
Webb, Thomas, scr A
Webb, Uriah, clo B
Webb, William, inn B
Webb, William, inn A123
Webb, William, vin B
Webster, Anthony, fou B
Webster, Godfrey kt, clo A
Webster, James, fou A
Webster, Joseph, wea A
Webster, Richard, bow B
Webster, Thomas, but A3
Webster, Thomas bt, clo A
Weedon, Thomas, vin B
Weeks, Israel, dis A
Weeks, John, hab A
Weeler, Francis, but B
Weight, William, bla B
Welch, John, clo A
Welch, Joseph, bri A
Welch, Joseph, bri A
Welch, Joseph, cur A
Welch, Samuel, joi B
Weldale, John, but B
Weldon, Charles, tai B
Welham, Robert, lor A
Wellbelloved, Philip, fru A
Wellington, Richard, sta B
Wellins, John, bre A
Wells, Benjamin, iro B
Wells, Dabby, lea A
Wells, James, uph B
Wells, John, dra B
Wells, John, fis A
Wells, John, lea A
Wells, Samuel, gls A
Wells, Samuel, iro A4B678
Wells, Thomas, bro A
Wells, Thomas, sad B
Wells, Thomas, vin B
Wells, William, sad B
Welter, William, sta B
Wenlock, Ralph, but B
Wentworth, Thomas, joi B
West, Aholiab, clo A
West, Edward, hab A
West, Edward, mer A
West, Francis, hab B
West, James, ski A
West, John, clo B
West, John, cor A
West, John, cp A
West, John, tai A
West, Joseph, ck A
West, Josiah, fis B
West, Matthew, gol A
West, Moses, pew A
West, Richard, fis A
West, Richard, gro A
West, Richard, pla B

125

West, Stephen, arm B
West, William, hab B
West, William, joi A
West, William, ski A
Westall, Daniel, mer A
Westbrook, John, pla B
Westbrooke, William, gro B
Westcott, Robert, vin B
Weste, George, bro B
Westfield, Edward, gro B
Westfield, John, dye A
Westfield, John, gro B
Westfield, William, gol A
Westfield, William, gro B
Westhall, Samuel, wax A
Westhorp, Samuel, hab A
Westley, Robert, tai B
Weston, Charles, gls A
Weston, Thomas, lea B
Westrag, George, tai B
Westwood, Jos, pew B
Weyfield *see* Wingfield
Whadcock, Charles, bar B
Whadcott, Simon, mer B
Whale, William, uph A23B68
Whalley, Jacob, dis A
Wharley, Daniel, glo A
Wharton, Edward, gol A124B6
Whatsmore, John, iro B
Wheatley, John, pai B
Wheatley, Thomas, pai B
Wheatly, John, dye A
Wheatly, John, glz A
Wheats, Thomas, ski A
Wheeler, John, bar B
Wheeler, John, lea A
Wheeler, Robert, fru B
Wheeler, Thomas, pla B
Wheeler, William, wea A
Wheler, George, bak B
Whelpdale, Andrew, tai B
Whichelow, Potter, glo B
Whiddon, Jacob, ski A
Whily, James, fru B
Whip, Richard, gol B
Whisker, Daniel, inn B
Whistler, Ralph, bar B
Whiston, Jos, dye A
Whitaker, Benjamin, pew B
Whitby, Jonas, inn B
Whitchand, Henry, fra B
Whitchcoat, Henry, iro A
Whitchurch, James, pai A
White, Alyffe, hab A
White, Amos, cut A123B6
White, Christopher, hab A
White, Edward, bla B
White, Edward, bla B
White, Edward, dye A
White, George, glo A

White, Henry, bri A
White, Henry, joi A124B6
White, James, gro A
White, John, bla B
White, John, bri A3B578
White, John, dis B
White, John, dra B
White, John, fou B
White, John, hab A
White, John, lea A
White, John, tai B
White, John, wea B
White, John, wea B
White, Jos, sal A
White, Peter, gol B
White, Richard, bak B
White, Richard, bla A
White, Richard sen, bla A
White, Richard, pew B
White, Samuel, bre B
White, Samuel, ski A
White, Thomas, bla A
White, Thomas, dra B
White, Thomas, dye A23B56
White, Thomas, gol A
White, Thomas, mer A
White, William, tur B
Whitebread, Benj, dra A13B78
Whitehall, Joseph, uph A
Whitehand, James, dis B
Whitehead, John, bla A
Whitehead, John, tai B
Whitehead, Samuel, ski B
Whitehead, William, clo B
Whitehorn, John, gro A
Whitehouse, Edward, wea B
Whiteing, John, gol A134B6
Whiteing, William, cp B
Whiteledge, Robert, sta B
Whitell, Joseph, fis A
Whiteman, George, tal A
Whitemore, Samuel, dis A
Whitfeild, Rob, bro A
Whitfeild, Samuel, gir A
Whitmay, William, fou B
Whitsey, Joseph, far A
Whittaker, Edward, pai A
Whittfield, Samuel, mer B
Whittingham, George, bla B
Whittington, Isaac, hab B
Whittle, George, dye B
Whittle, John, clo A
Whitworth, James, wea A
Whitworth, Miles, iro B
Wicker, Tobias, clo B
Wickes, Obediah, lea A
Wickham, Nathaniel, bar A
Wickham, Thomas, dis B
Wicks, Charles, uph B
Wicks, John, sal A

126

Wicks, William, gro B
Wiffen, John, pou A
Wiggins, Robert, cut A
Wiggins, Thomas, inn B
Wight, Daniel, dis A
Wigley, John, tal B
Wignell, John, uph B
Wigzell, John, wax A
Wilbraham, James, fru A
Wilch, Joshua, pla A
Wilcox, Daniel, sad B
Wilcox, John, glo A
Wilcox, Thomas, uph A
Wilcox, William, sad B
Wild, Benjamin, sta B
Wild, Edward, bow A
Wild, John, sta B
Wild, William, hab B
Wildboare, Nicholas, dra A
Wildbore, Joseph, mer A
Wilde, Ebenezer, bre A
Wilder, James, bak A
Wilder, John, vin B
Wildman, John, bla A
Wileman, Henry, clo B
Wilford, David, bla A134B6
Wilford, John, fis A
Wilkenson, John, tai B
Wilkes, John, dis A
Wilkes, John, plu A134
Wilkins, Abraham, car B
Wilkins, Chr, pla B
Wilkins, John, bro B
Wilkins, John, car B
Wilkins, Micha, bak A
Wilkins, Richard, sta B
Wilkinson, Christopher, sta A
Wilkinson, Edward, ck A
Wilkinson, John, dra A
Wilkinson, John, dye A
Wilkinson, John, tai B
Wilkinson, Richard, gol B
Wilkinson, Richard, ski A
Wilkinson, Samuel, dra A
Wilkinson, Samuel, iro A
Wilkinson, Thomas, bla B
Wilkinson, William, cor A
Wilks, Job, hab B
Wilks, John, arm A
Wilks, John, plu B
Willard, Joseph, arm A
Willcocks, William, pla A
Willcox, William, dra A
Willes, William, tai B
Willett, Charles, bak B
Willey, Noy, apo B
Willford, John, tal B
William, Charles, uph B
William, Daniel, far B
William, Joh kt, mer B568

William, Samuel, pai B
Williams, Christopher, inn A
Williams, David, gol A
Williams, Edward, cut A
Williams, James, dra A
Williams, Job, gir A
Williams, John, bro A
Williams, John, car A
Williams, John, glz B
Williams, John, inn B
Williams, Joseph, mer A
Williams, Joseph, uph B
Williams, Samuel, clo B
Williams, Thomas, ck B
Williamson, Daniel, hab A
Williamson, James, mer A
Williamson, Thomas, bar A234B7
Willice, John, vin B
Willing, Christopher, dis A
Willis, Benjamin, clo B
Willis, Henry, wax B
Willis, John, bla A
Willis, Samuel, wax A
Willmott, Benjamin, dye A
Willmott, Daniel, lor A
Willoby, George, dye A
Willoughby, Giles, hab B
Willoughby, Henry, cut A
Wills, Anthony, tur B
Wills, Edward kt, tai A
Wills, Henry, hab B
Willson, Bigley, vin A
Willson, Henry, gol A
Willson, Samuel, apo A
Wilmer, Thomas, clo A
Wilmer, Thomas, sta A
Wilmore, John, tai A
Wilmore, Thomas, car B
Wilmott, John, joi A
Wilmott, Nehemiah, gro A
Wilmott, Richard, clo A123B5
Wilshaw, Patrick, clo A
Wilson, Archibald, dye A
Wilson, Benjamin, cor A12B67
Wilson, Benjamin, far A
Wilson, Benjamin, lea A34B56
Wilson, Edward, vin B
Wilson, Francis, fou B58
Wilson, James, bri B
Wilson, Jeremy, wea A
Wilson, John, fle A
Wilson, John, lea B
Wilson, John, wea A2B678
Wilson, Joseph, cp A
Wilson, Richard, clo A
Wilson, Samuel, bak A
Wilson, Thomas, clo A
Wilson, Thomas, gir A
Wilton, Harward, bow A
Wimberly, Bartholomew, tal A

Wimpresse, Samuel, glz A
Winch, George, far B
Winch, Richard, cp A
Winch, Richard, lea B
Winchester, Daniel, ski B
Wincoat, Edward, bar B
Wind, John, sta A
Winde, James, uph A
Windfeild, George, dis A
Windlow, Rich, bro A
Windsor, Edward, joi A
Windsor, Isaac, ck A23B68
Windsor, Shadrach, mer B
Wingfield (Weyfield), Henry, hab A4B578
Winkfeild, George, bar A
Winkley, James, sal B
Winn, John, pla B
Winn, Thomas, wea A
Winnock, Edward, mer A
Winspear, Thomas, bla B
Winstanley, William, fou B
Winston, William, bla B
Winter, Rich, bro A
Winterburn, John, pla A124B6
Wintle, John, ski A4B678
Winton, Henry, uph B
Wintworth, Hugh, hab A
Wise, Daniel, cp A
Wise, John, plu B
Wise, Joseph, cp A
Wise, Theo, pla B
Wise, Thomas, mas B
Wise, William, clo B
Wise, William, clo B
Wise, William, coa B
Wise, William, mas B
Wiseman, Cave, wea B
Wiseman, Charles, bak B
Witchell, Nathaniel, glo A
Witchell, Nichol, glo A2B678
Witchelow, John, bla A
Witehell, John, glo A
Witherley, Nevil, tai B
Withers, Francis, bri A2B568
Withers, John, pla A
Withers, John, pou A34B56
Withers, Samuel, tal A
Withers, William, apo B
Withers, William kt, fis B
Witler, Thomas, sal B
Wittom, Robert, vin B
Wolfreys, Nathaniel, gol B
Wood, Charles, hab B
Wood, Edward, uph B
Wood, George, gro A12B78
Wood, Jeffry, hab A
Wood, John, bak A
Wood, John, cur A
Wood, John, dra A
Wood, John, far A34B58

Wood, Joseph, bar B
Wood, Nicholas, bri B
Wood, Richard, dis A
Wood, Robert, far B
Wood, Robert, far B568
Wood, Samuel, dra A
Wood, Seamour, hab A
Wood, Tho, tai B
Wood, William, bak B
Wood, William, cut B
Wood, William, gir B
Wood, William, joi B
Wood, William, joi A
Woodburn, George, bro A
Woodcock, Edward, dra B
Woodcock, Henry, vin A12B78
Wooddal, Randal, bla B
Woodfield, John, but A
Woodger, William, cp A
Wooding, Robert, joi A
Woodland, Jos, gls A
Woodland, William, lea A
Woodley, Henry, ski A14B56
Woodman, Matthew, iro A
Woodman, William, iro B
Woodman, William, mas B
Woodroff, John, bre B
Woodroff, Thomas, ski B
Woodrolf, Christopher, inn B
Woodroof, Daniel, uph B
Woodward, George, glz B
Woodward, John, joi A
Woodward, John, tur B
Woodward, Joseph, tal A
Woodward, Matthew, tal A
Woodward, Philip, clo A
Woodward, Samuel, inn A
Woodward, Thomas, tur B
Woolball, Henry, gro A
Wooldridge, Richard, lor A
Wooley, Edward, bro B
Woolf, Bartholomew, mas A12
Woolfe, John, dra A
Woolhead, Thomas, hab B
Woolhead, Thomas, tal A
Woolleston, William, tai A
Woolley, Arthur, gol A
Woolley, Francis, glo A
Woolley, Wight, mer A
Woolley, William, dye A
Woolley, William, gol A
Woolmer, Benjamin, fis A
Woolmer, Henry, dis B
Woolston, Benjamin, fle B
Wootton, Matthew, sta B
Worgin, Edward, tal B
Workman, James, but A
Worlidge, Richard, bla B
Wormell, Joseph, joi A
Wormlayton, John, bla A

128

Wormlayton, John, ski A
Worrel, Job, cut B
Worrell, Robert, lor A
Wrathall, Robert, inn A
Wray, Daniel, sal B78
Wray, Daniel, sal A
Wright, Benjamin, fou A
Wright, Broughton, ski B
Wright, George, apo A
Wright, George, tur A
Wright, John, arm A124B6
Wright, John, bar B
Wright, John, dye B
Wright, John, lor B
Wright, John, tai B
Wright, John, vin B
Wright, Leonard, bla B
Wright, Matthew, gro A
Wright, Michael, bro B
Wright, Thomas, gol B
Wright, Will, bro A
Wright, William, ck B
Wright, William, pai A
Wright, William, wea A
Wrightson, William, vin B
Wroughton, James, hab B
Wyat, Thomas, cut B
Wyat, Thomas, mus B
Wyatt, Rowland, fra A
Wyatt, Zedekiah, dra A
Wybarn, Anthony, pou A4B567
Wybird, John, tal B
Wyerdale, Benjamin, cut A
Wyeth, Joseph, glo A124B7
Wyman, Samuel, tur A
Wynde, John, sad A
Wynet, John, bro B
Wynne, John, wea B
Wyrill, Robert, tal B

Yalding, John, hab B
Yard, Warwick, mer A123B5
Yardly, Robert, lea A2B567
Yates, Andrew, glo B
Yates, James, tal A
Yates, Robert, hab B
Yates, William, hab B
Yeonard, George, cur B
Yerbury, Walter, clo A
Yerwood, Frances, joi B
Yexbury, William, sal B
Yoick, Thomas, bak B
York, Walter, lea A
Young, Daniel, but B
Young, Edward, dra B
Young, John, gro A
Young, John, lor A
Young, John, mas B
Young, John, mer A1B568
Young, John, vin B
Young, Joseph, iro A
Young, Joshua, bar A
Young, Lewis, ski A
Young, Peter, cp A
Young, Richard, cur A
Young, Robert, far A
Young, Roger, joi B
Young, Thomas, fis B
Young, Thomas, glz B
Young, Thomas, joi B
Young, William, dra B
Younge, George, bro B

Zachary, Thomas, ski A
Zouch, Francis, tai B
Zouch, George, tai A

LONDON RECORD SOCIETY

The London Record Society was founded in December 1964 to publish transcripts, abstracts and lists of the primary sources for the history of London, and generally to stimulate interest in archives relating to London. Membership is open to any individual or institution; the annual subscription is £5 ($12) for individuals and £8 ($20) for institutions, which entitles a member to receive one copy of each volume published during the year and to attend and vote at meetings of the Society. Prospective members should apply to the Hon. Secretary, Miss Heather Creaton, c/o Institute of Historical Research, Senate House, London, WC1E 7HU.

The following volumes have already been published:

1. *London Possessory Assizes: a calendar*, edited by Helena M. Chew (1965)
2. *London Inhabitants within the Walls, 1695*, with an introduction by D. V. Glass (1966)
3. *London Consistory Court Wills, 1492–1547*, edited by Ida Darlington (1967)
4. *Scriveners' Company Common Paper, 1357–1628, with a continuation to 1678*, edited by Francis W. Steer (1968)
5. *London Radicalism, 1830–1843: a selection from the papers of Francis Place*, edited by D. J. Rowe (1970)
6. *The London Eyre of 1244*, edited by Helena M. Chew and Martin Weinbaum (1970)
7. *The Cartulary of Holy Trinity Aldgate*, edited by Gerald A. J. Hodgett (1971)
8. *The Port and Trade of Early Elizabethan London: documents*, edited by Brian Dietz (1972)
9. *The Spanish Company*, by Pauline Croft (1973)
10. *London Assize of Nuisance, 1301–1431: a calendar*, edited by Helena M. Chew and William Kellaway (1973)
11. *Two Calvinistic Methodist Chapels, 1743–1811: the London Tabernacle and Spa Fields Chapel*, edited by Edwin Welch (1975)
12. *The London Eyre of 1276*, edited by Martin Weinbaum (1976)
13. *The Church in London, 1375–1392*, edited by A. K. McHardy (1977)
14. *Committees for Repeal of the Test and Corporation Acts: Minutes, 1786–90 and 1827–8*, edited by Thomas W. Davis (1978)
15. *Joshua Johnson's Letterbook, 1771–4: letters from a merchant in London to his partners in Maryland*, edited by Jacob M. Price (1979)
16. *London and Middlesex Chantry Certificate, 1548*, edited by C. J. Kitching (1980)
17. *London Politics, 1713–1717: Minutes of a Whig Club, 1714–17*, edited

130

by H. Horwitz; *London Pollbooks, 1713*, edited by W. A. Speck and W. A. Gray (1981)

All volumes are still in print; apply to Hon. Secretary. Price to individual members £5 ($12) each; to institutional members £8 ($20) each; and to non-members £10 ($25) each.